ABOLITION'S AXE

Beriah Green, ca. 1860. From *Beriah Green, Sermons and Other Discourses with Brief Biographical Hints*. New York: S. W. Green, 1860.

ABOLITION'S

BERIAH GREEN, ONEIDA INSTITUTE, AND THE BLACK FREEDOM STRUGGLE

MILTON C. SERNETT

Syracuse University Press

Copyright © 1986 Syracuse University Press
Syracuse, New York 13244-5160

All Rights Reserved

First Paperback Edition 2004
04   05   06   07   08   09   6   5   4   3   2   1

The paper used in this publication meets the minimum requirements of American National Standard for
Information Sciences—Permanence of Paper for Printed Library Materials, ANSI Z39.48-1984.∞™

Library of Congress Cataloging-in-Publication Data
Sernett, Milton C., 1942–
   Abolition's axe.

   (A New York State study)
   Bibliography: p.
   Includes index.
   1. Green, Beriah, 1795–1874.   2. Slavery—United
States—Anti-slavery movements.   3. Oneida Baptist
Institute—History.   4. Abolitionists—United States—
Biography. I. Title. II. Series.
E449.G79S47   1986   326'.092'4   86-5757
ISBN 0-8156-2370-4 (cloth); ISBN 0-8156-3022-0 (pbk. : alk. paper)

Manufactured in the United States of America

Milton C. Sernett is professor of African American studies and history and adjunct professor of religion at Syracuse University. In addition to *Abolition's Axe*, he is the author of *Black Religion and American Evangelicalism, Bound for the Promised Land: African American Religion and the Great Migration,* and *North Star Country: Upstate New York and the Crusade for African American Freedom* and editor of *African American Religious History: A Documentary Witness.*

CONTENTS

ILLUSTRATIONS

MAP

PREFACE

When the history of American emancipation is written, the name of Beriah Green will stand high on its roll of fame.[1] So prophesied Hiel Hollister in his history of Pawlet, Vermont, published in 1867. Hollister, the village chronicler, took pride in the fact that a young lad from a small community in the Green Mountains of Vermont had gone on to become a respected opponent of slavery and a passionate champion of the campaign to create a just society in which black Americans stood on an equal footing with white citizens, especially in access to educational opportunities.

Abolition's Axe first appeared in a cloth edition in 1986.[2] At that time both Green and his Oneida Institute, a radical abolitionist school located in Upstate New York, were relatively unknown to scholars and students of American social reform. I took up the challenge of recovering the story of the Rev. Beriah Green's role in the black freedom effort because of my own ignorance about where he should be placed in abolitionism's hall of fame. I found Green fascinating, a man worthy, despite his complex and often obdurate personality, of the accolades given him by those who came to study at his abolitionist school. As for that school, I did not then know that Oneida Institute (less than an hour's drive from my Upstate New York home), had earned first honors in its

---

1. Hiel Hollister, *Pawlet for One Hundred Years* (Albany, N.Y.: J. Munsell, 1867), 194.
2. Milton C. Sernett, *Abolition's Axe: Beriah Green, Oneida Institute and the Black Freedom Struggle* (Syracuse: Syracuse Univ. Press, 1986).

admission of African American students in the nineteenth century, educating more than the better-known Oberlin College of Ohio.

My invitation to write this preface to the paperback edition gives me the opportunity to reflect once more on the significance of Green's attempt to create a model egalitarian community at a time when the pall of a racial caste system supported by law and custom still blighted the American democratic experiment.

The Rev. Beriah Green picked up abolition's axe at a time when few white Americans dared to champion the cause of liberty and nearly two million African Americans suffered under the whip and the lash. In doing so, he assumed a burden of his own. To answer the cry for help of the slave was, Green asserted, a holy duty. As he said at the first anniversary meeting in 1834 of the founding of the American Anti-Slavery Society, "For, one, I cannot escape from the conviction that our Savior has presented to us this very case of our colored brethren, in the 25th of Matthew, and pointed them as his appropriate representatives. . . . And when we are called to give an account for not relieving these poor brethren, the plea of ignorance will be of little avail."[3]

Green's earnest morality and resolution to live a good and useful life was evident very early. In preparing this preface, I reviewed the research files I began compiling almost two decades ago. Perhaps the most prized original document they contain is the set of self-improvement resolutions Green wrote on April 25, 1816, at the age of 21. He posted them above his study table when he was a young scholar at Union Academy in Plainfield, New Hampshire. These "Proposita," which had been kept by Green's roommate J. Sessions after Beriah left for college, were given to Sessions' daughter, wife of one of the early missionaries to the Sandwich Islands. The "Proposita" rested in the archives of the library of the Hawaiian Mission Children's Society until passed on to me by an agent of the library. They form the earliest document discovered to date from Green's own pen. Though the classical Latin gave me difficulty at first, I managed to decipher enough of the spirit of these resolutions to confirm that even as a young man Beriah Green set himself on seeking the good as he understood it.

Green left Ohio's Western Reserve region in the summer of 1833 to come east and assume leadership of Oneida Institute, a manual labor school set alongside the Erie Canal a few miles east of the Village of Whitesboro in Oneida County, in the heart of New York State's famous Burned-over District. Fugitives on the run from the South's "peculiar institution" once found refuge in the college dormitories there, and Green's school was a magnet for African Americans who aspired to educational excellence in a nonprejudicial setting.

3. *American Anti-Slavery Reporter* 1 (June 1834): 89–90.

As a mature abolitionist, Green came to the conclusion that righteousness, Biblically grounded and informed by reason, was the sole good of human endeavor. He drew the conclusion that the civil order ought to be based on a theocratic model or at least that rulership should be placed in the hands of the righteous. This political philosophy would not fare well in American public opinion today. Nevertheless, we can learn from the young scholar who dedicated himself to always being directed by an informed conscience and a discipline of self that contributed to the public good.

"Abolition's Axe," as I have come to think of Beriah Green, became increasingly embittered and isolated as the Civil War approached. He lost faith in the political process and in democracy itself. In spite of Green's acerbic temperament, dogmatism, and idiosyncratic behavior in the last decades of his life, his admirers, female and male, black and white, remembered him with honor. William Allen, the black educator driven out of the United States because of an interracial romance, called Green "one of earth's noble spirits."[4]

Although *Abolition's Axe* received good reviews in academic circles in its original cloth edition eighteen years ago, it did not reach as wide an audience as I would have liked. The decision by Syracuse University Press to reprint *Abolition's Axe* in a paperback edition occurs in a climate of renewed interest in the pre-Civil War period and a groundswell of enthusiasm for local and regional history. Thus this first-time paperback edition should be of interest to a new generation of readers.

Abolitionist studies, once dismissed by some historians as a dormant subfield, has been enriched and enlivened by the publication of a plethora of new books, many focusing on the contributions of African Americans and women to the antislavery enterprise. Readers wishing to review more recent scholarship pertaining to the story told by *Abolition's Axe* should consult several books and essays published since 1986.[5] Were I writing today about Gerrit Smith's ties to Green and his school, for example, I would want to incorporate information from Norm Dann's new book, *Practical Dreamer: A Biography of Gerrit Smith* (Utica: Nicholas K. Burns Publishing Co., 2003). In

4. William G. Allen, "Remarks on Uncle Tom's Cabin," *Frederick Douglass' Paper,* May 20, 1852.

5. For example, Douglas M. Strong has written extensively and with great precision about the impact of the anti-slavery politics upon churches in New York State's old Burned-over District. See Strong, *Perfectionist Politics: Abolitionism and the Religious Tensions of American Democracy* (Syracuse: Syracuse Univ. Press, 1999). David Maldwyn Ellis explored the fractious spirit that erupted in Oneida County when Christians like those I write about in Whitesboro's Presbyterian church found that they could not agree on the means of ridding America of slavery. See Ellis, "Conflicts among Calvinists: Oneida Revivalists in the 1820s," *New York History* 71 (January 1990): 25–44.

addition, Syracuse University Press is about to publish *The Encyclopedia of New York State,* an important milestone that should spark additional interest in topics related to Green and his school.[6]

My own most recent contribution to New York State historical studies is *North Star Country: Upstate New York and the Crusade for African American Freedom,* published by Syracuse University Press in 2002. This book has a larger scope than *Abolition's Axe*; while it incorporates parts of my study about Green and his school, it takes a more comprehensive look at abolition in central and western New York, examining how the advocates of black freedom found fertile soil in the Burned-over District—so-called because of the waves of religious revivals inspired by the preaching of Rev. Charles G. Finney in the 1820s—and raised up a new reform movement in opposition to the country's cardinal sin: slavery.

In *North Star Country,* Green joins other notables of the region, such as Gerrit Smith, Samuel May, Frederick Douglass, Jermain Loguen, and Samuel R. Ward, in common cause. While working on the larger canvas of the *North Star Country,* I became familiar with figures not known to me when I wrote *Abolition's Axe*—people who had admired Green and sought his counsel and aid. I think, for example, of Thomas James. Born into slavery at Canajoharie, New York, in 1804, he obtained his freedom and became a clergyman of the African Methodist Episcopal Zion Church. In 1835, James came to Syracuse planning to organize a black congregation. When opponents of his plan set a trap for him by proposing a public discussion of the contentious abolitionist question, James, reluctant to face them alone, appealed to Beriah Green for help. Green, along with Gerrit Smith and Alvan Stewart, two reformers who figure prominently in *Abolition's Axe,* journeyed to Syracuse and stood beside James in a public debate that bested the anti-abolitionist forces.

James, like the black students who attended Oneida Institute, found Beriah Green to be a true friend, one of the few whites of the period who practiced the ideal of egalitarian Christianity. Cornel West, a close student of American progress in matters of race today, has commented that Alexander Crummell, one of Oneida Institute's most prominent black alumni, found in Beriah Green his "white significant other." Since writing *Abolition's Axe,* I have discovered others who experienced what Crummell and James so admired in Green.

Though I was interested during the research phase for *Abolition's Axe* in

6. In recent years, Syracuse University Press has renewed its commitment to publishing books of high quality on subjects pertaining to the history of the Empire State. I was especially pleased to see the press publish paper editions of Edgar J. McManus's ground-breaking *History of Negro Slavery in New York,* long out of print, and Austin Stewart's *Twenty-Two Years a Slave, Forty Years a Free Man,* edited by Graham R. Hodges.

how abolitionism and the women's rights campaign intersected in Upstate New York, the focus and structure of the book did not allow me to explore the topic. While writing *North Star Country* and in subsequent endeavors, I have discovered interesting links between the two reform movements that involve Green and his students. For example, Elizabeth Cady Stanton speaks appreciatively of Green in her reminiscences, *Eighty Years and More,*[7] while Harriet Smith Mills, the Syracuse-based women's rights activist, likewise acknowledged the importance of Green's efforts to do something practical for the freedom cause. (Her husband, C. D. B. Mills, attended Oneida Institute during Green's presidency.) Although Green's personal views on women's suffrage were decidedly conservative, he had the respect of many of the most vocal female reformers of the day.

In my current research for a book about the place of Harriet Tubman in the American memory, I've learned that Green knew of the famous "Moses of Her People." He once assisted Tubman by writing a letter on her behalf to introduce her to friends of humanity in New York Mills. Tubman was herself illiterate; she depended on admirers like Green who could provide her with letters of introduction to use when she went on her fund-raising tours.[8]

The historian's research task is made easier today by increased access to primary materials. When I was struggling in the early 1980s to piece together the story of Green and his school, I had to construct the narrative from scores of hard-to-find and rare documents housed in widely diverse places. I despaired at times of ever being able to rescue Green from the historical amnesia clouding his labors as abolitionist and educator.

I well recall the many miles I put on our Volkswagen Diesel Rabbit during the 1980s in search of information about Green. I found that memory of my subject's abolitionist career had all but vanished in those places where he took up the abolition's axe and used it to cut at the roots of American racism. Green had been a principal in a tumultuous academic controversy at Western Reserve College—the first of its kind in an American institution of higher education—wrestling against conservatives and colonizationalists under the new banner of Garrisonian immediatism. Yet when I first visited Hudson during a research trip to northeastern Ohio, no one could tell me much about him—or even which house had been his.

7. Elizabeth Cady Stanton, *Eighty Years and More: Reminiscences (1815–1897)* (London: T. Fisher Unwin, 1898), 144.

8. Letter, Beriah Green to Samuel Campbell, March 19, 1860, original in William C. Clements Library, University of Michigan. Copy sent to me by Kate Clifford Larson, whose new book on the life of Tubman is a landmark achievement. See Kate Clifford Larson, *Bound for the Promised Land: Harriet Tubman, Portrait of an American Hero* (New York: Ballantine Books, 2003).

Today, thanks to the Internet, anyone seeking information about Green and the young men who responded to his courageous call for "practical abolitionism" can find helpful resources with the click of a mouse.

The Whitesboro village historian told me in the early 1980s that all he knew of Oneida Institute was that it had failed. Green, said this custodian of communal memory, with a note of derision in his voice, was "something of a radical." Today, Green is better known and better thought of in places where he labored most intensely on behalf of freedom's cause. Unfortunately, the school buildings are long gone. A large funeral home stands on the front of the historic property where so many young men, white and black, took up abolitionism as their life's work.

In *Abolition's Axe,* I attempt to demonstrate how symbolically important Oneida Institute was to the American antislavery crusade, despite its ultimate failure as an institutional experiment.

The publication of *Abolition's Axe* in 1986 brought me into the company of an enthusiastic group of Green's descendants. Elizabeth Woodman Green of Newburyport, Massachusetts, welcomed my family into her home and told of how she became fascinated with the story of her great grandfather through her daughter's school assignment about Beriah's brother, Jonathan Green, the missionary to the Sandwich Islands (Hawaii), himself an abolitionist. John Underwood Green of Chicago, another descendent, wrote me that he had not known much about his ancestor and nothing at all about the early abolitionists until he read *Abolition's Axe,* which he described as "a runaway best seller among my family members."[9] He kindly sent me his transcription of an unpublished sermon Beriah Green delivered on the death of a granddaughter (infant sister of Harold Green Underwood). The sermon demonstrates a more pastoral and more empathetic side of "Abolition's Axe" than Green displays in many of the essays he wrote in the heat of the antislavery struggle. Other Green family members and genealogists, some of whom are mentioned in the notes to chapter 1, continued to enrich my knowledge of forebears and descendants of Beriah Green after reading *Abolition's Axe.*

In preparing the paperback edition, I have made a few minor corrections in addition to supplying this preface. Through the diligent research of Hugh Humphreys, for example, we now know that the daguerreotype of the fugitive slave convention reproduced on page 115 was taken in Cazenovia on August 22, 1851, and not two years earlier as I surmised in 1986.[10] Nevertheless, the

---

9. Undated personal correspondence, John Underwood Baker to Milton C. Sernett.

10. Hugh C. Humphreys, "'Agitate! Agitate! Agitate!': The Great Fugitive Slave Law Convention and Its Rare Daguerreotype," *Madison County Heritage* 19 (1994): 3–64.

text of this paperback edition is essentially unchanged from the original 1986 edition.

With the appearance of this edition of *Abolition's Axe,* readers interested in the story of Beriah Green and his beloved school will have another opportunity to judge whether or not the man who railed so strongly against injustice in the world as he knew it was able to work out his own salvation because he took up the cross-like yoke of the poor and the oppressed.

Cazenovia, New York   Milton C. Sernett
August 22, 2003

ACKNOWLEDGMENTS

Because of the elusive nature of the primary sources used in this volume, I wish here to express gratitude to many helping hands, personal and institutional. James M. Washington, Randall Burkett, and Richard Newman, of the Northeast Seminar on Black Religion, first challenged me to explore the influence that Beriah Green had on the black graduates of Oneida Institute who became important religious leaders. Carleton Mabee, Professor Emeritus of History at the State University of New York, New Paltz, graciously shared information he had gleaned on blacks at Oneida Institute and provided a model of careful research in his *Black Education in New York State*. Will Gravely of the University of Denver and David Smith, Professor Emeritus of Religion at Wesleyan University, likewise helped with the identification of black graduates.

Anyone who ventures onto the complex terrain of the "Burned-over District" soon discovers the formidable character of Charles Grandison Finney. The Reverend David K. McMillan hosted me at the Harvard Divinity School and regaled me with story after story on Finney, and he has supplied many valuable documents. Brother Joseph J. Britt, C.F.X., kindly sent me a copy of his thesis on Beriah Green and the Oneida Institute. William E. Biggleston, archivist of Oberlin College, also assisted in locating Finney materials.

Professor Bertram Wyatt-Brown, formerly Professor of History at Case Western Reserve University, provided encouragement and hospitality while I was investigating Green's Hudson years. The staff at the Western Reserve Historical Society, Case Western Reserve Archives, and Hudson Academy were likewise helpful.

My forays into upstate New York history proved truly enjoyable, primarily due to the very professional assistance afforded by the Oneida and Madison County historical societies. Mark Weimer and Carolyn Davis of the George Arents Research Library at Syracuse University gave useful counsel as I waded through the immense Gerrit Smith Papers collection. I also wish to thank the New York State Historical Society at Cooperstown and the New-York Historical Society in New York City for prompt responses to my inquiries.

Of the many special collections consulted, in addition to those already mentioned, I wish to acknowledge especially permission to use materials from the Boston Public Library, Library of Congress, Union Theological Seminary, Yale University, Harvard University, New York City Public Library, Cornell University, William L. Clements Library at the University of Michigan, Hamilton College Library, Berea College Library, the American Antiquarian Society, and the Presbyterian Historical Society.

Of the many fortunate and serendipitous experiences during my researches, I must mention discovering several descendants of Beriah Green and his brother Jonathan. Betsy H. Woodman of Newburyport, Massachusetts, William D. Green of Washington, D.C., and Newell Green of Ascutny, Vermont, proved enthusiastic and unfailingly helpful in sorting out the mysteries of family genealogy, and offered me the use of letters in their possession. Mary Jane Knight, librarian of the Hawaiian Mission Children's Society, Honolulu, discovered a very rare picture of Beriah and the earliest document from his pen.

I wish to acknowledge the expert services and kind assistance of all of the resident professionals in editing and production at Syracuse University Press for shepherding this book from manuscript to print. My colleagues in the Department of African American Studies have likewise offered an environment conducive to bringing my six-year quest to chronicle the odyssey of Beriah Green and his school to a happy conclusion.

Finally, my wife, Jan, and children, Rebecca and Matthew, should know that with the publication of *Abolition's Axe* I have been liberated from the study, though temporarily. The dedication is for Matthew, who once wondered why he was left out of the honors given in my *Black Religion and American Evangelicalism,* unmindful of the fact that he had not yet been born.

Syracuse, New York   Milton C. Sernett
Winter 1986

INTRODUCTION

I n the course of researching the story of Beriah Green and the Oneida
Institute, I have encountered numerous sympathetic persons whose
countenances brightened at the mention of "Oneida." Eager to
assist, they have generously offered sustenance from their well-
stocked larders concerning the Oneida Community of John Humphrey
Noyes. When I clarified my subject, however, their faces displayed
puzzlement rather than familiarity, and we usually switched to other intrigu-
ing aspects of New York State regional history. Owing perhaps to the elegant and absorbing studies of the nineteenth-century upstate New York
milieu by such prose poets as Carl Carmer, most contemporary readers
know this region for its visionaries who obeyed "voices speaking from no
visible mouths."[1] An excursion into Americana in what came to be known as
the Burned-over District, after the revival fires which blazed across the
region in the 1820s and 1830s, is something like venturing into grandmother's attic. There are curiosities aplenty, strange but compelling relics, and
ghosts from a time when mystics walked the land.

Though Beriah Green and his school at Whitesboro have received at
least passing notice in countless specialized and scholarly studies on American reform, the popular notoriety afforded other figures in the history of the
Burned-over District has eluded him. Green has been called one of the five
most important abolitionists in New York State, yet his name is far less
familiar than that of William Lloyd Garrison, Theodore Dwight Weld, Wendell Phillips, or even fellow New Yorker Gerrit Smith, all of whom have
received biographical appraisals.[2] After six years of painstaking searches for
primary sources, I am tempted to say that Green's heretofore obscurity
relates to the scattered and elusive nature of the material record. Historians, after all, cannot conjure up their subject out of thin air.

My own introduction to Beriah Green came many years ago when reading W. E. B. Du Bois' classic *Souls of Black Folk*. Du Bois records how impressed he was with the black patriarch and scholar Alexander Crummell and how fortunate the young Crummell had been to be exposed to the radical humanitarianism of Beriah Green while a student at Oneida Institute.[3] In my researches into the lives of other prominent nineteenth-century black American abolitionists and clergymen, I again encountered references to Green. Finally, curiosity gave way to a resolve to investigate just what manner of man this upstate New Yorker was and why he should be so fondly remembered by such important figures as Alexander Crummell.

The trajectory of Green's life simulates a parabolic curve. His New England origins, while significant in shaping the mature abolitionist, offer little drama. He enters from the wings onto center stage in the early 1830s, with the controversy at Western Reserve College over Garrison's call for immediate emancipation. He moves to the front during his ten years as president of Oneida Institute, America's first truly interracial "college," skirmishes with other actors in the tangled web of abolitionist politics in the late 1840s and 1850s, and then abruptly exits in the pre-Civil War years, when his radical vision of an egalitarian society was lost in the turmoil of sectionalism. He then occupied, by his own admission, a lonely rampart in reform circles. Even his abolitionist colleagues wearied of his fulminations and found him too ideologically idiosyncratic.

In rescuing Green from the corner of obscurity which he eventually occupied and, paradoxically, both cultivated and raged against, I by no means intend to explain away his personal idiosyncrasies. As Ronald G. Walters reminds us, opponents of the crusaders against slavery correctly pointed out that it was not "normal" in the 1830s to be an abolitionist. Unfortunately, some historians have busied themselves with attempting to explain the "abnormality" of individual abolitionists by reference to all sorts of inner demons and psychological dissections of their motives. While interesting and, to a certain point instructive, these efforts have tended to direct attention away from the central mission of the abolitionist crusade. Indeed, from the vantage point of present-day morality, as Walters cautions us, the truly "disturbed" individuals of the antebellum period were not the despised friends of the slave "but the respectable men who reacted emotionally and violently against them."[4]

What bound Beriah Green to the fate of American slaves was his strong and uncompromising conscience. But by sublimating his inner being into efforts to remove the pall of slavery from the land, he exposed himself to the prophet's curse. The American public proved indifferent to his pleas, particularly so because he dedicated himself to more than the dismantlement of the "peculiar institution." Green was in advance of many white abolitionists in that he sought to establish a truly biracial society, not simply to put an end to slavery. In this regard, his odyssey is exceptional, for the latent, and sometimes overt, racism of even the most prominent white abolitionists has been thoroughly documented by historians.

While the story that follows begins with Green's formative period in New England and moves to a consideration of his Western Reserve years, the major portion is played out in central New York. When Green arrived as president-elect of Oneida Institute in 1833, Whitesboro (sometimes referred to as Whitestown after the designation of the larger frontier tract) had a population of over four thousand, about half that of neighboring Utica, and was deemed prosperous and progressive. Oneida County and its environs were in the process of evolving from an economy based almost entirely on agriculture to one driven by the manufacture of textiles, iron mills, and glassworks. An emerging middle class took the lead in establishing religious, reform, and educational societies of an amazing number and complexity.[5] Green's transformation of Oneida Institute from a manual labor and literary academy, based on the study of the Greek and Roman classics, into a radical, interracial, abolitionist college dedicated to revolutionizing American society both drew on the religious and reform energies of the Burned-over District and tested them. In this regard, our story has translocal, indeed national significance, for upstate New York was a major center of abolitionist activity.

As I will argue, the abolitionists failed not in the justness of their cause nor in the zeal with which they fought the curse of slavery. They failed because they did not capture and hold enough of America's institutional power. To Green's credit, he saw the necessity of establishing a training center for young abolitionists and of erecting a school free of racial distinctions which could serve as a model for the country's other voluntary institutions, schools, churches, and the like. *Abolition's Axe* is as much the story of an institution as it is of a man. Oneida Institute deserves, as Elizur Wright, Jr., argued, "first honor" in the fight against racism and discrimination in American higher education.[6] With Green at the helm, it enrolled more African Americans than any other American college in the 1830s and early 1840s. The significance of this can only be understood when we realize how strongly blacks yearned to be free from the chains of ignorance that, as much as the iron fetters of the slave, held them in despair. Charles B. Ray, editor of the newspaper *Colored American* and a supporter of Oneida Institute, wrote in 1837: "Herein is our great deficiency. O! spirit of slavery, unholy prejudice against color, what hast thou done? Thou hast entered the colored man's intellectual world, and despoiled its inhabitants of the image of God. The repair of the ruins, brethren, is our citadel of strength. 'KNOWLEDGE IS POWER.' "[7]

In emphasizing the story of Oneida Institute, especially in the middle chapters, I consciously depart from biographical tradition. Apart from the difficulties of capturing fully the multifarious influences that shape anyone's daily existence, I have chosen to underscore what Green himself thought to be truly important. There is a chronological thread to what follows. Most chapters develop a theme out of a certain decade of Green's life, and the trajectory of the whole moves across his nearly four score years, which span the presidential administrations from George Washington to Ulysses S. Grant. Yet I have tried to measure the man by the yardstick he himself employed. Having accepted abolition as his sacred vocation, Green wished to be judged by his efforts "for dear Humanity's sake." Thus he first threw himself into battle as abolition's axe, then wielded it in the form of his school and his students, and finally turned it upon his fellow citizens and comrades-in-arms who had either retreated from the ramparts of primitive abolitionism or muted the voice of conscience with orthodox pieties.

I am not sure that I would have wanted Green as a neighbor, yet a world without his kind would be the poorer. His moral intensity bored with equal fervor upon friend and foe. With "luminous logic and merciless sarcasm," in the words of fellow abolitionist Henry B. Stanton, Green often made his contemporaries uncomfortable, no matter their station in life or ideological disposition.[8] In attempting to apply Christian ethics to the great moral issues of antebellum America, he did not wrestle with the question of whether he had a right to mix religion and politics. Those of us who suffer from the modern tendency to reduce religion to private and fragmented systems of ultimate meaning will have difficulty in understanding Green's world view, and Green's habit of subsuming all societal problems to the "Moral Government of God" would raise a host of complicated constitutional questions if pursued as public policy today.

Green practiced what Lee Benson once described as the Yankee "holy enterprise of minding other people's business."[9] He was a professional reformer who found his life's calling in the crusade against slavery and assumed that everyone else should demonstrate a zeal for righteousness equal to his own. When our neighbor dares to act upon the immutable promptings of conscience and expects us to do the same, there is a tendency to retreat behind the parody of the evangelistic sermon attributed to W. H. Auden, summarized in the line, "We are in the world to save all the people, but what all the other people are in the world for, we haven't the faintest idea."

The "other people" in Beriah Green's world included not only the slaveholders but Northern theocrats, church people, politicians, abolitionist colleagues, and, most significantly, African Americans, slave and free. Those bound by "the cord of caste" did not question his moral intensity, even when he drifted into an ideological conventicle of his own making and was deemed an oddity among his fellows. Blacks who as fugitives from "the peculiar institution" enjoyed the safety of the "Old Hive," Green's home in Whitesboro, or who as students earned an education at Oneida Institute, celebrated the nobility of the man, not his failures. His cantankerous personality struck them as justifiable holy zeal. That Green should feel so bound with them as to suffer willingly on their behalf went unquestioned by the blacks who knew him. Even when he became a self-professed misanthrope, they did not doubt his motivation, commitment, or sanity. Though the historian must be open to multiple explanations of human behavior, one is hardly obligated to explain away Beriah Green's moral fervor, given the plight of those for whom he fought and spoke.

A New England boyhood and education steeped in wakeful industry and earnest piety prepared the ground for Green's rebellion against the notion that one must accept societal injustice as a token of the fallen state of the world. His abolitionist awakening came in Ohio's Western Reserve region, a cultural extension of New England. Later, in Oneida County, another little New England, Green successfully transformed the Institute into a model biracial society. After its demise, he joined with others in the Burned-over District in an attempt at Bible politics. By the 1850s, he was "a voice in the wilderness," crying out for a restoration of civil or human government upon the basis of a theocratic model. The latter decades of Green's life, less well documented in the extant sources, are the most difficult to chronicle and understand. We will move with care across the inland ground of Green's mind and soul during the years when he had ascended to a "transcendental plane," as his brother Jonathan described it, and became "an amazing novelty—a very monster, to be classed with nobody knows whom or what."[10]

Green's sojourn from an orthodox New England religious and academic background to the radical theological views of his years in the Burned-over District seems to confirm Whitney Cross's observation: "Here appears the grand paradox of ultraism. Its truest, most consistent, most fanatical exponents, following the logic of events and of their faith, wound up at the opposite pole of religious belief."[11] Green was perhaps most faithful to his evangelical roots when he pursued his errand of mercy without regard to the restraints of theological dogma. Once committed to abolitionism as his sacred vocation, he pursued it with an elemental intensity which cannot be adequately explained except on its own terms. I have assumed that Beriah Green was as he appeared to those who knew him well, one of those rare souls who witnesses to the best within us while not immune to the tendency to want us to see the world through the zealot's eye.

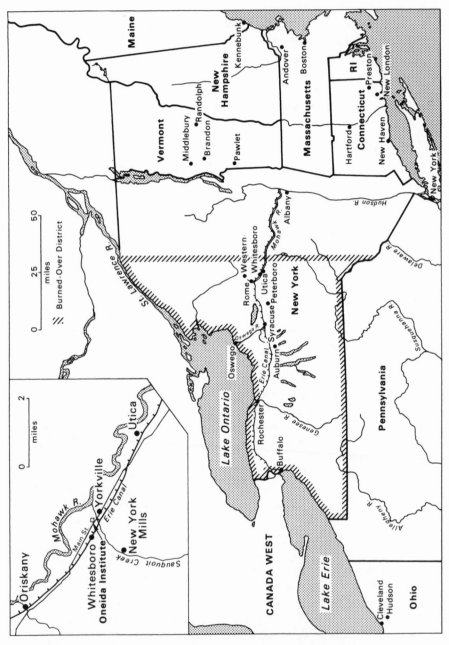

Beriah Green's reform career carried him from New England to the Western Reserve and then into the Burned-over District of central New York.
Inset: Oneida Institute, Whitesboro, and vicinity.

ABOLITION'S AXE

1

FORGED IN NEW ENGLAND

Beriah Green did not pick up abolition's axe until his late thirties, when he was far from the New England of his boyhood. However, he displayed the markings of being fired in New England's cultural forge throughout his seventy-nine years, and he honed, used, and eventually broke himself in the fight against slavery in cultural regions where much from his New England heritage had been transplanted.

The brief and only autobiographical remarks Green ever published begin, "I was born in New England on the lean soil and among the rocks and hills and streams of Connecticut. My infancy and childhood were spent among those who found wakeful industry, well conducted and strict frugality resolutely maintained, requisite to a livelihood."[1] We are truly pinched for specifics regarding Green's early years. No personal correspondence is extant from the New England period, and we have only scraps of testimony regarding his youthful character. Thus what follows necessarily draws in large measure on general portrayals of New England family life, education, religion, and culture during Beriah's formative years.

Genealogical searches, complicated by the commonness of the surname and by the existence of multiple Beriah Greens, have produced fairly trustworthy information on our Beriah's ancestry.[2] His mother Elizabeth (1771-1840) is thought to have been a sixth generation descendant of Elder William Brewster, who sailed on the Mayflower. The only daughter of Jonathan and Hannah Smith, she married Beriah Green (1774-1865) in 1793. His father, also named Beriah, fell into British hands while at sea during the Revolutionary War and never returned. Our Beriah's father built chairs, cabinets, clocks, and other household items, some of which survive among antique collectors. After Beriah's birth on March 24, 1795, at Preston, Connecticut, his father set up shop near the Lebanon, Connecticut, town meeting-house. After the addition of a second child, brother Jonathan in 1796, Beriah lived at Preston with his maternal grandparents from "eighteen months to fourteen years, nearly all the time."[3] Because of the itinerant nature of the cabinet-making trade, Beriah's parents moved from Lebanon to Windham to Lisbon, all towns in eastern Connecticut. Three sisters were added to the family during these years.

Moral earnestness emerges as the most important factor in Green's recollections of his New England ancestors and their world view. He described his mother as a "fair woman, very remarkable for her quiet, unobtrusive, tireless industry." She spun, wove, washed, baked, and mended, assuming, so her son recalled, "such responsibilities and labors as might well have occupied two or three woman." Elizabeth Green was a "still, modest, retiring woman," deeply pious and accustomed to attending religious meetings. Insofar as her son knew, she was "contented with the place allotted her" in life. Beriah recalled Grandmother Hannah Smith as vigorous, religious, industrious and upright. After her death in 1823, Grandfather Jonathan Smith, remembered as "a mild, quiet, religious man," sought out a new life in Connecticut's Western Reserve area, in what is now northeastern Ohio.

Beriah's father had already left Connecticut, in 1805. He drove an ox cart to Vermont and settled in the vicinity of Randolph, leaving, we suspect, some of his family, and certainly his eldest son in Preston. In 1810 he moved west to Pawlet in the Green Mountains, where the entire family was reunited. A declining regional economy and the immigrant fever eventually caused him also to move to the Western Reserve, where he settled at Twinsburg, Ohio. Small in physical stature, as were most males on the paternal side of the Green family tree, Beriah's father stood tall in his son's eyes for moral uprightness, physical energy, and practical piety.[4]

If the character of Beriah's childhood can be deduced from the temperament of the mature man, one suspects that he was schooled in strict self-discipline amidst material austerity. The future abolitionist and educator remembered that he was "inured to manual labor" at an early age.[5] Hard work had moral as well as economic benefits, for doing one's duty, even as a child, evidenced godliness. Historians of New England child-raising practices have chronicled the transition by 1800 from the older authoritarian Puritan style to a more evangelical one. Earlier generations attempted to combat the presumed propensity for evil in children by exterior constraints and punishment. Evangelical households stressed the inner life and integrity of the person. Children were to grow in faith and knowledge; their own conscience, not caning, was the route to responsible behavior.[6] Since Beriah spent his childhood at the knee of Grandmother Hannah Smith, perhaps he encountered attitudes and practices from the older school of thought.

Church folk on the small farms and in the villages of southeastern Connecticut took diligent care of the needs of the soul. Piety, self-reliance, and hatred of sin were the marks of the true Christian. Religious instruction began early. When about eight or nine, children were expected to show signs of "early piety" and to become subjects of "hopeful conversion." The post-Revolutionary inhabitants of Preston, situated among the irregular valleys and rounded hills of the eastern highlands, belonged to Connecticut's "Standing Order." Disestablishment of Congregationalism as the official religion would not come until 1818.

Nevertheless, much had changed since the days of the old Puritans. Almost three-quarters of the churches east of the Connecticut River had fallen before the mighty tide of the Great Awakening set in motion by George Whitefield, the Grand Itinerant of the 1740s and 1750s. Area preachers generally followed in the steps of Jonathan Edwards. Known as New Lights, they sought to save the Connecticut Valley by infusing traditional church structures with experimental religion or "vital piety." By stressing individual responsibility for "the New Birth" wrought in conversion, instead of the traditional theology of salvation via the covenanted community of the religious elect, they contributed to the decline of the old order.

New Divinity preachers arose in the 1790s to revive the fortunes of the evangelical movement, which had flagged during the War for Independence. In the Second Awakening, the churches in and around Preston solidified their separatist identity. New Divinity clergy held Samuel Hopkins in high esteem. Green tells us that as a youth he was taught to repeat Hopkins' name "with veneration."[7] In *System of Doctrines* (1793), Hopkins codified the Edwardian legacy for a generation that wished to face the future of the young republic with more optimism about human possibilities than the older Calvinist worldview afforded. Hopkins equated sin with self-love and virtue with disinterested benevolence and taught that conversion necessarily led to demonstrations of one's new birth in Christ through practical reform.

Green also learned to appreciate Hopkinsian theology through his exposure to the views of Nathanael Emmons. Emmons championed New Divinity ideas for more than half a century from a rural parish at Franklin, Massachusetts. Known as the "Farmer Metaphysician," he asserted that sin is in the sinning. It is an act of will and not, as the Old Calvinists taught, the result of a prior disposition or an inherently sinful nature. Here again the emphasis was on individual responsibility. Emmons' idiosyncratic lifestyle and original mind portended Green's own. Beriah remembered listening to preachers expounding Emmons' pragmatic Calvinism "eagerly and gladly."[8]

Though Beriah came of age under the influence of New Divinity preachers, we miss any reference in his recollections to a conversion experience akin to the kind sought by Charles Finney in the Burned-over District in the 1820s. By the time of Green's coming-of-age, New Englanders generally viewed conversion as a gradual process. The young were more likely to become communicant members of a local congregation after a period of "growth in grace," rather than as the consequence of a dramatic and instantaneous conversion experience. Nurtured in a pious household, Beriah must have taken in religion as naturally as he did nourishment of the body. Like many who championed social reform in post-Revolutionary America, he grew to accept the world as neither hopelessly profane nor wholly sacred. It was a battleground on which the regenerate fought the good fight of faith.

The paucity of primary sources pertaining to Green's youth precludes a satisfactory assessment of the state of his religious development when he left Connecticut for the hill country of western Vermont. He was, however, to find familiar forms of piety and practice in Pawlet, a small village some twenty miles southwest of Rutland in the Green Mountains. Most settlers in the longitudinal valleys presided over by forested hills hailed from Connecticut and were of the New Divinity persuasion. They organized Congregational churches, as did the inhabitants of Pawlet in 1781, and struggled to overcome the paroxysms of radical sectarianism so pronounced in the 1770s and 1780s. When Beriah rejoined the family in 1810, the region was enjoying "the zenith of prosperity and the flowering of its Antifederalist culture."[9] Pawlet boasted the Pawlet Academy, a manual labor school in which young men and women combined book learning with physical exercise in useful work. Beriah was put to work in his father's cabinet and chair-making shop but may have attended the academy when not needed at home. At about eighteen, he became an apprentice in a machine shop.

While learning the machinist's trade, Beriah mused about a higher calling. The vocational question ranked second in importance only to the search for religious assurance among New England youth. In contrast to their fathers, these products of evangelical households had more vocational options and therefore more personal wrestling over which course to pursue. Unlike the earlier generations, even young men from poor families could aspire to college due to the emergence of provincial schools and the democratization of higher education. Individuals who evidenced an aptitude for study and pious habits were encouraged to "fit for college." Those who expressed interest in the ministry were encouraged to seek the requisite college and seminary training.

In 1816 Beriah went off to prepare for college at the Kimball Union Academy in Plainfield, New Hampshire. The earliest extant document in Green's handwriting is a set of five resolutions (*"Proposita"*) and a brief prayer which he posted above his desk at the academy. We can image that Green took these promises, here translated from the original Latin, quite seriously.

I decree that in the study of Mathematics, I will remember each rule in order.

I desire knowledge of the Sciences, which I attend to daily, especially the useful ones.

I will go in the place [room] of no student on some pretext without business.

I will go for a walk at least twice on every clear day to preserve the health of the body and by breathing [hard] to restore the mind.

I [will] look to temperance in eating my food. I will preserve moderation in all things.

Make these resolutions, O Heavenly Father, for my benefit, I pray thee, at length.

Watch over [them] until change or necessity makes them unneedful.

After Beriah left for Middlebury College in 1817, his roommate retrieved the *Proposita* and preserved them with a note that Green had been "a faithful student & eminent Christian" while at the Union Academy.[10]

Chartered in 1800 with encouragement from President Timothy Dwight of Yale, Middlebury College was established in opposition to the University of Vermont, where Ethan Allen's deism had taken root. Middlebury stood solidly, Green testified, "in the course usually preferred in the religious circles to which I belonged."[11] It offered a traditional classical curriculum infused with New Divinity piety and theology.

Exactly when Beriah made the decision to prepare for the ministry is not known, though it likely occurred during his stay at Middlebury. He was doubtless motivated by the same forces which propelled so many young men from evangelical households into the ministry. Parents, clergy, college mentors, and their peers impressed the belief upon them that a meaningful life involved doing something for the betterment of the human condition. Many a pious and bright youth from the farms of New England sought personal fulfillment and a resolution of the vocational question by preparing for duty with the American Board of Commissioners for Foreign Missions.

The missionary spirit was strong at Middlebury College during Beriah's student days. He graduated in August 1819 with a B.A., the valedictorian of a class of nineteen, with the intent of seeking advanced theological preparation for the foreign mission field.[12] Beriah might have sought out Yale, but it did not have a divinity school until 1822. Princeton Seminary, founded in 1812, belonged to the Presbyterians. Harvard College, the mother lode of New England Congregationalism, no longer attracted the orthodox who opposed its Unitarian leanings. Thus Beriah decided upon Andover Seminary, located in Andover, Massachusetts, north of Boston.

Green enrolled in the fall of 1819 to find the seminary soundly established as a school for those of evangelical disposition. Founded by an alliance of New Divinity and Old Calvinist leaders in 1808, Andover was hailed as the "West Point of Orthodoxy." It attracted New Divinity students who wished to spread the Gospel at home and abroad. A group of the more zealous organized a missionary society which evolved into the American Board of Commissioners for Foreign Missions. Scores of Andover graduates took evangelical Christianity and the New England cultural ethos to the spiritually benighted on the American frontier. They were especially instrumental in shaping the New England character of regions important to Beriah's future abolitionist career—the Western Reserve of northeastern Ohio and the Burned-over District of upstate New York. Andover boasted heavy orthodox artillery on its faculty. Moses Stuart, an important ideological foe to Green in later years, commanded the latest in German biblical criticism but used it to buttress orthodox doctrine. Leonard Woods had already earned high marks among New Divinity clergy for his public opposition to the Unitarian heresies of Harvard and for his defense of the views of Nathanael Emmons.

Pinched by poverty, Green had to quit a regular course of study after a year or so to teach at Phillip's Academy, a preparatory school in Andover. He very likely continued his seminary studies on a private basis, perhaps attending lectures when possible. This was not unusual, for the Andover curriculum at the time allowed students to matriculate and, in essence, graduate on the basis of private study and counsel with the faculty. He soon found trying to teach and study at the same time physically and emotionally debilitating. In a letter written in support of the Society for Promoting Manual Labor in Literary Institutions, Beriah commented that he customarily took no recreation, studied late, and rose early. He tried to regain the full use of his mental powers through vigorous exercise in the wood-pile. "I passed from my books and my desk, 'on the run', to the saw and the axe. Whether in exercise or in study, I felt continually hurried. Every nerve was strained. I did not pause to inquire whether I was well or sick—sinking or rising."[13] The new regimen was to no avail. Green began to have problems with his eyes. When he tried to read, he noticed "a strange appearance in the atmosphere" between his eyes and the printed page. Alarmed, he threw down his books and fled to Boston for medical advice and assistance.

The Boston physician, in keeping with the primitive medical therapy of the day, tried the universal pallative. He treated Beriah with leeches, blisters, and "the blue pill." The patient's condition worsened. Now dark spots, "some of them fantastical enough," appeared before Beriah's eyes. So he threw away the leeches and pill box and adopted, so he recalled, "such methods as might subserve my health generally."[14] He found salvation cutting firewood. Eventually his nerves became "orderly and strong" and his vision cleared. This experience taught Green the singular lesson that physical exercise was as necessary as study to any future reformer or missionary. He withdrew from Andover Seminary in 1821 for fear of precipitating another breakdown.

Though not a graduate of Andover Seminary in the formal sense, Beriah had demonstrated his readiness for ministry. He was eager for a call and a place to begin a family. In January of 1821, he married Marcia Deming, whom he had courted while a student at Middlebury College. Little is known of her background, except that she was born in 1798 and was from a pious and respectable Middlebury family. The young couple waited upon an assignment from the American Board of Commissioners for Foreign Missions, but none was immediately forthcoming. Beriah accepted a temporary call to a small church on Long Island and then became acting pastor of a congregation at East Lyme, Connecticut. There the candidate and his wife rejoiced over the birth of their first child, Samuel, on May 9, 1822. More than fifty years later, the father recalled the happy event: "It was a sunny morning in 1822. I was so glad—I hope thankful, that the cherished young mother lived thro' the struggle—was still spared to me and with a Son—our Son—our Firstborn at her bosom."[15] It would not be long before Green had cause to grieve over "the cherished young mother."

Beriah's health deteriorated again, this time to the point of spitting blood. A doctor pronounced him "within reach of consumption, or gloomy dyspepsia." His friends regarded him "near the end" of his race.[16] Once again he sought an antidote in physical exercise. He turned to a wood lathe in an unoccupied shop. After long sessions away from his study, he recovered sufficiently to conduct an occasional worship service. But this brush with permanent debility or perhaps even death scared Green to the point that he concluded that his physical constitution simply was not up to the rigors of a foreign mission field, so he withdrew from the auspices of the American Board.

The First Congregational Church of Brandon, Vermont, some twenty miles north of Pawlet, needed a permanent minister. Green accepted an invitation to preach a trial sermon in the summer of 1822. As they would in the decades to come, his oratorical skills stood him in good stead. Beriah returned to East Lyme, gathered up his possessions and family, and brought everything some two hundred miles back to Brandon in a plain, one-horse wagon.[17] He now had a place to exercise ministry, though he admitted that it was but a remote village in the Vermont hills. The final step in Green's credentialing for the public ministry took place on April 16, 1823. The Reverend John Hough, Professor of Divinity at Middlebury College, came to Brandon to deliver the ordination sermon. He warned Beriah that clergymen who honestly and forthrightly declared what they believed to be "the voice of Heaven" should not expect popular acclaim.[18]

Hough's admonition reflects the decline in status with which New England clergy had to deal in the 1820s. Occupants of the sacred office in the days of high Puritanism exercised both pastoral and magisterial authority. Their high social standing derived from their role as mainstays of communal order among God's covenanted people. After the Revolutionary War, however, the clergy's role as the guardians of communal order became less central because of the rise of the politics of party. With the rise of denominationalism and decline of state support, as Donald Scott has argued, the New England clergy experienced a transition "from office to profession."[19] No longer able to rest comfortably with an ascribed status, preachers had to establish their importance by virtue of individual earnestness. In short, the clergy of the early 1820s stood this side of the fissure which separated the world of Yankee individualism from the organic, heirarchical Puritan state.

Green felt uneasy about the public devaluation of the ministerial office. He did not want to be taken as a pious anachronism by his fellows. He bristled when a joiner, amused by Green's mistake in describing a certain tool, made the observation, "Ministers have all kinds of sense except *common* sense." Green felt that he had as much right as "worldly wise men" to comment on secular affairs and reminded readers of the *Vermont Chronicle* of the Puritan preachers whose counsel was sought by all in the community. He waxed indignant after reading a letter from a Philadelphia judge who averred that the clergy had become mere custodians of theological mysteries, and he attacked the disciples of David Hume, the Scottish empiricist, for their assertions that theology was nothing but "mysterious jargon."[20] Emotionally at least, Green clung to the office of the seventeenth century Puritan divine who could pilot the fragile bark of community order through life's stormy seas with unquestioned authority.

Though Beriah bemoaned the transformation of the ministry from office to profession, he acknowledged that the changing times demanded a new style of ministry. He threw himself into the Brandon pastorate with the nervous energy and compulsion for ministerial excellence of one who recognized that what once passed for clerical authority no longer prevailed. When overtaxed, he took to the woodpile, interspersing stints with the axe with sessions, standing, at his desk. He preferred the study to tramping about Brandon, calling on parishoners. Green once wrote that he "set his face like flint" toward needless interruptions and responded coldly to idle questions from those whom he described as experts "in the sublime enterprise of wasting time."[21] He held a high view of the pulpit and carefully prepared every sermon. On the Sabbath, at least, he would have a captive audience, though even here he recognized that the congregation would not be content with any kind of preaching. Excellence had to be demonstrated.

Green acknowledged that parishoners no longer appreciated sermons with their "wearisome monotony and disgusting tone." An effective preacher could not rely simply on the majesty of the pulpit: he needed to interest and persuade, to speak "with pleasure to himself and acceptance to his hearers." He counseled other clergy to redeem their time through diligent study of the Hebrew and Greek originals and regular use of the best biblical commentaries.[22] When actually delivering the product of these long and careful mental exertions, the preacher was to dispense with the old, spiritually deadening method of reading manuscripts.

Green counseled against the use of elaborate outlines and clever but opaque classical illusions and urged fellow homileticians to adopt a natural direct style, not unlike "the manner in which shrewd children express their wishes." "You may tell," he admonished his clerical peers, "of *deducing consequences from premises by rigid and irresistible ratiocination,* and some simpleton may stand aghast at your college learning; but those who hunger and thirst for 'the bread of life,' will break their teeth upon the bones you are dealing out."[23] In recommending the free use of Saxon English and the extemporary pulpit method, Green did not mean to exhalt a careless, loose, or vulgar style. He bemoaned the reluctance of some publishers to accept books of good sermons while they catered to a public which, in his words, ran "mad after the light literature which is now-a-days afloat in the form of novels, 'keep-sakes,' [and] ladies magazines."[24] But Green recognized that his hearers were also consumers, hungry souls who were to be fed. "The extempore preacher," he urged, "takes the posture of transacting business with his audience."[25] The plainest Christian could discern both sloth and artificiality in the pulpit. Good preaching taxed one's physical and emotional energies.

Changes in Green's domestic circle added to the emotional burdens of his Brandon pastorate. On January 18, 1824, his wife gave birth to their second child, Ann Parker Green. Ann was not quite two or her brother

Samuel four when their mother became seriously ill. On March 21, 1826, Beriah wrote in great alarm to Hannah Deming, his mother-in-law: "We *do* think, my dear wife very, very sick. We seriously fear she is on the brink of the grave."[26] He requested a consulting physician from Middlebury, but Marcia rapidly declined and died ten days later. Her husband buried her in the graveyard behind the Brandon church. Six months later he remarried. Daraxa Foote, a native of Middlebury, bore Beriah two children during the remaining years at Brandon, with five more to come in subsequent years. Though we know nothing of the exact circumstances of their courtship and very little about Daxara, we can surmise that this second marriage was thought neither hasty or unwise. A clergyman with two young children and many responsibilities needed a helpmate. Beriah was already extending his influence beyond Brandon and could continue to do so only with someone to manage affairs in the parsonage while he promoted the work of the church.

Green collected subscriptions for and helped organize auxiliaries of the American Board of Commissioners for Foreign Missions in neighboring congregations. In 1826 he told the members of the Rutland County Missionary Society that *their* best interests could only be promoted by the performance of their duty to the heathen.[27] In other words, the fulfillment of Christian duty reflected on the state of grace of the actor. This theme, later popularized by the holiness churches and essential to an understanding of Green's abolitionism, had emerged in the new evangelical understanding of Christian conversion. In the older Puritan community, the saints were recognized by their organic link to the covenant between God and the chosen people. Now Christians sought full assurance of God's work of grace in them as *individuals* through the exercise of duty in a fallen world. Confirmation of their conversion came in proportion to the performance of "disinterested benevolence" among the heathen abroad as well as the unchurched on the American frontier. All Christians, Green argued, were bound together in one great evangelical enterprise. Professed Christians in all walks of life were duty-bound to support the brave souls who left for foreign fields with their prayers and their purses.[28]

Beriah's brother Jonathan, about two years his junior, was one of several members in the Brandon congregation who heeded the call to foreign missions. He graduated from Andover Seminary in September 1827 and, while waiting a specific charge, returned to Brandon, where he organized a Sunday school and stood for ordination in October. Beriah preached the sermon, urging his brother to cultivate piety, zeal, and "disinterested, well-directed labors." Echoing the admonition received at his own ordination, he warned Jonathan to expect "injurious treatment" from those whose "love of lucre, impurity, and self-complacency set them against all holy endeavors."[29] Jonathan and his wife Theodotia sailed from Boston in

November with the Third Company of the American Board bound for the Sandwich Islands and arrived at Honolulu in March 1828. Jonathan became known as the "father of wheat culture" in the islands and was an educator and abolitionist in his own right.[30]

We can only speculate on Beriah's emotions as he bade farewell to his brother. Perhaps it was with some envy, for his post in Brandon was not as much of a leap into the inspiring unknown as was Jonathan's venture. Did he regret having resigned from the American Board? We suspect so, for he compensated by engaging in a host of voluntary enterprises in which Christians who could not serve in foreign fields labored mightily to redeem their own communities and the nation at large for the Lord. The evangelical network of voluntary agencies, products of the new ministerial consciousness, became Beriah's surrogate mission station. Even in the local parish, one as small and remote as Brandon, a clergyman of the 1820s could assume a larger and translocal ministry. He could seek to influence the world by advocating support of mission, education, tract, temperance, and Sabbath school societies. Parish clergy with the requisite intellectual gifts and sufficient energy could reach out to evangelical audiences by writing tracts and essays for the religious press.[31]

Green both acted as an agent for several agencies and wrote extensively to support the "benevolent empire" of interdenominational organizations. On behalf of the American Home Mission Society, he urged that New England's evangelical emissaries fan out in the Great Valley of the Mississippi and not rest from their labors until every settlement had become a bastion of virtue and piety. He organized monthly "concerts of prayer" within his and neighboring churches. At these midweek meetings, the faithful prayed that God would accomplish the millennial age. He also spoke and wrote on behalf of the American Education Society. Organized as a national agency in 1826, it sought to assist the many pauper students who were willing to study for the ministry. Green cast an eye to the plight of pastorless emigrants from New England in the West and called upon his readers and hearers to "urge forward with irresistible force and accelerated movement the triumphal car of our Messiah" by supporting the education society.[32]

While participation in the national agencies placed a local pastor's name before a wide audience, congregations of the New Divinity persuasion in the 1820s were most apt to judge clerical competence by the ability of their preachers to conduct revivals and garner new members. Green agreed in principal with the need for revivals, urging in several published sermons that sinners repent and seek the Lord while they still had opportunity.[33] According to a local historian who drew on the memories of individuals who knew Green, he initially impressed the congregation as "a young man of much promise and an interesting speaker." But he failed to light the revival fires. Brandon's previous resident pastor had brought in more than 120 converts during a revival in 1816 and 1817. During the whole of Green's stay, slightly more than six years, there were only 25 additions by letter and profession. This gain was almost totally offset by 24 excommunications, an unusually high ratio. We can surmise that Green's strict discipline and either neglect of the pastoral aspect of his ministry or lack of interest in promoting revivals lost him the confidence of the congregation. We find the following epitaph for his Brandon, Vermont, ministry in an early Rutland Country history: "He was more a preacher than a pastor, and remained here a trifle more than six years, being dismissed on the 11th day of May, 1829."[34]

While serving at Brandon, Green became more widely known through his published essays and sermons. He tells us that he received a number of overtures to accept a professorship in "one and another theological seminary." Several congregations in New England also tried to woo him away from Vermont's Green Mountains. He finally settled in 1829 upon what he termed a "distinctly orthodox" church in Kennebunk, Maine, situated south of Portland near the Atlantic coast.[35] He remained there less than a year, and then, at the urging of President Charles B. Storrs of Western Reserve College, in Hudson, Ohio, accepted a call to a newly created professorship in Sacred Literature, which also entailed serving as college chaplain. Had Green, then nearly thirty-five, foreseen the firestorm which would engulf him at Western Reserve, he might have had second thoughts. But in the summer of 1830, as his family packed for the long trek to Ohio, all was calm. William Lloyd Garrison was still in Baltimore and the nation slept.

Though the primary sources are limited, the picture here drawn of Green's New England period reveals nothing of the radical abolitionism to come. Nevertheless, the outlines are in place. As he later asserted, he had been "decided, wide-awake, outspoken" on behalf of the principles to which he subscribed and the organizations he supported.[36] He possessed the true reformer's confidence that divine providence and human history course together. He believed that individuals who demonstrate willing obedience to a holy errand help to work out the divine will in this vale of tears. He understood that life entailed struggle, be it against the weaknesses of one's own mind and body or against those who opposed the exercise of Christian duty. The character traits forged in New England—a sensitive conscience, intellectual acuteness, wakeful industry, moral earnestness, an inclination to look for opposition, and a fear of nervous prostration—all became more pronounced in the tumultuous decades of Green's anti-slavery career.

Environment may explain as much about why Green did not become an abolitionist while in New England as it does to explain why he would on the Western Reserve. The aggressive anti-slavery sentiment which occasioned, for example, the formation of the Connecticut Anti-Slavery Society in 1790, had dissipated prior to Green's formative years. The American Colonization Society, founded in Washington, D.C., in December 1816, when Beriah was preparing for college, served as a surrogate for abolitionism and eased New England's conscience. Samuel Hopkins, known as "the father of African colonization," viewed colonization as the perfect nexus between social and religious reform. By sending Afro-Americans to Liberia, white Christians furthered missions and did something about slavery, or so they thought. In actuality, the colonizationists were motivated by anxiety over the growing free black population, especially in the border states, and, like Thomas Jefferson, had concluded that a biracial society was impossible. Green did not take an active role in Colonization Society activities, but he urged church members to read colonizationist publications in order to provide informed support.[37]

Historians have sought in specific psychological distresses and family problems an explanation for why some and not others made abolitionism their vocation. Though this approach can prove interesting, there is, in the final analysis, no accounting for individuality. Ronald Walters reminds us that the anti-slavery immediatists were "less unique in their anxieties and hopes than in the embodiment they found for those anxieties and hopes."[38] Having acknowledged this, we can still place Beriah Green within the general portrait of future abolitionists. In an analysis of the New England cultural impact on its youth, Bertram Wyatt-Brown has persuasively argued that "almost by definition, missionaries and reformers were untranquil souls" and has listed some of the formative influences they shared:

> *a common upbringing under strict, orthodox, evangelical parents; a conversion experience of rich personal meaning; a sense of special destiny; the product of compulsive application to study; a post-parental subjection to pious, admired superiors and elder friends who stirred religious ambitions; and finally a common decision to seek a risk-taking course for the sake of God and personal fulfillment.*[39]

Brother Jonathan found his course early; eventually the missionary became an abolitionist. Beriah too had the missionary disposition, though he would never sail the high seas or roam the American frontier. He was, as it were, still a missionary awaiting assignment in 1830. Not until he picked up the abolitionist's axe on the Western Reserve and applied it to the root-evil of American society would he too set off into a glorious, risk-filled unknown.

On the evening of August 16, 1826, the Reverend Beriah Green of Brandon, Vermont, stood before the associated alumni of Middlebury College. Commencement that day had capped the college careers of yet another crop of young men from New England's farms and villages. Green reminded them that the purpose of education was to unite vigor of intellect with moral affections. Since graduating from Middlebury, he had learned something of the subtle interplay between the mind and what he termed "the animal spirits." The mind and body worked in tandem; neglect of the one affected the other. He urged the new graduates not to venture into public life without "a system of operation" by which the mental and physical might be disciplined and brought into harmony.[40]

Not a man of wealth, from no family of influence, living at a time when the ministry had passed from office to profession, Beriah Green possessed but one weapon in the fight against slavery and racism—his mind, and by extension, his voice and his pen. But as men and women of superior intellect and sensitive conscience have always discovered, the mind is encapsulated in a mortal, often fragile, husk. To protect and preserve the powers of the mind, Beriah Green began early to resort to one of the oldest of human tools. "The axe has always been my favorite instrument," he wrote in October 1832, from the Western Reserve. "Were I, as I am not, a poet, I would celebrate its virtues in song."[41]

2

AXE-HONING ON THE WESTERN RESERVE

olklore has it that if an Ohio town erected a Congregational church and a college, it was of New England origin. But if it had a Presbyterian church and a distillery, it had been settled by Virginians. Hudson, located about twenty-five miles southeast of Cleveland, bore a distinctly New England character when Beriah Green arrived in 1830. Founded in 1799 by David Hudson, a native of Connecticut, the town emerged as a singular seat of piety, learning, and good order in the vast wilderness of the Western Reserve. Most inhabitants were transplanted New Englanders. Others hailed from western New York, an important intermediate stop on the cultural trail linking New England with northeastern Ohio. Sometimes called "New Connecticut," the Western Reserve exhibited many of the marks of cultural domestication by the time the Green family arrived from Maine. With its commons, Congregational church, stores, and substantial homes, Hudson was more like the New England ideal than many towns in Connecticut and Massachusetts.

Pioneering families decided early to build schools rather than send their first-born back to New England. In 1805 the Erie Literary Society opened an academy in Burton, a village about twenty miles northeast of Hudson. Because of swampy conditions, the trustees determined to move the school to a more elevated site and purchased land about a third of a mile northeast of Hudson, near the farm and home of David Hudson. In April 1826, the local citizenry celebrated the chartering of Western Reserve College and the laying of the cornerstone of the first building, known as Middle College. Trustee Stephen I. Bradstreet intoned with predictable hyperbole: "The forests have yielded their places to cultivated farms; in these very spots, where but yesterday the fierce sons of nature prowled in all the wanton sport of savage wilderness, are now spacious mansions, elegant churches, and seminaries of learning."[1] Bradstreet's rhetoric notwithstanding, Western Reserve College took shape in fits and starts. Its entrance requirements and curriculum were modeled after Yale College, but students were required to earn their keep and develop moral character by performing manual labor.

The trustees appointed Charles Backus Storrs Professor of Sacred Theology in 1828. A Massachusetts native and contemporary of Green at Andover Theological Seminary, Storrs settled in Ohio in 1822 after a stint as an evangelist in South Carolina, where he saw slavery at close range. In 1829, Elizur Wright, Jr., accepted the professorship of Mathematics and Natural Philosophy. Born in Connecticut in 1804, a Phi Beta Kappa Yale graduate and former colporteur for the American Tract Society, Elizur decided upon teaching rather than the ministry after duty at Lawrence Academy, Groton, Massachusetts. The third faculty member present in 1830, when Green arrived, was the Reverend Rufus Nutting, Professor of Ancient Languages and head of the library, who had graduated from Dartmouth.

Hudson's *Observer and Telegraph* hailed the election of the Green to the faculty as "peculiarly auspicious."[2] The college needed someone competent in biblical studies and the sacred languages. The name of the thirty-five year old preacher and scholar had come before the trustees upon the recommendation of Storrs, then president *pro tem*. Storrs felt that Green's expertise would make it possible to attract young men interested in the ministry. With a population of nearly one hundred thousand, many of whom were said to live in abounding wickedness, the vast Western Reserve tract demanded pastors and missionaries. President Storrs spoke of the challenge before Western Reserve College in an October address reported in the Hudson *Observer and Telegraph*. "At the East it is regarded as the hope of the West and the only institution in the great Western Valley which is destined to rank with the first grade of our eastern colleges."[3] Local boosters bragged that Storrs fledgling enterprise would become "the Yale of the West." Beriah, his wife, and four children took up residence in Hudson late in the summer of 1830, barely giving him time to prepare for the beginning of the college's fifth academic year. Green found a house large enough to board several of the theological students and soon took up his classroom duties.

In 1804 and 1807 the state of Ohio had introduced various Black Codes in order to restrict the rights of free blacks to settle, own property, and testify against whites in the courts. The Western Reserve generally had a reputation for being more "pro-Negro" than other parts of Ohio, but the inhabitants viewed colonization as a reasonable remedy to the problems attendant to a growing population of free blacks in the North. In the 1820s, Storrs led in the formation of a branch of the American Colonization Society at Ravenna, and Elizur Wright, Jr., wrote favorably concerning the Society for the *Observer and Telegraph*, which was partly owned by the Portage Presbytery and edited by Warren Isham, an ardent colonizationist. The college trustees and area clergy, like their counterparts in New England, were comfortable with colonization as a surrogate for abolitionism.

Hudson's inhabitants, however, kept a watchful eye on events back east. Isham's *Observer and Telegraph* carried a story about William Lloyd Garrison's imprisonment in Baltimore in April 1830 on charges of libel. Garrison, then co-editor of *The Genius of Universal Emancipation*, had been sued for accusing Francis Todd of Massachusetts of allowing his ships to transport slaves to New Orleans. Conversations in the religious circles of the Western Reserve began turning on Garrison's character and the merits of his case. In September, just as Green was settling in, Isham's paper gave space to Garrison's prospectus for the publication of *The Liberator*, the opening salvo in the attack upon the colonization enterprise by the immediatists, advocates of rapid and complete emancipation.[4]

It was not long before Garrison's paper reached Western Reserve College. After the Christmas recess of Green's first term, Isaac Bigelow, a student from Massachusetts, returned to campus to tell of an interview with Garrison and to distribute copies of *The Liberator*. Bigelow called upon President Storrs and, seeing a copy of Garrison's paper already in his possession, asked him for an opinion of its views. Storrs is said to have replied, "I do not see how they can be refuted."[5] Storrs met with Wright and Green in the following weeks to discuss Garrison's attack on the American Colonization Society. On February 9, 1831, Storrs delivered his inaugural address, in which he invoked the spirit of the English abolitionist William Wilbeforce and asked, "What shall remove from the vitals of the nation the oppressive load which the guilt of slave-holding has imposed?"[6]

Interest in the debate between the immediatists and the colonizationists accelerated. Trustees, faculty, and students began to choose sides. The slave insurrection led by Nat Turner of Virginia in July of 1831 hardened conservative opposition. Those inclined toward Garrison's views planned a county-wide antislavery meeting for December for the purpose of discussing the abolition of slavery in the District of Columbia, which they believed to be subject to federal, as opposed to state, remedy. The majority of the Presbyterians and Congregationalists in Portage County exhibited little enthusiasm for the idea, or for Garrison's call for immediate emancipation. The college trustees and regular clergy in the Hudson area were generally of the "Old School" New England tradition and socially conservative.

The "New School" professors, Green, Storrs, and Wright, were

The Western Reserve College campus in a view from the southwest, an 1856 wood-cut appearing in the *College City Venture* newspaper, published in Hudson. The building at the extreme right is South College, built in 1830. The basement contained the college chapel, where Green preached his four abolition sermons.

products of New England's evangelical awakening and more open to applied Christianity and social reform. Rufus Nutting was the only faculty member to share the older generation's easy conscience with regard to the American Colonization Society. He could be counted upon to keep the debate out of the classroom. Storrs, so the conservatives believed, could be relied upon not to let passion replace reason, but Elizur Wright, Jr., was already suspect because of his liberal views on the reconciliation of science and religion in interpreting the Genesis creation story. As of late 1831, anyway, Beriah Green remained an enigma. His Old Testament theology ran in orthodox channels, but he would bear watching lest his views on reform course too strongly in sympathy with the plight of the American slave.

Garrison's *Thoughts on African Colonization*, full of material documenting the racist premises behind efforts to export American free blacks to Liberia, appeared in 1832. Green, Wright, and Storrs, as well as many of the students, read it with interest, for never before had the true motives behind the colonization scheme been exposed with such damning clarity. In July 1832, Wright, whose thinking had developed quite as far as Garrison's, began a series of articles in the *Observer and Telegraph* favoring immediate emancipation. Conservatives demanded that Wright desist, and Isham closed his paper to the views of the immediatists. Wright held firm to the position that, like the sheep dog which sleeps with the wolf, the colonizationists gave moral encouragement to the predators who guarded slavery's evil den.[7]

Western Reserve's campus rapidly became the center of the local controversy. A student auxiliary to the parent American Colonization Society had existed since the fall of 1830. In March 1832, some twenty or twenty-five students described as "professedly abolitionist" declared themselves in opposition to the sixty or seventy who still espoused colonization. Since the total number of students in 1832, inclusive of the college and preparatory divisions, numbered ninety-four, nearly all had taken sides. During the summer Green and Wright asked sophomore Amos P. Hawley to prepare a colloquy or skit for August's commencement under the title, "The Recaptured Slave."[8] This converted additional students. Green and Wright met privately with those wavering between colonization and immediate abolition and won them over, as they did with Theodore Dwight Weld (then a student at Oneida Institute and protégé of George Gale) when he passed through the Western Reserve lecturing on the manual labor movement.[9] Sometime in October, students organized their own abolition society. Two students still favoring colonization wrote back east to Ralph R. Gurley, Secretary of the American Colonization Society, concerning the "recent revolution of sentiment" at Western Reserve. They asserted that Garrison's *Liberator* had been instrumental in causing the majority of their fellow students to consider "the old and well-received doctrine of African colonization ultra and paradoxical."[10]

The student informants also reported that two of their ablest professors had become "bold & even warring advocates" of the "new-fangled" theory of immediatism. Because of their learning and station, these professors (doubtless Wright and Green) were able to "awe into silence those who would otherwise oppose them."[11] In early November, Green announced that the weekly rhetorical exercises, mandatory for all students, would take the form of a debate on "the points which separate the patrons of the American Colonization Society from the advocates of immediate emancipation."[12] No record of the outcome survives, but as a result of the debates, Green decided to carry the question beyond the classroom and into the chapel pulpit. He professed to have been radicalized by the folly of the colonizationist arguments presented in the disputations:

> *Apologies were made for the present race of slaveholders, under pretense that the evils beneath which they are placed, and from which, it is said, they long to break way, were entailed upon them. But it was especially*

*insisted on, that against the colored American, a prejudice, arising from
his complexion, was universally cherished, as effective and invincible, as
a constitutional tendency, which must forever exclude him from the affection and regard, and withhold from him the rights and privileges of his
white neighbors. Those who claimed to be free from this prejudice, it was
alleged, could hardly be regarded as sincere.*[13]

This may be the closest we can come to the moment of Beriah's public
commitment to abolitionism, for once the last vestiges of antislavery Laeodi-
ceanism fell away in his confrontation which the student colonizationists, he
gave himself totally to the sacred vocation of abolitionism.

Green had been at Hudson just over two years, during which time he
had supported a variety of benevolent causes and agencies akin to those he
had favored in his New England years. These included the Prison Discipline
Society, domestic and foreign missions, manual labor schools, and Christian
education. In addition, he had protested the Indian Removal Act with which
the Jacksonians covered their crimes against the Creeks of Georgia.[14] But
defending the humanity of the slave now became his all-consuming passion.
He vowed to do his duty "to expose the noxious tendencies and counteract
the deadly influence of such doctrines" as were subversive to the first
principles of Christian truth.[15]

Like a gladiator preparing for the coliseum, Green honed both body
and mind for the battle to come. He exercised at the woodpile more frequently and subjected himself to a morning ritual of ablutions with cold
water and rubbings with a coarse woolen cloth. He had decided to take the
battle into the chapel pulpit, for which he had responsibility. On November
5, 1832, Green wrote Simeon S. Jocelyn, a white minister of a black congregation in New Haven, Connecticut, and an early convert to Garrisonian
abolitionism, that a "great change" had come over Western Reserve College. President Storrs, Elizur Wright, Jr., and trustee Deacon Wright, Elizur's father, had come out for abolitionism, as had many of the students.
All were ready "to give arm and soul" to the cause. Green requested aid
from the New England Anti-Slavery Society: "We want facts—facts—
FACTS." "We have a great struggle to go through," he confessed, "the
strength of public prejudice, as such openly avowed, is awaking."[16]

As students, faculty, and guests filed into the college chapel on November 18th, Green may have spotted one or more of the four "fullblooded colored" students said to have been part of the preparatory
department in 1832.[17] Their presence would have heightened the emotional
impact of his sermon. Green cared little for those who bemoaned the plight
of the distant slave but discriminated against the African American within
arm's reach. As analysis of Green's sermons on four successive Sabbaths

will reveal, he used the college pulpit to reshape the whole debate over slavery. Green felt that reform began at home. Until his friends, colleagues, neighbors, and fellow citizens complied with the demands of morality, he would not lay down abolition's axe. As long as the discredited colonization scheme had advocates at Western Reserve College, the school was in conspiracy with the slaveholder against both humanity and God.

In the first antislavery sermon, Green hoped to demonstrate that Christians who based moral reform upon "an accurate discrimination between right and wrong, had good reasons to expect success." He attacked those who distinguished between "what is right and what is practicable." Extensive footnotes to the printed text castigate agents of the American Colonization Society whose "political wisdom" entailed efforts not to disturb the prejudices of slaveholders. Green argued that once the nefarious facts of slavery were brought to the attention of the Christian, expediency offered no refuge. By what measure was evil ascertained? He answered, "Heaven's revealed will." Green's optimism turned on the hub of his understanding of the relationship between divine revelation and the science of human nature. God imprinted the divine will on the human conscience. The reformer merely brought these original tendencies to bear upon the "prejudices and beloved habits of man's acquired character." "The guilty bosom," Green confidently proclaimed, "will be wrung with remorse—will be tortured with anticipated pangs of eternal damnation."[18]

Turning directly to the *"loathsome crime of slave-holding,"* Green argued that chattel slavery broke the bonds of marriage, fostered unchecked licentiousness, and created conditions against which "the black sinewy arm" would surely rise in righteous vengeance. Slavery also concealed the key of knowledge, keeping both the black slave and freeman in ignorance. It exposed the philanthropist, though a thousand miles distant, to contempt and disgrace. Green called upon his hearers "to open the eyes of the infatuated slaveholders on the tremendous perils . . . gathering around them" and to convince them to "let the people go."[19] Here was an appeal to conscience not unlike that of the revivalists. Expose sin, describe the loathsome facts, and the sinner must respond, repent, and change. The conscience was the fulcrum point, the eternal abiding place of the "principles of rectitude"—the ineradicable and reflective will of God.

Though cast in the idiom of traditional evangelical revivalism, Green's first sermon incensed some of his hearers. They walked out complaining that Western Reserve's Professor of Sacred Literature had desecrated the chapel pulpit. Though urged to desist immediately, Green occupied the chapel pulpit again on the following Sabbath. He chose the theme "Progress of Sin," based on the warning of Jesus to the scribes and pharisees in Matthew 29:13. He spoke of the cumulative effect of the shedding of right-

Elizur Wright, Jr., 1841. From Philip Green Wright and Elizabeth Q. Wright, *Elizur Wright: The Father of Life Insurance* (Chicago: University of Chicago Press, 1937), opposite p. 139.

eous blood upon each generation and contemptuously dismissed the slave-holders' argument that their guilt was diminished by being entailed or inherited. He painted a grim portrait of every increasing iniquity: "Pause, I beseech you, pause. Draw not down upon your heads the threatening ruins of a thousand generations. Warned by the plagues of others, escape to the arms of mercy."[20]

On December 2nd, Green preached for a third time. He chose to expound on a theme which brought the accusatory finger even closer to those in the pews before him. *"The judgment, which men form on subjects of practical interest, is greatly affected by the state of their affections."* He cited situations in which self-interest disqualified an individual from making a fair judgment, as when an officer of the court decides a case to which he is a party. Green discussed the reasoning process by which one arrives at judgments based on inductive logic. Selfish affections clouded human reasoning. No one filled with prejudice against the character of his colored brethren, Green concluded, was fit to judge the claims of African Americans—"A wolf might as well be trusted to devise a plan to protect the sheep."[21]

News of Green's alarming sermons spread throughout the Western Reserve, but he continued, taking to the pulpit one last time on December 11, 1832. He spared no one. On the basis of 1 John 4:20, Green announced his thesis: *"The regard, which we manifest for man, is a fair test and just measure, of our regard for God."* His hearers doubtless winced at verbal pictures of the judgment seat of Christ before which they would be found wanting for having failed to plead the cause of the least of the children of God. Green warned that all sympathizers with colonization would hear the words: "I was a colored man, and you maintained a cruel prejudice against me; enslaved, and you apologized for my oppressor; torn with whips, and you refused to pity me; deprived of the bread of life, and you alleged that expediency required me to submit to starvation; and at length, forced from my native country to a foreign shore, and you assisted in the enterprise."[22] Green now retired from the pulpit. But the abolitionist engine he helped set in motion could not be throttled down.

Western Reserve College, though far from the New England maelstrom, thus became the first American college to debate Garrison's immediatism seriously. Two days after Green's last sermon, Wright wrote Garrison that his colleague's rhetoric had smoked out the opposition.[23] Wright also informed Theodore Dwight Weld of the impact of Green's four sermons: "Abolitionism has assumed a far deeper interest that it had when you left us."[24] As evidence of their deeper interest in immediatism, some of the more ardent students forsook their books to conduct rallies in nearby villages. Green himself preached on abolition in neighboring towns. Though shut out of most congregations by their opponents, the abolitionists intended to spread the doctrine of immediate, universal emancipation throughout the Western Reserve. "We now very clearly see what is before us," Wright confided to Weld, "nor do we see how we could have avoided the onset with safe conscience, and we are taking in breath for the *long pull.*"[25]

The Christmas holidays offered a brief respite to the campus. Students went home with the news of the rumpus Green had created, and Green busied himself with preparing his four sermons for publication. Storrs reported on developments to Arthur Tappan, a silk importer in New York City and prominent layman in evangelical reform circles. Tappan promised financial assistance. Wright wrote Weld that influential men, "especially two on the board of trustees," intended to put a stop to Green's "magnanimous work" by calling forth public sentiment against him. Green added a note which, in retrospect, assumes momentous significance. He requested a copy of Weld's report on manual labor in literary institutions and remarked, "Could I see you, I should ask a good many questions about Onei[da] Institute. Can you say any thing to me about it?"[26]

Long after the protagonists cannonaded their last salvos at each other, Elizur Wright claimed that "the high ecclesiastical" trustees were dissatisfied with him, Green, and Storrs prior to the college controversy. These conservatives, Wright alleged, had been gathering documentary evidence on the three faculty "not so much from what they did preach as what they did not."[27] Wright's geology lectures may have made him previously suspect, but Green had not given the trustees cause to censure him until the debate over colonization erupted. Of the twelve trustees, only Deacon Wright sided with the abolitionist faculty. Two of the most conservative trustees, Caleb Pitkin and Harvey Coe, decided to rid Western Reserve of Green in the wake of his four chapel sermons. Pitkin chaired a prudential committee charged with assessing the general state of the college.

The prudential committee turned the sensitive matter of Green's fate over to an ad hoc committee of six trustees. Seeking to calm the troubled waters, the investigating committee deplored the "unyielding, self-justifying disposition" on both sides and termed the whole controversy "a very lamentable instance of human infirmity."[28] It refused to censure the offending faculty but hinted at serious repercussions if the abolitionists did not keep quiet. Trustees Coe, Pitkin, and David Hudson, upset by the committee's gentle reprimand, met secretly with some of the other conservatives to demand Green's ouster. Storrs showed up unexpectedly and defended his faculty's right to speak on abolition. Green, having learned of an attempt to replace him as college chaplain, resolved not to honor the committee's recommendation to keep silent in regard to "the agitated subject" and became even more determined.

The conservatives vented their frustration upon Storrs. Coe began spreading rumors that Storrs had abandoned his office, that the college "was fast sinking," and that it was "threatened with destruction by the mismanagement of the faculty."[29] Diary notes kept by Storrs reveal his inability to assist the offending faculty. Though he had allied himself with Green and Wright, he bemoaned the fact that "nothing is done in [the] college but discuss abolition and colonization."[30] He was losing control. Students debated among themselves and circulated petitions regarding the character of preaching in the college chapel. The hoped-for calm did not materialize. Trustees Hudson, Pitkin, and Coe used the *Observer and Telegraph* to absolve themselves of any neglect of duty with regard to what was transpiring and pointedly disavowed Green's preaching.[31] He refused to recognize their authority and responded, "Do they imagine that I can know them as legislators, when our board is not in session?"[32]

Encouragement came from the East. William Lloyd Garrison applauded Green's sermons and expressed his understanding of what was at stake in the Western Reserve controversy: "It now is palpable as the sun in heaven, that the slaveholders and the colonization party are united together to suppress the freedom of speech and of the press and even to exclude from the pulpits of our land those who plead for the immediate abolition of slavery."[33] Green informed Garrison in early March, 1833, "Pres. Storrs is fully, cordially, powerfully with us—We are likely to have troubles with a few of the trustees." He reiterated the central point of his objections to colonization. It was "an act of high-handed tyranny for any master to impose upon them (the slaves) the necessity of going to Liberia or continuing in servitude."[34] Sometime in late spring, Green's four sermons appeared in print, and were widely distributed and even extracted in such papers as *The Abolitionist*. Now many beyond the Western Reserve would know the gospel of immediatism according to the Reverend Beriah Green.

Now that Green had set a course from which he would not retreat, he committed more and more of his inner being to the cause of black freedom. "I have lately felt," he informed a critic, "unutterable throes in contemplating the condition and prospects of my colored brethren."[35] This strong empathy for the oppressed underlies the psychology of commitment, which is hardened in turn by the cycle of attack and counterattack between the reformer and his critics. Green's own experiences at the hands of the conservative trustees led him to become more radical. Emotional stress once again drove him to the woodpile, where in April he cut his foot. Elizur Wright, Jr., informed his wife that Green's injury was not serious, and that their friend still intended to celebrate his "favorite instrument" in poetic verse.[36]

Toward the end of April, Green wrote Wright, then in New York City conferring with fellow immediatists and debating representatives of the American Colonization Society, about possibly leaving Western Reserve. He had recently received a letter from the trustees of Oneida Institute, urging him to accept leadership of their manual labor school in Whitesboro, Oneida County, New York. Green's scholarly credentials were well known in central New York. Many families in the Western Reserve had relatives in the Whitesboro-Utica area, and the religious press in central and western New York had carried reports on the controversy at Western Reserve. Theodore Dwight Weld, who was a student at Oneida Institute, urged Green's candidacy, as did the Reverend John Frost, a prominent member of Oneida's governing board. Green demurred at first, for he was torn between seeing the battle through at Western Reserve and the opportunity to start fresh with an institution where the lines had not been drawn over the issue of abolition. In subsequent correspondence, Green noted the one condition upon which he would consider leaving Western Reserve College for Oneida Institute. "I am assured," he told Wright, "that Africa shall lose nothing in the exchange of stations, which I am urged to venture on. I am even as-

William Lloyd Garrison. From the *Dictionary of American Portraits* (New York: Dover Publications, 1967).

sured that the Trustees will help me in my efforts to 'strike the chains' from colored limbs, etc." Then, hinting at his intentions, Green confided to Wright that the upstate New York institution might be transformed into a "school like we talked about."[37]

Green submitted his resignation as an act of protest to the June meeting of the trustees. The board deferred action on his case until July but granted President Storrs, who had contracted pulmonary tuberculosis, a leave of absence. Storrs died of consumption six months later. The Quaker abolitionist John Greenleaf Whittier marked Storrs' death in poetic verse, describing him as "martyred of the Lord," the first fallen soldier of the immediatist campaign.[38]

Upon hearing of Green's intent to resign, Wright wrote on June 7, 1833, "I feel sad at the thought of your leaving our college. But the Lord's will be done. It will probably decide the question of my own stay."[39] Before Green departed Hudson, he fired off one last round at the conservative trustees, who were already claiming victory. Denied access to the college chapel, he resorted to the local Congregational church to deliver a farewell sermon on the theme "Remember those who are in bonds as bound with them."[40] In September, Wright wrote Weld of Green's last days: "Bro. Green, as you have doubtless heard, has left us to fill the Presidency of Oneida Institute. His farewell addresses here were very happy for the cause he so much loved. They came near to banishing the last shreds of 'patchwork morality' from this college. Only half a dozen now remain who pretend to support the Colonization scheme."[41] Wright also resigned by the end of the summer.

A tutor by the name of Ralph Walker did assist some students in keeping antislavery sentiment alive at Western Reserve after the departure of Green and Wright. But the school gradually came under the total control of the conservatives. In November, Deacon Wright wrote his son that Pitkin was "yet indefatigable in attempts to curtail free discussion on the important question [of abolitionism] among the students" but that the students debated among themselves anyway.[42] The more radical ones left for Oberlin College, located about thirty miles to the west. Wright, Storrs, and Green may have won the battle at Western Reserve in the sense that they had not compromised with colonization, but the larger war was still ahead.

Like the conservatives in Hudson, most white Northerners preferred social and institutional stability to debates over slavery. Though Green could claim to have kept the immediatist flag untrammeled only by carrying it to new ground, his Western Reserve experience had been instructive. He had tested the evangelical doctrine of immediate repentance of sin and found that many hypocritically failed to apply it to slavery. "We see it both naturally and morally impossible," Coe and Pitkin contended, "in a moment of a year, to set all blacks in our land free and raise them to an equality of intellectual power and privilege with the whites."[43] If pressed, Green would have admitted that the call for immediate emancipation really meant that one's evangelical duty was to *begin* immediately the *process* of dismantling the system of slavery. This involved not only preaching and lecturing against slavery, known as moral suasion, but also doing something practical. Western Reserve helped Beriah hone abolition's axe, but he needed another little New England in which to apply it fully. When he went to Hudson from New England, Green was a missionary awaiting assignment. When he left for Oneida Institute, he at last had a clear sense of his divine call.

The concept of a sacred vocation is helpful as a means of gauging the intensity of Green's commitment to abolitionism. As Donald Scott has argued, the immediatists of the 1830s understood abolitionism as a form of evangelicalism. Just as their missionary counterparts fought against spiritual blindness among the heathen, so they served as evangelists to those who were blind to the sin of slavery. "Immediatism," Scott reminds us, "was less a program of what to do about slavery then, in evangelical terms, a 'disposition,' a state of being in which the heart and will were set irrevocably against slavery.''[44]

Green's conversion to immediatism while at Western Reserve caused him to see slavery as symbolic of all the evil in the world. Because of Green's faith in moral progress, stemming from the millennial overtones of the evangelical Christianity which had shaped him, slavery represented all that was morally retrogressive. More than any other social ill, it robbed the individual of the freedom to respond to the dictates of his or her own conscience. The slave had to submit to the demands of an earthly master, often in violation of the will of God. By inserting himself between the slave and God, the master subverted the moral government of God, which Green felt was the basis of all human institutions, such as the family.

The abolitionist mandate which Green accepted in the 1830s was not just another star in the evangelical night sky, as was, for example, prison reform. In the moral universe which he now occupied, abolitionism was the preeminent issue; all other necessary and worthy reforms were secondary. We will not understand Green's radicalism nor his intemperate style unless we appreciate the centrality of antislavery activism to his understanding of self and sacred vocation. No matter what the future held, Beriah could no more escape the radicalizing influence of the gospel of immediatism than his brother Jonathan could ignore the obligations of Christianity on the missionary field.

3

HEWING ONEIDA INSTITUTE

B eriah, his wife Daraxa, and the six children, Samuel, Ann, Marcia, Elizabeth, Jonathan, and Mary left Hudson on July 27, 1833. The family journeyed to Cleveland, where Green preached, and then boarded the steamboat Henry Clay for the twenty-two hour trip across Lake Erie to Buffalo. At Buffalo the Greens transferred to the line boat Genesee, which took them as far as Rochester, where they stayed several nights and Beriah delivered sermons in prominent Presbyterian churches. On Monday, August 5th, everyone boarded the packet North America, which traveled the Erie Canal into the heart of Oneida County. When it arrived at Whitesboro on August 7th, Mrs. Green was sick with cholera morbus, and the children were weary. Once his family had secured lodging, Beriah set out to inspect Oneida Institute.[1]

Present-day visitors to the Mohawk flats bordering Sauquoit Creek, about four miles west of Utica, will find no historical marker on the former grounds of Oneida Institute. Nothing memorializes the site where Oneida's students worked, studied, and, in the little free time allotted them, watched the passing of boats on the Great Western (Erie) Canal. All that the rather bleak landscape now contains is a deteriorating brick factory which once housed the Anchor Knitting Mill and in front of which stands a newly erected mortuary of startling proportions. The town of Whitesboro, with its New England–like village green, is now but a bedroom community, an appendage to Utica. But in 1833 the town ranked with the best in New England in its cultural advantages. Carved out of the vast Whitestown tract and settled in 1784 by Hugh White of Middletown, Connecticut, Whitesboro (or Whitesborough) was no longer just a Yankee outpost on the frontier.

Whitesboro of the 1830s was at the heart of a post-frontier region imbued with New England values and dominated by a middle class that prized communal order, piety, education, and commercial prosperity. Yankee entrepreneurs had established textile mills along the Sauquoit and Oriskany streams. Whitesboro's citizens had been avid promoters of the Erie Canal and hailed its completion in 1825 as a boon to the local economy and another sign that the community was destined for greatness. They erected churches and schools and organized voluntary reform societies similar to those of New England. In short, Green and family were to find that Whitesboro, like Hudson, was New England transplanted.

Oneida Institute was already six years old when Green became its president-elect. He replaced the Reverend George Washington Gale, the school's founder and retiring principal. Formerly a Presbyterian pastor in Adams, New York, Gale was an enthusiastic supporter of the religious revivals which swept central and western New York in the 1820s and resulted in the appellation "the Burned-over District." The lawyer and self-professed skeptic Charles Grandison Finney heard Gale preach, experienced conversion in 1821, and sped like a spiritual fireball across the "Burnt districts" igniting religious revivals. Finney's use of protracted "inquiry meetings," in which even longtime church members were asked to consider whether or not they had been truly saved, use of the "anxious bench" for potential converts, encouragement of females to testify during revivals, and popular, passionate, and direct style of preaching upset traditional religious leaders. His emphasis on the human production of conversions and belief in the possibility of entire holiness or sanctification troubled the orthodox and brought criticism even from Lyman Beecher, the New England patron of revivals.

As Finney captured one city after another, including Utica in 1826, Gale gathered Finney's recruits for practical theological training. He brought seven young enthusiasts to a small farm near Western, nine miles north of Rome, in an effort to train them as emissaries of the new revivalism. The young Finneyites united academics and manual labor under Gale's watchful eye, though the established clergy who supported Hamilton College and Auburn Seminary, the traditional route to the Presbyterian ministry, thought that Gale's plan was theologically shallow and designed to circumvent the longer and more rigorous programs of ministerial preparation.[2] Gale defended his educational experiment as a happy medium between the cold, formal curriculum of the traditionalists and the anti-education bias of Finney's most enthusiastic converts.

Gale soon needed more space than available at his farm and searched much of the Burned-over District for a new location. He finally decided upon Whitesboro as the best in the region, obtained the support of the

Charles Grandison Finney, the "Grand Itinerant." Courtesy of the Oneida County Historical Society.

Oneida Presbytery, and in May 1827 opened Oneida Academy in the old Hugh White farmhouse on 115 acres just east of the village. There Gale sought to unite classical education with agricultural, horticultural, and mechanical labor. His school eventually became the most widely known American version of the social regeneration idea of education combining learning

George Washington Gale, founder of the Oneida Institute. *McClure's Magazine,*
April 1895.

and labor, pioneered in Europe for poor youth by Phillip Emmanuel von
Fellenberg, the Swiss educator and philanthropist, in the early 1800s.

Twenty-seven of Finney's holy band arrived in Whitesboro for the
school's first term to find a campus consisting of a converted farmhouse and
several outbuildings. Theodore Dwight Weld, later a passionate abolitionist
and social reformer, was among the first students. At twenty-four, he was
older than most of the fledgling scholars and quickly became their leader,
assigned to supervise the milking crew. Like the others, Weld had looked
into Finney's "great staring eyes" and experienced conversion. The son of
a Presbyterian clergyman in Fabius township, some forty miles south of
Utica, Weld had briefly but unofficially attended Hamilton College after leaving Andover Academy in New England. He became an enthusiastic supporter of the manual labor idea and spent his vacations traveling about
soliciting funds for Gale's school.[3]

Earliest sketch of the Oneida Institute, southwest view. Original source: *Historical Collections of the State of New York* (New York: S. Tuttle, 1841). Courtesy of the Oneida County Historical Society.

The Whitesboro institution was chartered in 1829 as the Oneida Institute of Science and Industry.[4] Five hundred prospective students had to be turned away in 1830 for lack of space. Those who could be accommodated received their board, room, and laundry in exchange for labor on the farm and in the wagon, carpenter, and blacksmith shops. Despite periodically flooded fields, cramped facilities, and a chronic shortage of funds, the students remained optimistic. They were, after all, engaged in a holy enterprise, the unifying of mind and body for the spiritual reformation of the nation. Leaders of Whitesboro's religious establishment, such as the Reverend John Frost of First Presbyterian, shared the students' millennial vision and served as trustees of the Oneida Institute. Benjamin Walcott, a local textile manufacturer, likewise supported Gale's enterprises.[5]

Though Gale failed to obtain coadjutors, Oneida Institute continued to grow. The original farmhouse was expanded, and new buildings were erected and shops added where students could practice carpentry and harness-making. Gale required that his pupils, most of whom were at least sixteen, work twenty-one hours a week to defray costs and simultaneously derive the physiological and emotional benefits of physical exercise deemed important not only for good health but also as a means of demonstrating kinship with common people. In January 1831, obligatory manual labor was reduced to eighteen hours, figured at six cents an hour. So many young men eager to prepare for the millennial struggle enrolled that dormitory space became a problem. Of the eighty students who came in 1831, only fifty-six could be housed on campus. Enrollment peaked while Gale was principal in the spring term of 1832; many students had to take lodging in the village or in makeshift rented quarters. Despite a cholera outbreak, seventy young men returned for the fall term. Gale declared, "our school is prosperous."[6]

Gale soon found the burden of being the school's chief instructor and administrator too taxing. His interest in building up the Institute waned as he became more deeply involved with promoting the manual labor philosophy in other regions. More of a pastor than a theologian, and lacking the dynamic personality of a Finney, Gale privately desired to turn the reigns of leadership over to someone else. He tried to lure Finney from the revival circuit, appealing to him in 1830, "Shall the Institution which is doing more for the education of youth in its influence directly and otherwise—for the education of youth for the ministry than any other in the land, fall under the hammer of the auctioneer?"[7] The revivalist was more interested in capturing Auburn Seminary, the traditional Presbyterian route to the ministry, located at Auburn in Cayuga County. Gale also failed to attract Nathan S. S. Beman, a "New Measures" Presbyterian clergyman, to a proposed theological professorship.[8]

Several of Oneida's trustees began looking for someone with weightier academic credentials and fresh enthusiasm. In March 1832, the Reverend S. C. Aiken of Utica appealed to Finney, "My object in writing to you at this time is to enlist your cooperation in obtaining a Principal for the Oneida Institute in the place of Bro. Gale."[9] Gale assisted in the search, for he was anxious to be relieved by a new principal with better health and better qualifications.[10] Students were grumbling that though a pious man, he did not inspire them to meet the challenges of the millennial age.[11] They possessed the zeal of new recruits, Gale the caution of a weary veteran. In autobiographical reflections, Gale passed judgment on his Oneida years: "I had done enough, expanded means and labor enough to bring the Institution to its maturity and tested the practicability of combining labor and study, and the carrying forward of the enterprise might now devolve on someone else."[12]

Perhaps Gale left Whitesboro in part because he foresaw that the abolition controversy would erupt at Oneida Institute as it had at Western Reserve College. In July 1832, a month prior to Green's arrival, thirty-five students at Oneida Institute formed an antislavery society on immediatist principles, the first in New York State. Thirty-four opposing students organized an auxiliary colonization society in August.[13] The student abolitionists applauded the election of a president who had placed himself solidly in opposition to the American Colonization Society. Student leaders and several abolitionist-minded citizens of Oneida County issued a public challenge to the colonizationists: "The only proper remedy for the sin of slaveholding must be found in the *immediate, full, heartfelt respect of those rights* in the invasion of which this monstrous crime consists. Every slave ought immediately and unconditionally to be emancipated."[14] Thus Green stepped into a supercharged atmosphere, one filled with debate over the proper course of action regarding the issue of slavery.

In September, Green delivered a ringing inaugural address, much to the discomfort of the student colonizationists and the more conservative trustees. He called for immediate, unconditional, and uncompensated emancipation. "Perish the cord of cast [sic]," he intoned with somber intensity. Here was a radically new mission for Oneida Institute. Green wanted to raise up an abolitionist phalanx, young reformers who would identify with human weal and woe in every form. To this end, he advocated a revision of the curriculum so that students might study the Bible in its original languages, rather than read the spiritually deadening and impractical Greek and Roman classics. He urged the students, faculty, and trustees to do something practical on behalf of "dear humanity."[15] A few weeks after Green's installation, a student wrote William Goodell:

> *Our leader here is President Green, than whom we want no better. His efforts in the cause of the colored man are untiring. He has begun a course of lectures (by request of the students) on slavery and attendant evils, which is listened to with the utmost interest by not only those connected with the Institute but by many from the neighborhood—I am as confident of a final triumph as I am that the Millennium will dawn upon the earth.*[16]

Green demonstrated his commitment to practical abolition by joining with fellow immediatists in organizing a national society. On the evening of December 3, 1833, some twenty or thirty abolitionists met in Philadelphia to make arrangements for the first convention of the American Anti-Slavery Society. The Reverend Samuel May, a Unitarian from Boston who later became a prominent abolitionist in Syracuse, recalled that the group thought it best to obtain the consent of a native Philadelphian to preside over the convention. Such a stratagem, May felt, would guarantee the public that "we were not the reckless band of incendiaries that the newspapers represented us to be." A committee called on an antislavery member of the Philadelphia Society of Friends. He excused himself, whereupon the small group retreated. On the steps outside, Green turned "somewhat abruptly" to the others and said, "Don't you feel small? I do. This hunting about for a President! Why, if there isn't timber enough in our Convention to make a President of, let us go without one!" The next morning, the convention elected him as its presiding officer. May testified that Green "proved to be a man in whom there was 'timber' enough to make half a dozen Presidents, if the Convention had needed so many."[17] Another delegate, the Quaker poet and abolitionist John G. Whittier remembered Oneida's president as "a fresh-faced, sandy-haired, rather common-looking man, but who had the reputation of an able and eloquent speaker."[18] Green closed the assembly with "a solemn, sublime and thrilling speech" in which he remarked on how happy and united the delegates were but warned of the difficulties to come.[19]

When the American Anti-Slavery Society met for its second convention in New York City in 1834, Green was one of those present. Again he addressed the gathering, this time on the need for the abolitionists to exhibit fraternal sympathy and effective aid "to our colored brethren" as a biblical requirement. The "poor, distressed and abject slave," Green argued, was the Divine Judge "in disguise." The delegates applauded Beriah's efforts to transform Oneida Institute into an abolitionist school and sent him home with the following token of support: "We trust that friends of the oppressed will not be slow to support an institution which promises so much to the cause of humanity in its struggle with prejudice and the foul spirit of caste."[20] Green was elected one of the society's vice-presidents, a largely honorary position.

When Green was but a professor in Hudson, he had only his voice and pen as weapons in the battle to liberate the slave. Now he had a school. He but needed to hew it into shape and did so with dogged persistence and little regard for the misgivings of the faint of heart. The student colonizationists at the Institute disbanded in August 1834. They could not hope to withstand Green's withering onslaught against their parent body—in the classroom, from the chapel pulpit, and in a steady stream of public lectures as an agent of the American Anti-Slavery Society. Oneida Institute soon lost its predominantly "Presbygational" identity. As Charles Denison informed William Lloyd Garrison in 1834, it was "every hour becoming more and more an abolition school."[21] The more conservative trustees, who were upset by Green's efforts to *institutionalize* radical abolitionism, were soon up in arms over what was happening on campus. As tensions increased, Beriah received an encouraging letter from Elizur Wright, Jr., who had become secretary for domestic correspondence of the American Anti-Slavery Society, reminding him of the Hudson years.

> *I wish you could raise such a storm in every city and village in the land. If the Lord should let loose upon you Pitkins and Coes enough to turn you out of your present situation, I should more than acquiesce in the providence . . . I know that Oneida Institute is an important post, and it*

Theodore Dwight Weld. From the *Dictionary of American Portraits* (New York, Dover Publications, 1967).

ought to be held for the good of our cause, but if it cannot, then I am clear our Society ought to pledge you a comfortable support and let you work as a general agent.[22]

Unlike the events at Hudson, the conservatives resigned, leaving the field to Green and his supporters. Wright urged Garrison and his colleagues to abandon plans for a manual labor school for "colored Americans" in New England (which never materialized, in part due to black opposition to segregated education) and concentrate the strength of the abolition band upon the Institute.[23]

Green used his school as a command post from which to carry the abolitionist flag into new and ever-expanding territory. He helped organize antislavery societies in Syracuse and Rochester and used invitations to preach as occasions to spread the gospel of immediatism. When the Reverend Joshua N. Danforth, permanent agent of the American Colonization Society for New York and New England, appeared in Utica, Green engaged him in a series of public debates. Even the pro-colonization Utica press remarked on the power and persuasiveness of Oneida Institute's president.[24] A mob element disrupted the debates and hung Green in effigy. Utica's Common Council passed an ordinance prohibiting further agitation on the slavery question. Nevertheless, Green triumphed. Danforth gave up efforts to solicit monies for the American Colonization Society in Oneida County.

Green saw his students as living epistles, extensions of himself. The 1834 academic year began with sixty-nine freshmen and twenty-one sophomores. Most hailed from the Mohawk Valley, though some came from New England and the Canadian provinces. Green hoped to keep the older students at the Institute by adding junior and senior classes and introducing theological courses for the pre-ministerial candidates. Green did not want to see a repeat of the exodus of older students who followed Theodore Dwight Weld out to Cincinnati and the fledgling Lane Seminary, an educational outpost in the West, founded on manual labor and evangelical principles. Twenty-four of the forty members of Lane's first theological class were Oneida boys, many of whom had rafted down the French and Allegheny Rivers in 1833 for Cincinnati. The former Oneidans, who had been disenchanted with Gale's leadership and the lack of regular theological courses at the Institute, took the lead in debates at Lane over slavery and colonization in February 1834. Rebuffed by the trustees and faculty, who wanted no political activity to disturb the peace of the Seminary, the student rebels withdrew almost en masse for the Oberlin Collegiate Institute in northern Ohio. One can only speculate on how Green's labors to transform Oneida Institute might have been eased had such zealous young reformers as Weld, Henry Stanton, and John Alvord remained. The Oneida boys at Oberlin endorsed its manual labor system and, in the spirit of Green, sought changes in the old classical curriculum so as to introduce educational reforms more conducive to the reform challenges of what they perceived to be the millenial age.

Fully conscious of Oberlin's growing reputation within evangelical and abolitionist circles, Green redoubled his efforts to build up Oneida. He soon discovered that Gale had misled him concerning the Institute's financial health, largely dependent on private donations in the early years. He felt that he needed one hundred thousand dollars to furnish ground for a fair experiment of his plans. Because contributions had fallen off, Green had to rely more on the manual labor arrangements by which his young charges earned part of their expenses. Students furnished their own beds, books, light, and fuel. By laboring three hours each day, they came near to earning enough to pay for their board. Tuition, room rent, and contingent expenses amounted to $34 in 1834. Students rose long before sunrise, had chapel, classes, and then worked to subdue the flesh in service to the spirit. Green rhapsodized about the moral benefits of manual labor, but he realized that the system was also an economic necessity for the many students from poor families.[25]

The 1834 school year began the second Thursday of February and continued for forty weeks. In order to be admitted to the upper division, a candidate had to be at least fifteen, be able to furnish proof of a good intellectual and moral character, be of sound health, and demonstrate competence to teach a common or elementary school and recite the Greek grammar. Forty-eight younger boys were enrolled in the juvenile department, which served as a preparatory school academy. During the three-month winter vacation, the older students taught common school to replenish their purses, while the younger ones returned home, hoping that their parents or some benefactor would come to their aid for the following term.[26]

The students' difficulties multiplied when the Presbyterian Education Society struck Oneida Institute from its list of approved schools in 1834. One of the society's directors, under the pseudonym "Pax," accused Green of introducing "a NOVEL plan of study" by dropping the classics.[27] This disqualified Oneida Institute, "Pax" argued, from Presbyterian benevolence directed at the pauper scholars of literary institutions. The American Education Society followed suit, citing the action of its Presbyterian counterpart. It refused students further assistance on the grounds that "in the common acceptance of the terms, Oneida Institute [is] neither an Academy, nor a College, nor a Theological Seminary,"[28] Though the Oneida Presbytery tried to compensate for the loss of support from the national agencies, Green viewed the matter as more than just a question of money. He was willing to debate the curricular issue, but he accused those in charge of the educational agencies of trying to embarrass the Institute because of its position on human rights—an embarrassment revealed, he said, in "the eager and indecent haste with which we were driven away from the table ecclesiastic."[29] The educational societies, run by conservatives, had lost interest in the manual labor idea and feared losing contributions because of Oneida's radical reputation.

Green needed friends with the financial resources necessary to sustain his "poor boy's school." He looked to Gerrit Smith, of nearby Peterboro, in Madison County, who possessed considerable wealth and enough land to be embarrassed by it. Smith's father, Peter Smith, had been a partner of John Jacob Astor in the fur trade and other enterprises. Gerrit took control of a sizeable portion of his father's business and immense land holdings in 1819. After a religious conversion in 1826, he saw himself as a steward of the Lord and gave liberally to many reform causes.

Contemporaries described Gerrit Smith as majestic in personal appearance. One visitor to Peterboro rhapsodized about the owner of the only mansion in the village: "Tall, magnificently built and magnificently proportioned, his large head superbly set upon his shoulders he might have served as a model for a Greek God in the days when man deified beauty and worshiped it."[30] Beriah Green, Elizur Wright tells us, was "a man of not more than middling stature, earnestly stooping forward [with] a strongly marked, nervous face."[31] Smith impressed friend and foe alike as disarmingly gracious and affectionate, the epitome of the evangelical Christian. By contrast, Green appeared severe and altogether too earnest. Upon returning from a visit to Whitesboro, a New England abolitionist described him as "ugly and clerical."[32] Despite physical and temperamental differences, Green and Smith were yoked in common cause for nearly four decades.

Smith attracted Green's interest because he too had shown concern for the education of "colored youth." As early as 1827, Smith floated a proposal for a school in Peterboro which would prepare American blacks to go to Africa as missionaries under the auspices of the American Colonization Society. He seems to have abandoned the plan until 1834, when he announced the opening of a manual labor "high school" at Peterboro. Smith wrote Leonard Bacon, a colonizationist leader, "I hope my first class, limited to 15 will have members who will go to Africa with a sound education of head and heart."[33] A handful actually came. Housed in a small frame structure, the Peterboro Manual Labor School had but one instructor, Colquhoun Grant, brother to one of Green's faculty. Supported only by Smith's benevolence, the school closed in 1835. Green gave a sigh of relief, for he had written Smith a year earlier: "For one I am from principal opposed to charity which excludes either color; I am opposed to the cord of caste wherever it may appear. Away with caste! It has strangled its thousands. . . . Till we have white and black together in our schools, the cord of caste will remain."[34]

Though well-intentioned, Gerrit Smith had not yet climbed aboard the abolitionist wagon. A generous supporter of the American Colonization Society, he complained about the immediatists who "by violent, bitter and fanatical writing in their publications supporting emancipation, turned public sentiment against colonizationists."[35] In 1834 he wrote in his journal, "I think I cannot join the Antislavery Society as long as the War is kept up between it and the American Colonization Society—a war, however, for which the American Colonization Society is as much to blame as the other Society."[36] Did this portend wavering on Smith's part? Elizur Wright, Jr., thought so. He saw Smith as "making his last effort to reform the poor old colonization hobby. It is the creation of his imagination he clings to—not the odious reality."[37] Green appealed to Smith to join with the abolitionists who were planning on meeting in Utica in October 1835 for the purpose of organizing a state antislavery society. Smith hesitated, but Beriah kept after him: "I feel a confidence, which my heart refuses to let go, that you will, sometime or other, give us your heart and your hand."[38]

Nearly six hundred abolitionists converged upon Utica on October 21st for a meeting at Bleecker Street Presbyterian Church. By coincidence, Gerrit Smith and wife were overnighting in the city en route to visit his father in Schenectady. More out of curiosity than conviction, Smith attended the opening session of the New York Anti-Slavery Convention. He had barely taken his seat when a group of about eighty men stormed the church shouting, "Open the way! Break down the doors! Damn the fanatics! Stop your damn stuff!"[39] Mob members belonged by and large to a commercial and professional class in Utica which feared that the abolitionists intended to sow the seeds of communal disorder and social revolution. As the meeting broke up in confusion, Smith's "resonant and pervasive voice" rose above the clamor. He appealed for fairness and free speech, though he declared that he was "no abolitionist."[40] Insulted by the mob's behavior, he invited the delegates to reassemble in the safety of his Peterboro estate, some fourteen miles to the southwest of Utica.

More than half of the abolitionists reconvened at Peterboro on the following day. By force of circumstances, Smith now assumed a prominent role in the deliberations. He later declared that the mobbing at Utica had been "an instructive providence."[41] Smith now saw that however radical their views, the abolitionists had a right to be heard.

The enormous and insolent demands of the South, sustained, I am deeply ashamed to say, by craven and mercenary spirits at the North, manifest beyond all dispute, that the question now is not merely, nor mainly, whether the blacks of the South shall remain slaves—but whether the whites at the North shall become slaves also.[42]

Here was a pattern repeated many times in the North. Once whites felt the long arm of slavery reaching into their personal lives, whether by mob action, economic threats, restrictions on freedom of speech or assembly, opposition in the churches, or denials of the right to petition government, they stopped temporizing. Smith wrote Abraham Cox, secretary of the American Anti-Slavery Society, on November 12, 1835, asking that his name be added to the membership rolls.[43] He then resigned from the colonization society, notifying its secretary that his decision had been motivated by the "recent alarming attacks" on the right of free discussion.[44] Upon hearing of Smith's conversion, Green wrote him, "I rejoice to know that your thoughts and heart are so much with the oppressed."[45]

Now that they were allies, Green urged Smith to view Oneida Institute as "a special object of solicitude and of patronage." If friends of the slave allowed the school to fall, abolitionism would suffer embarrassment and ridicule. Green had his wish list all prepared—water power for the workshops, scientific apparatus for chemistry and physics, and an endowment to cushion the manual labor experiment. Smith was still a trustee of Hamilton College in Clinton, his alma mater, and gave liberally to Oneida's rival. Green argued that the Institute offered a more effective means to "subserve the glory of our Savior and the interests of His Kingdom."[46] Smith eventually resigned from Hamilton's board on the grounds that the school was insufficiently antislavery and became a trustee of the Institute. Though he missed many meetings, Smith assured Green, "Because of the simple, straight-forward honesty inculcated in it [Oneida Institute], it is dearer to my heart than any School with which I am acquainted."[47]

The Institute was becoming more and more a hotbed of antislavery activity. Green's eldest son Samuel was one of the 130 students enrolled in 1835. He wrote Grandmother Hanna Deming, "Here at Oneida Institute we are all abolitionists to a man—Trustees—Faculty—& Students."[48] The Institute was indeed an abolitionist training camp. Students printed numerous abolition tracts and reports on the college press and took over responsibility for publishing *The Friend of Man*, an abolitionist paper begun at Utica by William Goodell to serve the New York Anti-Slavery Society.[49] They fanned out into the churches of central New York with the gospel of immediatism according to President Green. Green welcomed the abolitionist zealotry of his energetic scholars. To his way of thinking, an education which was not harnessed to the celestial chariot of reform was no education at all.

We can further gauge the depth of Green's impact on Oneida Institute by examining his essays on reform published in 1835 and 1836. Conservative theologians were attempting to thwart abolitionism by erecting a wall of separation between religion and politics. Leonard Woods, one of Green's theological mentors at Andover Seminary, had censured the abolitionists for meddling in the fundamental institutions of civil government and religion with "rash and unbidden hands." Green invoked the legacies of Luther, Clavin, Knox, and even Jesus himself, in defense of the proposition that the great reformers all had disturbed worldly arrangements for the sake of doing good. He argued that every man, woman, and child had a sacred obligation to oppose sin with righteousness, despite slurs that reformers were radicals, fanatics, incendiaries, and "black Mormons of the East." In a circle continually widening until "scores, hundreds, thousands" occupied common ground, the reformer laid "the axe to the roots of the evil." In the timid ecclesiastics of the North, Green saw "foul apostasy from the Christian cause" and racism masking itself in unctuous defense of civil order. He chided Woods, "He, who hates the Negro, will never love their reprovers. We may as well throw ourselves on the mercy of the negro-stealer of the South as the negro-hater of the North."[50]

Woods depicted Green as belonging to a company of "dark and grim visaged" radicals, like the zealots who turned the French Revolution into a bloodbath. He saw himself as the reasonable reformer and Green as the ultraist, not unlike the temperance advocate whose hatred of alcohol led him to abandon the use of the fermented grape in the Lord's Supper. Green responded by pointing to the hypocrisy of the conservative reformers who regarded "the brown and ragged wood-sawer with his coarse jug of cheap whiskey with abhorrence but with 'manly patience and religious composure' " kept their place among wealthy and refined winebibbers. He likewise pointed to the hypocrisy of those who condemned the African slave-trader as a "dark minded wretch" but extended forbearance and paternal love toward "the intelligent, genteel, *chivalrous* slave grower and soul driver of the South." Green admitted that true reformers had been regarded as "perverters of the people," "pestilent fellows," and "ultraists and radicals" by "courtly conservatives" ever since Christ's crucifixion. What would it take to silence him? Green challenged Woods to prove that the Negro was not a man, that he could be held as a piece of property without sin, and that Christians could without risk to their own souls blind themselves to a system which promoted theft, adultery, and murder.[51]

In June 1836, Green put pen to paper, incensed at having read an attack upon the abolitionists by the Reverend John C. Rice, D.D., Professor of Christian Theology at Union Theological Seminary in Virginia. Here was a perfect foil—a doctor of divinity, supporter of the American Colonization Society, and an advocate of the doctrine of expediency. Though a Southerner, Rice was held in high regard by conservative theocrats in the North and was regarded as a liberal in his native region. Like Woods, Rice tried to separate religion and politics. His solution to the problem of slavery was to wait for a transformation of the public will that would cause the slaveholders spontaneously to free those kept in captivity. He denounced the abolitionists for meddling with slavery and argued that the church would be "carried along" in the river of righteousness once the whole mass of the community had been set in motion. Green countered that the church had been carried along "like dead fish in a filthy stream!"[52] He believed it necessary to proclaim to Christians everywhere: *"To be saved, we must come into conformity with the relations we sustain to God and our neighbor."*[53] Green was not one to let his piety suffocate his humanity.

We see this clearly in his most widely disseminated antislavery essay, *Things for Northern Men to Do.* Delivered on a Sabbath evening in July, 1836, at the First Presbyterian Church in Whitesboro, it directs the accusatory finger at Northerners themselves. Had they not displayed prejudice against the complexion of the African American? Did they not tolerate the sale of human beings in the District of Columbia? Who among them had aided the fugitive slave? Where were they when assaults were made upon the civil rights of abolitionist lecturers? Green suggested that there were individuals in First Presbyterian itself who had profited, albeit indirectly, from the misery of the slave. He called for a clean break with the denominations which tolerated slaveholding members. Slavery was the "pet-sin" of the church; she must be aroused to her guilt before God's blighting cures wasted and withered her. The republic, Green warned, would rot in the same dishonored tomb unless northern Christians did something practical to end slavery.[54]

Green gave so much of himself to the abolitionist cause in the mid-1830s that he had precious little time for his large and growing family. It occupied a gambrel-roofed house with large maples in the yard, located across from the Institute grounds. Family members took pride in the fact that their home, which they dubbed "the Old Hive," was the first framed house in Oneida County.[55] Beriah's seventh child was born in August 1835 and named Charles Stuart Green, indicative of Green's respect and affection for Charles Stuart, the West Indian-born British abolitionist who had taught a boys' school in Utica. Mrs. Green remained in feeble health through much of 1836, causing her husband great anguish. He also worried constantly about his family's financial plight. The two oldest children, Samuel and Ann, stayed periodically with the Smiths in Peterboro to allow their mother more rest and reduce the number present at the dinner table. Beriah was constantly on the run between home, school, and speaking engagements in churches and abolitionist meetings. Thus he agonized over not being able to give more time to his family and came close to emotional and physical collapse trying to juggle the demands of home and school.

The Institute burgeoned to 136 students in 1836 and was about to graduate the first class of seniors.[56] The school was now abolitionist to the core, more so than any other American college. Consequently, its enemies took counsel and sought ways to rein in the Oneida radicals. State Senator David Wager of Utica introduced a resolution in 1836 requesting the Senate Committee on Literature to consider the propriety of denying Oneida Institute its share of a fund distributed to regent approved schools to assist with salaries and instructional equipment. A conservative Whig and anti-abolitionist, Wager derided the Institute as a "hot-bed of sedition" and complained that Green had encouraged his students to lobby for abolitionism at the polls. Beriah counterattacked by calling for a mass protest in Utica.[57] He viewed Wager's legislative maneuver as a stalking-horse for slavery and a threat to freedom of thought and speech. "It is time for us, fellow citizens," he told those who assembled in Utica on April 20th, "to rouse up; to examine our conditions and prospects and under God to assert our rights! Let us tear the mask from the face of tyranny!"[58] Gerrit Smith and others spoke in defense of Oneida Institute; none denied its abolitionist character. Donations from among the 165 friends of humanity in attendance amounted to nearly five thousand dollars.

Though Wager's attempt to punish the Institute failed, it clearly demonstrated that Green had been successful in hewing the school into shape. It had become an extension of himself, more powerful than voice or pen. But Oneida Institute was more than an institution in which abolitionism thrived. Had it become only a training center for young reformers, Green would have considered it a failure. In chronicling Oneida's transformation from a manual labor school in which pious enthusiasts were trained under Gale, to an abolitionist school of the prophets under Green, we have told but half the story.

Green accepted the presidency in 1833 under two conditions. He must be free to preach immediatism. He was also to be allowed to admit students regardless of race. This last and equally important objective was, in the final analysis, much more radical than remolding the Institute into an abolitionist institution. Green envisioned his school as a model biracial and prejudice-free community. Interracial education was to be the acid test of his abolitionism. If abolitionists themselves could not demonstrate the practicality of Christian egalitarian principles, then their fulminations against the slaveholders were hollow and hypocritical. In the face of the hated and enslaved black, Beriah Green saw Christ on the Day of Judgment, inquiring concerning his stewardship of love.[59] Many white abolitionists were content to love the enslaved black at a distance; their abolitionism had little to do with how they treated African Americans in their own communities. Beriah Green's abolitionism began where that of other opponents of chattel slavery ended.

4

"TO CUT THE CORD OF CASTE"

Only "a crank and an abolitionist" like Beriah Green, W. E. B. Du Bois asserts in *The Souls of Black Folk*, would have dared in the mid-1830s to admit black youth to Oneida Institute. Du Bois went on to describe the effect of Green upon Alexander Crummell, one of the African American alumni. "Before the bluff, kindhearted man, the shadow [of racism's veil] seemed less dark."[1] The mature Crummell remembered Oneida Institute's president as "that master-thinker and teacher." He pointedly recalled "3 years of perfect equality with upwards to 100 white students, of different denominations, at Oneida Institute."[2] A collective portrait of the African Americans at Oneida Institute will demonstrate just how effectively Green broke "the cord of caste" in American education and helped to lift the veil of racism about which Du Bois wrote so eloquently in 1903.

In the 1830s and 1840s, black leaders sought racial elevation by stressing individual self-improvement. They campaigned within the black community for literacy, hard work, temperance, piety, frugality, and respectability. An editorial in *Freedom's Journal*, an important black newspaper, stated: "Educate our youth, and you remove the moral infection that exists among the lower classes of our people—you elevate the intellect and excite an oppressed and injured people, to honorable and successful endeavors after virtue and competency. This is the whole secret of amelioration."[3] This emphasis on education and moral improvement complemented the abolitionist crusade. Black leaders felt it important to undercut the proslavery argument that the race was incapable of handling freedom. "It is for us," the editor of *Freedom's Journal* argued, "to convince the world by uniform

49

propriety of conduct, industry and economy, that we are worthy of esteem and patronage."[4] As Daniel Alexander Payne, the great African Methodist bishop and educator, learned in his youth, the only difference between the master and the slave was "superior knowledge."[5] Like many other black leaders, he dedicated himself to the proposition that "knowledge is power."

Northern blacks sought "mental improvement" by organizing Sabbath schools and literary societies with libraries, lectures, and discussions. One such group, known as the Phoenix Society, existed in Utica prior to Green's arrival at Oneida Institute.[6] But blacks lacked the financial resources to establish institutions that might afford more than a rudimentary education. In 1830 several in the black convention movement attempted to found their own college in New Haven but were forced to abandon the plan because of white prejudice. In an age when most Northern blacks had no formal education at all, or had to be content with charity schools run by whites, higher education was a dream deferred. Several New England colleges tolerated the presence of a black or two. Amherst, Bowdoin, and Dartmouth had each graduated one black by 1830. But these were exceptional cases. More commonly, colleges denied admission to promising black students— Wesleyan College to Charles B. Ray, Brown to Thomas Paul, Sr., and Columbia to J. McCune Smith.

White hostility toward interracial education increased with the emergency of immediatism. Northern whites might be antislavery in principle, but they shuddered at the prospect of having their sons and daughters educated with free blacks. The Quaker Prudence Crandall's troubles began which she received a black girl into her boarding school at Canterbury, Connecticut in 1833. The local citizens created such an uproar that Miss Crandall had to close her school in 1834. Mob action also shut down the integrated Noyes Academy at Canaan, New Hampshire, in 1835, after only a year's operation. Whites would tolerate charity schools only if they were designed to educate blacks separately.

Thus Beriah Green's plans to offer higher education to blacks in an interracial setting at Oneida Institute must be reckoned as both daring and historically significant. The New England Anti-Slavery Society applauded his pioneering efforts. It introduced a resolution in 1836 urging financial support of Oneida Institute, because it was the only literary institution east of Ohio which made students of color feel welcome. The resolution noted that while some other colleges may not have had official policies barring blacks, they "encouraged a prejudice which created an atmosphere in which a colored student could not live."[7] Oberlin College, Oneida's rival for first honor in interracial higher education, admitted several blacks to Sheffield Institute, its preparatory division, in 1835. But the Ohio school did not graduate its first African American (George B. Vashon) until 1844, when Green's experiment had ended.

Information concerning the African Americans who attended Oneida Institute is elusive and scattered. Class rosters, usually appended to school catalogues, do not identify students by race and are extant for only the first four years of Green's ten years as president.[8] Many of his personal letters and papers turned to ashes in a house fire in September 1843, six months prior to Oneida Institute's closing. Those that survived or were accumulated thereafter give scant reference to individual students, black or white. Green himself seemed unconcerned about the exact number of African Americans who attended his school. In 1840, fellow abolitionist Amos Phelps, eager to wave Oneida Institute's flag against that of Oberlin's supporters at the forthcoming world assembly of abolitionists in London, asked Green about the number of blacks at the Whitesboro school. He responded, "I know not what number of colored students we have had. We have at this time, including those of Indian blood, about 20."[9]

Beriah's inability to provide an exact tabulation of black students at Oneida is indicative of the philosophy with which he approached interracial education. He was not so much interested in numbers as in creating an egalitarian community of youthful reformers. He welcomed fugitive slaves to his home and to the campus, where students hid them in their dormitory rooms. He defended the rights of free blacks, and accepted students whether of African, Native-American, or Anglo-Saxon origin because it was right to do so. Interracial education was a self-authenticating right, a test of the inner connections between immediatist principles and practice. Already despised as a haven for the "foul abomination of abolitionism," Oneida Institute became known as the "Negro school," not because black students ever outnumbered whites, but because blacks took their rightful place alongside students from all classes, races, and backgrounds.[10] Witness the testimony of Josiah B. Grinnell (later a prominent Iowa politician and namesake of Grinnell College). He recalled that when he entered Oneida Institute about 1841, it had "a heavy brain at its head" and an open door policy which resulted in "a motley company" of

> *emancipator's boys from Cuba; mulattoes; a Spanish student [from the Island of Minorca]; an Indian named Kunkapot; black men who had served as sailors, or as city hackmen, also the purest Africans escaped from slavery; sons of American radicals, Bible students scanning Hebrew verse with ease, in the place of Latin odes; enthusiasts, plowboys and printers; also real students of elegant tastes, captured by the genius of President Green.*[11]

Green, it will be recalled, accepted the presidential office on the condition that discrimination bar no one from entering Oneida Institute, in the hope that he could do something *practical* in the fight against slavery. After obtaining assurances from the board of trustees, in March 1834, that it would not oppose his efforts, Beriah spread the word that black students should apply. Elizur Wright, Jr., happily informed William Lloyd Garrison in June that Green intended to make the Institute "the focus of light to the minds of colored Americans."[12] Despite the reservations of some of Oneida's supporters, Green advanced his plan. He wrote Amos Phelps on September 4, 1834, "I hope God will send us a goodly number of colored students to begin the next year with. We have 3. Two of them are quite promising. The third is young and boyish somewhat; & I think will leave us."[13] The precise number of Afro-Americans who attended Oneida Institute during Green's ten-year presidency cannot be determined. However, on the basis of a wide variety of elusive sources, we know of the following fourteen: Samuel A. Jackson; William D. Forten; Amos G. Beman; Amos N. Freeman; Alexander Crummell; Henry Highland Garnet; Thomas S. Sidney; Garrett A. Cantine; Augustus Washington; Elymas P. Rogers; Jermain W. Loguen; William G. Allen; John V. DeGrasse; and Jacob A. Prime.

Students of African American history will readily recognize several of these names. Garnet and Loguen, for example, have found their way into accounts of black abolitionism. Crummell achieved prominence in the colonization movement of the 1850s, when American blacks viewed Liberia as a positive alternative to oppression in this country. But others, such as Samuel A. Jackson and Garrett A. Cantine, led relatively obscure lives after their Oneida years. Thus a collective portrait of the black Oneidans is difficult. We can, however, say something about their background, reasons for enrolling, experiences at Green's school, and later careers. When a definitive history of the northern black free community of the pre-Civil War era is written, the blacks who came to Whitesboro in pursuit of liberation through education will doubtless assume the recognition due them.

Given the minuscule number of blacks living in central New York in the 1830s, it is noteworthy that the first African American to enroll at the Institute came from Onondaga Hollow, a settlement south of Syracuse. Admitted to the First Presbyterian Church of Whitesboro in October 1834 by letter of transfer, Samuel A. Jackson started his studies that fall. He gave up his books in 1835 to serve as Institute steward, suggesting that he may have been the immature candidate of whom Green wrote Phelps. Jackson rejoined the freshman class in 1836, shared quarters with Alexander Crummell in 1837, but is not listed on the student rosters for 1838 and 1839. While at Oneida, he worked with Utica's small black population in organizing a celebration of emancipation in the British West Indies. Jackson thus set a precedent for future black Oneidan's by involving himself with local blacks while still a student.[14]

William D. Forten is more typical of the black Oneidans in that he came from an urban area with a significant black population. The youngest child of a prominent Philadelphia sailmaker, William arrived at Whitesboro in 1835 to join the first year men in the upper division. Perhaps because of some deficiency in academic preparation, he transferred to the English and Preparatory Department the following year. This was not atypical. Henry Highland Garnet also had difficulties handling the college curriculum. Having been denied academic opportunities at the high school level, at a time when universal public education still eluded whites, several of Oneida's black students needed to begin with the younger classes. As Forten's name does not appear among any of the 1837 classes, he probably left Oneida Institute and returned to Philadelphia.

Three other blacks enrolled in 1835—Amos G. Beman, Amos N. Freeman, and Alexander Crummell. They apparently did well. Green would later testify, "Mr. A. G. Beman has won the confidence, found the love, and raised the hopes of his affectionate instructors."[15] Pelatiah Rawson, Professor of Mathematics, and Innes Grant, Professor of Greek and Hebrew Languages, confirmed that Beman had "sustained the character of a good and regular student" during his years at the Whitesboro institution.[16] Beman's cordial reception among the Oneidans contrasted starkly with the hostility he had encountered at Wesleyan College in Middletown, Connecticut. The forced departure in 1832 of Charles B. Ray devastated Beman's hopes of also enrolling at Wesleyan. A sympathetic white student began tutoring him, but anonymous letters threatening bodily violence drove him to Massachusetts, where he taught a common school until enrolling at Oneida Institute.

Beman (1812-1874) left the Institute in 1837 and became a Congregational clergyman. He pastored the Temple Street Colored Church in New Haven, Connecticut, for nearly two decades. In pursuing a ministerial career, Beman, like the many of the black Oneidans, availed himself of one of the few professions open to members of his race in antebellum America. Beman's labors on behalf of black suffrage, civil rights, fugitive slaves, the American Missionary Association, and the freedmen exemplified the kind of reform career Green intended for his students.

Amos N. Freeman, a native of New York, spent three years at Oneida. He first roomed with fellow blacks, but when on-campus facilities became overcrowded in 1837, he boarded in the village of Whitesboro, certainly something of a novelty among the white citizens. In 1838 Jackson left to establish a "colored" school in New Brunswick, New Jersey, but soon found his true calling in the ministry. Amos Beman apparently recommended Freeman to the Abyssinian Congregational Church in Portland,

Maine. As Beman had previously pastored there and helped to install Freeman, we can only conclude that Oneida Institute served as something of a
"old boys" network for blacks. Having known one another as students,
they sustained fraternal bonds after leaving Green's school. For example,
Beman, Freeman, Rogers, Garnet, and Prime were active in the Evangelical Association of (African American) Presbyterian and Congregational
Churches, a kind of black caucus in a white religious tradition.[17]

Alexander Crummell, the fourth African American to enroll in 1835,
was surely one of the most noteworthy alumni of Green's school, black or
white. Born in 1819 of free parents in Brooklyn, he went with Henry Highland
Garnet and Thomas S. Sidney to Canaan, New Hampshire, to enroll at
William Scales's Noyes Academy. But, as Crummell tells us, "the Democracy of the State could not endure what they called a 'Nigger School' on the
soil of New Hampshire." Farmers with ninety yoke of oxen dragged the
academy building off into a swamp. So the three frustrated scholars returned home for a few months. Then, according to Crummell, "information
was received that Oneida Institute, at Whitesboro, a Manual Labor Seminary, had opened its doors to colored boys. Thither we three New York
boys at once repaired, and spent three years under the instruction of that
Master-thinker and teacher, Rev. Beriah Green."[18] Du Bois more than adequately summed up Crummell's experience at Oneida—"to the lonely boy
came a new dawn of sympathy and inspiration."[19]

While a student Crummell sent a most revealing letter to Elizur
Wright which underscores Du Bois' conclusion. It recounts Crummell's
"profession of Religion" shortly after arriving at Oneida and specifically
mentions the president's chapel Bible classes. At one session, Green was
endeavoring to inculcate the principle that "the man who would not submit
to evidence had the elements of lying in him." This so struck the
seventeen-year old that he wrote to Wright to confess "a palpable false-
hood" regarding the circumstances under which a rocking chair had been
broken. While delivering the chair to Wright's home, Crummell had driven
too fast and the chair fell off the wagon. Though he had denied responsibility
for the broken chair at the time of the incident, Crummell wrote Wright
after hearing Green lecture, "Henceforth my aim and endeavor shall be to
be a man of Principle; convinced that nothing but principle and honesty in
every department of life, will make a man—a man of usefulness."[20] Green
could not have said it better.

Crummell graduated in November 1838 and returned to New York
City, where he and Thomas Sidney planned to open a school for poor black
youth. The same year he was appointed ward commander for the New York
Association for the Political Improvement of Colored People. He soon set
his sights upon the Episcopal ministry, but General Theological Seminary

refused him admission. Former classmates at Oneida Institute held a meeting to protest Crummell's exclusion.[21] Crummell eventually obtained private tutoring in Rhode Island and was consecrated a deacon in 1842 and a priest in 1844. In 1848 he traveled to England, where friends arranged for his matriculation in Queen's College, Cambridge, which awarded him the B. A. degree in 1853. In 1892 the *Washington Bee* hailed Crummell as the "most educated Negro in American."[22] He had spent two decades as a missionary in Liberia and advocate of the uplift of Africa through civilization and Christianity. He served a quarter century as the rector of St. Luke's Episcopal Church in Washington, D.C., and died in 1898.

Henry Highland Garnet's parents escaped from a Maryland plantation to Wilmington, Delaware, in 1824, when he was nine. They settled in New York City, where their son received a grammar school education in the African Free School. He served as a cabin boy on two voyages to Cuba, only to return to find that his family and home had been broken up by slave hunters. Quakers on Long Island took him in as an indentured servant for two years. In 1831 Garnet began studying at the High School for Colored Youth, where he was introduced to the Latin and Greek classics. News that Noyes Academy was prepared to admit "colored youth of good character on equal terms with white of like character" raised Garnet's hopes.[23] He left New Hampshire bitterly disappointed. On the trip home, Crummell and Sidney feared for their friend's life.

Garnet's intellectual qualities, Crummell recalled, were distinguished by intuition, wit, brilliance, and power. But Crummell felt that his friend's "early, long continued illness broke up the systematic training of the schools; and so he was never the deep-plodding, laborious student"[24] This may explain Garnet's demotion in 1836 to Oneida's Preparatory Department. In any case, he went on to demonstrate his native abilities, especially in public debate. He once turned upon a heckler, who had thrown a squash upon the stage during Garnet's class oration, with the retort, "My good friends, do not be alarmed, it is only a soft pumpkin; some gentleman has thrown away his head and lo! his brains are dashed out."[25] After graduating in 1839, he served the Liberty Street Presbyterian Church in Troy, joined the American and Foreign Anti-Slavery Society, backed the Liberty Party, fought for the elective franchise in New York State, led in the formation of African American state conventions, harbored fugitive slaves and was active in the free produce movement, which sold only products not tainted by the "peculiar institution."

Perhaps the most radical of the black Oneidans, Garnet saw little hope for freeing the slaves except by their own efforts. "If you must bleed," he counseled his brethren in chains, "let it all come at once—rather *die freemen, then live to be slaves*."[26] His own straining against the "cord of

Henry Highland Garnet. From William J. Simmons, *Men of Mark* (Cleveland: Geo. M. Rewell & Co., 1887).

caste" took him to various pulpits in this country, then to Great Britain, Scotland, the West Indies, and, in 1854, to Liberia, West Africa, where he was appointed Minister Resident. He, like Crummell, promoted the African Civilization Society. Garnet was pastor of Shiloh Presbyterian Church in New York City but returned to Liberia in 1881 as United States minister resident. He died a year later.

We know very little of Thomas Sidney, the third refugee from the Noyes Academy outrage who found a safe haven at Oneida Institute. He died in 1841 when only twenty-three. Dr. James McCune Smith, the prominent African American physician and abolitionist, memorialized Sidney in fulsome phrase: "The wit, the pure patriot, the almost self-taught scholar, cut off alas! in the very bloom of his promising youth."[27] After leaving the Institute, Sidney served as a ward commander and as corresponding secretary of the newly formed Association for the Political Improvement of People of Color in New York City. He taught briefly at the New York Select

Alexander Crummell. From William J. Simmons, *Men of Mark* (Cleveland: Geo. M. Rewell & Co., 1887).

Academy, which had an all-black board of trustees and conducted classes in the basement of the famous abolitionist-supported Broadway Tabernacle. Despite a short public life, Sidney identified himself, as did all of the African Americans who attended Beriah Green's school, with the struggle for civil liberties and racial equality.[28]

Of Garrett A. Cantine, listed as a member of the Preparatory Department in 1837, we know even less than we do of Sidney. He too came from New York City. The *San Francisco Elevator,* an African American newspaper, made reference to a Garrett A. Cantine who served as principal of the Nevada City Colored School during the 1860s.[29] This is very likely the same individual who attended Oneida in 1837. Were we able to identify all students by race on the class rosters, we would doubtless discover other blacks who like Cantine studied at Oneida Institute but did not achieve the prominence of Crummell or Garnet.

The costs of tuition, room, and board at Oneida Institute, though modest because of the manual labor emphasis, proved an impediment to the very poor. Augustus Washington enrolled in 1837, but after one year found himself two hundred dollars in debt. He moved to Brooklyn, where he clerked in a drugstore, studied Latin and Greek privately, and eventually paid off every cent. A self-described practical abolitionist, he served as an agent of the *Colored American* and became involved in campaigns for black suffrage and temperance. He taught in Brooklyn's African Public School No. 1 for about three years and then applied to the American Education Society for assistance in completing college. It refused him on the grounds that Oneida Institute had dropped the study of Latin. Washington then spent two years at Kimball Union Academy in New Hampshire, which Green attended in his youth.[30] Washington's case was not unique. Black leaders recognized that want of pecuniary means prevented many of the very poor from attending the Institute. Robert Purvis and James Forten, Sr., offered in 1839 to purchase a scholarship or right to ten years of tuition and room rent for indigent black youth at Oneida Institute.[31]

Like Garnet and Crummell, Washington supported African colonization. In the wake of the Fugitive Slave Act of 1850, he redoubled his efforts to convince fellow African Americans that whatever may have been their objections to colonization in former times, the reality of the racial situation in the 1850s made emigration to Africa both necessary and morally defensible. "Who but educated and pious colored men," he exclaimed in a long essay written for the *New York Tribune,* "are to lead on the van of the sacramental host of God's elect; to conquer by love, and bring Africa, with her trackless regions, under the dominion of our Savior."[32] Washington emigrated to Liberia, where in 1862 he was reported to have "risen to eminence having been several times a legislator and now one of the judges."[33]

In December 1834, Gerrit Smith, whose wealth and abolitionist sympathies brought many appeals from or on behalf of indigent blacks, received a letter of reference from Thomas H. Gallaudet, a clergyman of Hartford, Connecticut. Gallaudet wrote of "a pious & unceasingly well-behaved young man" of about twenty years of age who had "a good mind and [was] very anxious to improve."[34] This was Elymas P. Rogers, yet another of Oneida's African American students. He spent one year at Smith's manual labor high school in Peterboro and then enrolled at Oneida in 1837. In a eulogy delivered upon Rogers' death in 1861, Henry Highland Garnet stated that his former classmate completed his studies at Oneida in 1841 and then began to teach in Trenton, New Jersey.[35] Since Rogers entered only as a preparatory student in 1837, he must have completed an accelerated program in order to graduate four years later from the college division. In 1846 he moved to Newark and assumed the pastorate of an African Presbyterian church. He united with temperance forces and penned a lengthy poetic broadside in 1845 entitled "Alcohol Personified." He also earned a reputation for having done much to mitigate the pro-slavery feelings of Newark's white citizens. Under the sponsorship of the American Colonization Society, Rogers journeyed to West Africa in 1861, but died within a few weeks of arriving, a victim of tropical fever.[36]

While at Oneida, Rogers taught a "colored school" in Rochester during summers and vacations. He recruited a hotel porter at the Rochester House by the name of Jermain Loguen for Oneida Institute. Born in Tennessee of a white father and a slave mother, he had escaped around 1834 to Canada, where he tried his hand at farming. After creditors seized the farm, Loguen settled in Rochester. With Rogers' encouragement, he enrolled at the Institute in 1839 and soon won the confidence and esteem of both students and faculty, despite his lack of formal education. In his last year at Oneida, he started a school for the black children of Utica who were excluded from the public system[37]

In 1841, Loguen settled in Syracuse and opened another school. He soon received a license to preach from the African Methodist Episcopal Zion denomination. At various times he ministered in Bath, Ithaca, and Troy, New York, but Loguen's energies were more devoted to abolitionism than the pastoral ministry. He constructed an apartment for fugitive slaves in his home, gave abolition lectures, and became known as the "General Superintendent of the Underground Railroad" in the Syracuse area. In October 1851 Loguen participated in the famous "Jerry Rescue," in which local black and white abolitionists snatched a fugitive slave known as William Henry, or "Jerry," from federal authorities and spirited him to Canada.[38] Loguen eventually rose to the rank of bishop in the African Methodist Episcopal Zion denomination. After the Civil War he took an active interest in the welfare of the ex-slaves. He died in Syracuse in 1872.

The twelfth African American whose attendance at Oneida Institute can be documented was born in Virginia about 1820 of a free mulatto mother and a Welshman. William G. Allen was adopted by a free black family of Fortress Monroe, where he caught the eye of the Reverend William Hall, a New Yorker who conducted a black elementary school. Hall wrote Gerrit Smith in 1839, urging him to sponsor Allen's education in New York State.[39] In 1840 Green sent Allen to Smith with an accompanying letter describing the young man's character and financial plight. Though poorly clad, Allen had already earned high marks in his studies and was well spoken-of for his good conduct, accomplishments on the flute, with which he assisted the chapel choir, and service as clerk to the Institute's superintendent and treasurer.[40] Allen spent the summer of 1841 teaching in a school which Hiram Wilson, a white alumnus, had established among fugitive slaves in

Jermain W. Loguen. From *The Rev. J.W. Loguen as a Slave and as a Freeman* (New York: J.G.K. Truair & Co., 1859).

Upper Canada. He graduated in 1844 with Oneida's last class, then moved to Troy, where he taught school and assisted Garnet in editing the *National Watchman,* an abolitionist and temperance paper for African Americans.

William Allen is probably best remembered because of his appointment in 1850 to New York Central College in McGrawville, Cortland County. After Oneida Institute closed, Gerrit Smith and other antislavery philanthropists turned their attention to this interracial and coeducational institution, chartered in 1849 by the American Baptist Free Mission Society. Allen served as Professor of Greek and German Languages and of Rhetoric and Belles Lettres. He thus became only the second African American to teach at a predominantly white American college. (Charles L. Reason was already on the faculty.) In 1852 Allen announced his intention to marry one of his white students, Mary King, of Fulton, New York. Incensed by this interracial professor-student romance, the local white citizenry threatened mob action in the neighboring village of Phillipsville, where Allen and Miss King were visiting friends. Allen's fiancee was taken back to Fulton and he under protective guard to Syracuse. The couple eventually went to New York City, where they married secretly on March 30, 1852. New York Central College, always at the point of financial collapse, would tolerate no further embarrassment, so Allen resigned and took his wife to England. There he wrote a stinging indictment of American racism. Yet he recalled with fondness the years he spent at Oneida Institute. He praised Green as one of the chosen few, "a profound scholar, an original thinker, and better and greater than all these, a sincere and devoted Christian."[41]

John V. DeGrasse enrolled at Oneida Institute in 1840. George De-Grasse, his father, was one of the few "colored aliens" to receive naturalization papers in the early 1800s. John was born in New York City in 1825 and attended school there until coming to Whitesboro. He remained only one year because Oneida did not offer Latin. He then entered Clinton Seminary, the Free Will Baptist school in nearby Clinton. DeGrasse went to France in 1843 to study for two years, thereafter returning to New York for private training in medicine. After additional medical study at Bowdoin College in Maine, DeGrasse returned to Europe and the hospitals of Paris. Eventually he practiced in Boston and achieved the honor of being admitted to the Massachusetts Medical Society.[42]

Jacob A. Prime, the fourteenth and last African American known to have attended Oneida Institute, represents a number of others, not identifiable by name, who witnessed the end of Green's experiment. Born about 1809 at Kinderhook, New York, Prime probably enrolled in 1842 or 1843. He was one of a handful who desired to remain at Whitesboro after the Free Will Baptists purchased the grounds of Oneida Institute in 1844. Prime is listed as a member of the Middle Class in the catalogue of Whitestown Seminary for the year ending July 1846.[43] Few facts are known of his post-Whitestown Seminary years. According to a certificate of ordination in the handwriting of Amos Beman, he was set apart "to the work of the gospel ministry" at Geneva, New York, in October 1849 during the Convocation of Christian Brethren.[44] Prime served Presbyterian congregations in Buffalo and Troy. While pastor of Liberty or Seventh Street Presbyterian in Troy, he engaged in efforts to open the public schools to African Americans and participated in the black state convention movement.

Further research may extend the list of African Americans at Oneida beyond the fourteen who have been positively identified. Since no catalogues were published beyond 1837, with the possible exception of one for 1839, now nonexistent, identification of additional African American students is difficult. Some questions may never be adequately answered. For example, does Samuel R. Ward's ambiguous reference to Oneida Institute as "the alma mater of several of my dear schoolfellows, among them Henry Highland Garnet and Alexander Crummell" mean that he actually studied there? Ward's autobiographical testimony to "the profound, the learned, the original Beriah Green" at the very least suggests considerable contact with Oneida's president.[45] The racial identity of students listed as being from the settlements of Upper Canada or Canada West, if known, could possibly add several names to our list, since large numbers of slave and free African Americans sought refuge there.

We do know that fellow abolitionists directed promising free black youth and fugitive slaves desirous of an education to Green's doorstep. Gerrit Smith inquired in 1835 about finding a place with Green for one of his beneficiaries, a certain James Glocester.[46] Elizur Wright, Jr., wrote Green in 1842 about the possibility of putting Henry Scott, recently rescued from Virginia, "with some good abolitionist of Oneida County."[47] The previous year he had informed his old friend about George Putnam's son, "one of our proscribed brethren," who had been denied a grammar school position in Boston. Dissatisfied with being restricted to monitoring a "colored school," the younger Putnam wished to attend Oneida.[48] No confirmation of Putnam's enrollment could be found.

Unless evidence appears to the contrary, Beriah Green's decade-long experiment in interracial education must be remembered as furthering the aspirations of more African Americans than any other American college in the 1830s and early 1840s. There is no way to measure adequately the impact Oneida Institute made upon the lives of the students, black and white, who passed through it portals to share Beriah Green's vision of equality and justice in a society borne down by the weight of caste and class distinctions. Given the educational philosophy and mission of Oneida Institute, we can assume that its alumni went on to lives of usefulness. Certainly the known black graduates fulfilled Green's hopes for them. His white students too took an active role amidst the world's "weal and woe." Some became abolitionists, reformers, and educators in their own right, following in the footsteps of Theodore Dwight Weld.

Green sat down in 1843 to review something of the character, claims, and conditions of ten years as Oneida Institute's president. "The elevation of the colored people to their proper position in society," he wrote ". . . entered into the very heart of Oneida Institute."[49] Three years earlier, in a report to the Regents of the University of New York, Green had passionately defended offering the advantages of his school "with like cordiality and on the same conditions, to applicants from all quarters, and of all complexions." He wrote:

The red sons of the Western forest, the sable sons of the sunny South have here found a home together, and amidst their various tasks, manual and mental, have lived in peace and love with their pale-faced and blue-eyed brethren. Nor has the one fallen short of the other in the integrity, enterprise and attainments. We could maintain no other position without violence to our best convictions.[50]

5

WEAPONS OF THE MIND

T hose who knew Beriah Green remember him not only for his self-sacrificing labors on behalf of the victims of prejudice, but also for the intellectual acumen with which he attacked the very foundations of American racism. Alexander Crummell described him as the "master thinker and teacher," a tribute echoed in Josiah Bush Grinnell's assertion that Oneida Institute had a "heavy brain" at its head. The *Colored American* praised Green's love of deep learning, and Green's white abolitionist colleagues looked to him for intellectual leadership. Gerrit Smith boasted that President Green's intellect was "not surpassed in the whole range of my acquaintance." James Gillespie Birney recorded in his diary, "Of all my friends and acquaintances in the abolition ranks—and they certainly contain a great deal of talent—Beriah Green's arguments strike me as most forcible and convincing."[1] These plaudits invite consideration of Green's use of the mind as a weapon in the fight against slavery.

The intellectual underpinnings of American abolitionism are equally as important as a narrative account of antislavery activism. We cannot truly understand Beriah Green unless we wrestle with his world of thought. Just as contemporary Americans argue about principles and ideas when engaged in social reform, so the abolitionists of the 1830s knew that they had to bring about a revolution in consciousness about how to *think* about slavery if they were to free a single slave. From the enlightened vantage point of the late twentieth century, the following elucidation of Green's intellectual argument against slavery may appear obvious. What is self-evident to the modern mind was not so to Green's generation. He had to make a case against slavery using the philosophical and theological traditions of his era in order to discredit slavery's apologists in the best academic and religious circles.

Personal experience taught Beriah that mental exertions were no less taxing than hard, physical labor. Just as the body could be corrupted by intemperance and other evil habits and needed to be cleansed and strengthened through physical exercise, so the mind was subject to the pollution of wrong principles. Once Green secured the presidency of Oneida Institute, he used its classrooms as zealously as its workshops to train and discipline those who were to comprise his abolitionist phalanx. Oneida's founders had been primarily interested in preparing evangelists for the rigors of the frontier. Gale had shortened but not substantially altered the classical curriculum common to American literary institutions in the 1830s. Green needed allies in the fight against slavery, so he took Oneida's manual labor program and subserved it to the preparation of practical-minded reformers.

Oneida's students welcomed their president's intellectual intensity and shared his millennial vision of a new age in which justice and righteousness would triumph over the evils of Jacksonian America. They were willing to take up the manual labor regimen and endure the spartan lifestyle at Oneida for the sake of a *practical* education. One disgruntled, abolitionist-minded student wrote when Gale was still principal, "I cannot see what good it will be to study Latin and Greek. If I were the best linquist in the universe it would not aid me in telling a heathen sinner the way to go to the Savior's feet."[2] Once Green became president, he urged his pupils to whet their reform axes upon Isaiah, not Ovid, Virgil, or Homer. Green scorned the idea that mere education was the mark of an educated man. He substituted Hebrew and New Testament Greek for Latin and classical Greek, because he felt that only the Bible could serve as a charter for the new social order.[3]

Green also revamped Oneida's curriculum by giving greater attention to the study of ethics or moral philosophy than was the case during Gale's tenure, or indeed at most American colleges in the 1830s, where courses in moral philosophy, usually taught by the college president, were designed to examine the motives, rules, and actions of individual behavior. They were targeted at students in the senior class who were about to graduate and, so it was thought, assume the burden of moral leadership among the general public. As John Dewey once observed, these senior ethics courses were intended to be "a kind of intellectual coping to the structure erected in earlier years or, at least, as the insertion of the key-stone of the arch."[4]

At once distinct from theology, with its appeal to Scripture, and related to religion in the area of ethics, moral philosophy was thought of as a "science." The academic moralists, armed too with insights from intellectual or mental philosophy, which Green also taught, studied the motives and rules of human action in a fashion similar to the astronomer studying the universe. They then drew conclusions about duty or right behavior for individuals and, in a related area known as political economy (another of Green's specialties), for society as a whole. Green felt that examination of the moral constitution of man was far too important a subject to be left for the senior year. So as Professor of Mental and Moral Philosophy, he redistributed courses traditionally in a student's last year among the different classes at Oneida Institute. He wanted to make sure that all students had *"a full conviction of the truths of Christianity"* as early as possible.[5]

The student scholars at Oneida had more formal exposure to their president's views about Christian beliefs, values, and duty than did young men in the traditional institutions. Though they had other instructors, their school was dominated by Green's personality and views and became widely known simply as "President Green's school." In November 1833, a few weeks after his installation, Green began to work on the students with a course of public lectures on slavery, also attended by community residents. In addition, he used the chapel pulpit to disseminate his views on education, temperance, abolitionism, and other moral reform causes. Each fall he delivered a valedictory address to the graduating seniors which assessed the state of affairs at the Institute in relation to some dominant theme, such as the place of the reformer in American life, the basis of a sound reputation, or the Christian principles of true success. At the request of the students, the addresses were printed on the Institute press and distributed beyond the campus. Green also invited students to his home, where he continued their ethical instruction in a more intimate fashion.[6]

Green found none of the traditional textbooks on academic moral philosophy wholly satisfactory in dealing with the demands of a generation harnessed to the engine of reform and confronted with the sin of slavery. By 1835 he had dispensed with the standard textbook approach and lectured on the basis of his own notes, a method reflecting his disdain for slavish attachment to textbooks and the older catechetical mode of instruction. Green's own moral philosophy was becoming increasing eclectic. He decided that none of the academic moralists dealt adequately with the challenges facing an abolitionist-minded student body. Green was the only academic moral philosopher among the immediatists of the 1830s. This is striking on several counts. Academic moral philosophers, like systematic theologians, tend to be of a conservative nature, for they serve as the custodians of a community's values and traditions. They love system and order.

Francis Wayland, America's most widely read moral philosopher in the 1830s, exemplifies this point. His textbook *Elements of Moral Science* appeared in 1835 and became standard fare in American colleges. President of

Brown University, Wayland was a moderate Calvinist whose evangelical leanings led him to examine social problems in the light of moral philosophy. One's moral duty was based not upon self-interest—that is, upon the fear of hell and hope of heaven—but upon distinctions between right and wrong which arose in uniquely moral relations. Green was heavily influenced by this intuitive approach and wrote frequently of the self-evident principles of reason in his early essays and sermons. He too taught a kind of moral realism derived from common sense philosophy. He believed that moral truths have some kind of independent ontological status and can be known by introspection and by reflection upon the relationships one has with other moral beings. As D. H. Meyer has observed, the academic moralists "made a great display of 'discovering' these truths as empirical 'facts' in their own consciousness, and from these drew inferences about society, nature, and the moral universe."[7]

Wayland's reflections on the self and moral relations led him to conclude that the Creator had endowed every man with the right "to use his *body* as he will" so long as he did not interfere with the rights of his neighbor. The section on personal liberty in *Elements of Moral Science* quotes the Declaration of Independence: "We hold these truths to be self-evident: that all men are created equal; that they are endowed by their Creator with certain inalienable rights; that among these are life, liberty, and the pursuit of happiness."[8] This led Wayland to acknowledge slavery as a violation of personal liberty, since it allowed a master to control the physical and intellectual life of the slave.

Wayland's good reputation among abolitionists did not last long, for in 1838 he published *Limitations of Human Responsibility,* in which his basically conservative temperament and love of social order triumphed over his intuitionist moral philosophy. Though he still thought slavery morally wrong, Wayland now argued that the abolitionists, either as citizens of the United States or as human beings under the moral government of God, had no right to tamper with the existing institution of slavery. Wayland admitted that the general ethical teachings of the New Testament were subversive of slavery, but finding no explicit condemnation of slavery, he equivocated. "Whether slavery be bad or good," he wrote in *Limitations of Human Responsibility,* "we wash our hands of it, inasmuch as it is a matter which the providence of God has never placed within our jurisdiction." "We have no right," he told those who hoped that he might lead fellow Northerners out of the wilderness of moral indifference, "to force our instructions upon them [the slaveholders] either by conversation, or by lectures, or by the mail."[9]

Green's conversion to abolitionism as his sacred vocation allowed for no artificial distinction between moral truth and moral duty. His moral philosophy was intellectually traditional yet socially radical. Like Wayland, he began with introspection and discovered self-evident principles of moral obligation which he felt were rationally justifiable and normative for all:

> *Reason whether it shine on the face of God or be reflected from the soul of man is Reason—the same clear, certain, unerring light throughout the Universe. The principles, which in this light command our ready, unhesitating, full assent, are everywhere and at all times the same. Truth, justice, disinterested love are recognized as much wherever and whenever they may be exhibited. The equality of the principle method embodied in the Golden Rule not more surely finds an echo in the bosom of the saint than in the bosom of the savage.*[10]

But Green's observations of the world about him and the way in which people actually behaved led him to conclude that human passions, or self-interest, clouded individual moral judgment. "Selfishness," he asserted, "throws all things into disorder." Those who were blind to the sin of slavery had closed their "eyes against the light of reason, and turn[ed] away from the inspired volume."[11]

Green viewed the conscience as the "faculty" by which we know that the world without and the world within correspond, analogous to the function of the senses and understanding in informing us of the physical universe. In this he hewed closely to the views of the British poet and moralist, Samuel Taylor Coleridge. Coleridge described the conscience as the eternal abiding place of the "principles of rectitude"—the ineradicable and reflective will of God. "The conscience is neither reason, religion, or will," Coleridge wrote in his *Aids to Reflection,* "but an experience *sui generis* of the coincidence of the human will with reason and religion."[12] Green shared Coleridge's notion of the "republication" of divine principles in the conscience. He believed that when the conscience, reason, and will were in perfect harmony, right action would surely follow.[13]

Green's optimism was tempered by the plain fact that people did not always choose good over evil; indeed, many had become confirmed in their sin. The slaveholder, for example, sincerely believed in the righteousness of his actions. Green attributed this to the evils of the "acquired character." The duty of the reformer was to awaken the conscience, to bring to life the principles which were "in every man's bosom." This demanded ceaseless opposition to iniquity by any means short of violence, which would be contrary to the New Testament ethic to love one's enemies. Wayland had warned against direct confrontation. But Green could not see how the slaveholder was to be convinced of his sin without bringing the "celestial truth" directly to bear upon his conscience.[14]

For two centuries American Christianity had accommodated itself to slavery by seeing it as the bad fruit of the primal fall from grace. Like physical suffering and natural catastrophes, slavery was a token of original sin, a reminder that human perfection since the Fall was impossible. Though he rejected the heady utopianism of the communal perfectionists, such as that of John Humphrey Noyes, the founder of the Oneida Community located to the west of Whitesboro, Green believed in liberation from the consequences of man's sinful nature.[15] Be it the demon of alcohol or of slavery, the sinner was to cast off evil, repent, and don the seamless garment of Christ's righteousness. Green could not approve, however, of the tendency of perfectionists like Noyes to withdraw from the world and leave its sufferers to the mercy of their oppressors.

In the late 1830s, Green became preoccupied with answering the "grave and learned ecclesiastics" of the North. He tried to dispel the myth that the slavery controversy was merely a difference of opinion among "good men," men "orthodox, enterprising, zealous," and remarkable for their religious activity but given to quarrelsome debate over theological trivia. Green maintained that every other issue paled by comparison with the question of the humanity and rights of the slave:

> *The very vitals of Humanity are concerned in this strife. If the yoke of the enslaved is broken, Humanity will escape from the incubus by which she has been well nigh suffocated—she will breathe freely again. If the pledged auxiliaries of the oppressor triumph, Humanity must bleed at every pore, and can escape from her insatiate foes only by some special intervention of Almighty Power.*[16]

The "main pillars which prop up the old Bastille" of slavery, Beriah felt, had their foundation in the North, for Southern planters needed Northern markets. The contest was between men of principle and men of no principle. Green made no distinction between the ecclesiastics who complained about the stiff, unyielding spirit of abolitionist "firebrands" and the mobs which threatened the very lives of the friends of the slaves.

The martyrdom of Elijah Lovejoy reinforced Green's view of the anti-abolitionists as united in a conspiracy against the friends of humanity. Lovejoy, a newspaper editor, had been hounded out of Missouri because of his antislavery editorials. He moved to Alton, Illinois, where his printing presses were destroyed three times. An armed mob, incited by a well-organized nucleus of proslavery and colonizationist citizens of prominence, surrounded a warehouse containing another press on November 7, 1837. When a riverfront tough attempted to raise a ladder from which to torch the building, Lovejoy, who had armed himself with the approval of Alton's mayor, rushed out and raised his pistol at the man. The anti-abolitionists then shot him. Lovejoy's death sent shock waves throughout abolitionist circles.

The American Anti-Slavery Society immediately saw him as a martyr to liberty and sought someone to compose a fitting memorial. At the urging of Elizur Wright and others, Green took on the task, setting aside his most pressing responsibilities at the Institute to commemorate the fallen hero. He journeyed to New York City to deliver the tribute in a memorial service held at Broadway Tabernacle, the reformist citadel of Lewis and Arthur Tappan. After returning to Whitesboro, Green wrote Smith that he had been so *"exceedingly* opressed with the solemn work" of delivering Lovejoy's memorial that he had *"staggered at every step."*[17] Green repeated the discourse at Bleecker Street Presbyterian Church in Utica, site of the anti-abolitionist riot of 1835.

The memorial begins with a review of the moral truths imprinted on the conscience which the reformer is duty-bound to proclaim. It attributes the actions of the Alton mob to the influence of those who had prostrated themselves to "the altar of animalism." Green placed Lovejoy in the book of martyrs alongside God's faithful witnesses in all ages and predicted that the editor's death would arouse many of the indifferent to the claims of the enslaved. In keeping with his conspiracy theory, Green argued that guilt for Lovejoy's death had to be laid upon the "heads of law-abiding, public-spirited, and useful citizens" who were "instigators and abettors of the intoxicated rabble."[18]

Lovejoy's use of a gun, though an act of self-defense, troubled many nonviolent moral suasionists and provided fodder for their enemies. Green's discourse does not explicitly refer to Lovejoy's use of "a carnal weapon," as Garrison put it, but treats the question as to whether or not Lovejoy was "imprudent." Green was an advocate of "peace principles," but he had not sworn himself to the abolitionist ethic of nonresistance. Like Lewis Tappan, he concluded that Lovejoy was justified in attempting to defend himself against the mob: "It was the only point where his rights *could* be defended. Abandoned there, they must give place to the yoke of slavery."[19]

Green had always assumed that the moral law and the divine law as revealed in the Bible were in perfect harmony. His abolitionist argument customarily begins with an appeal to moral values and the transcendent or divine law that sustained them. By basing virtue upon a rationally defensible moral law, he thought he had left no excuse for slavery unchallenged, either from the converted or the unconverted, since Christian and non-Christian alike were to honor the self-evident principles of reason. When "the grave and learned ecclesiastics," even in the face of such atrocities as Lovejoy's murder, appealed to Scripture in defense of their political quietism, Green found the debate over slavery shifting ground.

Southerners, counting upon the public's reverence for the Bible as a cultural icon, sought to portray their critics as Bible-doubters. The Southern Presbyterian theologian Robert L. Dabney wrote his brother, "Here is our policy, then, to push the Bible argument continually, drive abolitionism to the wall, to compel it to assume an anti-Christian position. By so doing we compel the whole Christianity of the North to array itself on our side." Proslavery writers marshalled proof-texts from the Old and New Testaments in defense of slavery as an institution. Richard Fuller, a Southern evangelical, emphatically declared: "WHAT GOD SANCTIONED IN THE OLD TESTAMENT, AND PERMITTED IN THE NEW, CANNOT BE SIN."[20]

The Southern strategy forced the abolitionists to search the Scriptures, for now the argument was not about self-evident principles but about God's revealed or "naked will." This demanded skills in biblical interpretation, for the pro-slavery theologians liked to quibble over the meaning of specific passages, the translation of key Hebrew and Greek words, and the nature of slavery among the ancient Jews as well as in the time of Jesus. Theodore Dwight Weld tried his hand at the Old Testament but felt that someone more qualified should examine the New Testament case against slavery and urged the task upon Green.[21]

Green had quoted liberally from the Scriptures in earlier abolitionist essays. But his use of biblical texts generally embellished a line of argument which was rooted in the notion that slavery violated rational and self-evident principles of justice and equality. Now he was invited to conduct a sustained exegetical examination of those passages from the letters of St. Paul used frequently by the defenders of slavery or their allies, the Northern fence-sitters who bemoaned the plight of the American slave but excused themselves on the grounds that Scripture sanctioned the institution of chattel slavery. Green sensed that he was about to move into difficult and controversial territory. He complained that he was "a poor, overwrought creature" whose many duties did not allow enough concentrated study to do an adequate job. Nevertheless, he proposed a plan of attack and sent his friends a sort of prospectus. He wanted, he wrote, "to prove that a System of Religion, which is by the way of eminence and emphasis THE TRUTH does not lend its function to a most horrible lie!"[22] He needed to demonstrate that God's "naked will" in Scripture could not be set in opposition to the axioms derived from moral intuition or Reason.

Though well versed in the grammatical-historical method of biblical interpretation imported from Europe, Green proposed an alternative hermeneutic. He wrote Wright and Weld, "We are not only authorized, then, but required to bring the light of Reason to shine on every problem, which with the N. T. in our hand we are required to dispose of.''[23] This hardly sounds like the radical Protestant principle of letting Scripture interpret Scripture. Green intended to measure Scripture against the self-evident truths of Reason. What if the New Testament should be found wanting? Green would admit of no such possibility, but he did hint at a potential explanation of what he knew to be one of the major conundrums. There was no explicit condemnation of slavery either from the lips of Jesus, whom he called "the perfection of Reason," or the pens of the apostolic writers. He made the preliminary observation that the character of domestic life among the Jews might have modified the particular teachings of Jesus and averred that the disciples, being mortal men, might have failed to draw out the full implications of the Gospel with regard to social conditions.

Green did not begin writing until late November 1837. Then he began tentatively, sending Weld and Reuben Hough, the Institute's superintendent and treasurer, a copy of the first page of what would become *The Chattel Principle*. He admitted to being a slow writer: "My bump of caution hangs heavily on my pen; little as superficial readers think so.''[24] He wrote Weld asking for more samples of the writings of Moses Stuart and Charles Hodge. In purposely choosing these two Northern critics of anti-slavery activism, Green was, in effect, chopping away at the theological traditions which had nurtured him. Moses Stuart, Professor of Sacred Literature at Andover Seminary when Green was a student, was America's most respected scholar of the latest techniques of Biblical criticism. Charles Hodge dominated Princeton Seminary and was, after the denominational split of 1837, the chief theologian of the Old School Presbyterians.

Green's rebuttal to Hodge and Stuart ran to seventy-one pages and appeared later in 1839 as number seven of *The Anti-Slavery Examiner*, a series of pamphlets sponsored by the American Anti-Slavery Society. *The Chattel Principle* bore the subtitle, *The Abhorrence of Jesus Christ and the Apostles, or, No Refuge for American Slavery in the New Testament*. Indicative of the belief that the New Testament would be found to republish the truths of Reason, the treatise begins with the Jeffersonian declaration: "We hold these truths to be SELF-EVIDENT, that all men are created equal; that they are endowed by their Creator with certain inalienable rights; that among these are life, LIBERTY, and the pursuit of happiness." It then cites the minutes of the Presbyterian general Assembly for 1818: "Slavery creates a paradox in the moral system—it exhibits rational, accountable, and immortal beings, in such circumstances as scarcely to leave them the power for moral action." Both church and state, Green concluded, had condemned slavery. Why then, did "theological professors at the North—professors of sacred literature at our oldest divinity schools" defend slavery?[25]

Charles Hodge. From the *Dictionary of American Portraits* (New York: Dover Publications, 1967).

Before directly answering the question, Green summarized his opponents' views, beginning with Moses Stuart. Stuart had contended that slavery existed in a worse form among the Greeks and Romans during the time of Jesus and the Apostles than in the American South. He concluded from the alleged silence of the New Testament concerning this crueler form of slavery that Christians had no business meddling with the South's "peculiar institution." Stuart admitted that Christianity would ultimately destroy slavery; *ad interim*, Christians were to concentrate on things spiritual, not political.

For the sake of argument, Green first allowed Stuart's hypothesis about the nature of slavery in New Testament times. But he countered that Stuart's assumption set Jesus in opposition to himself, for Jesus preached glad tidings to the poor and identified with the outcasts of society. Green acknowledged that Jesus did not condemn slavery by name, but he refused to conclude from this silence that Jesus condoned it.[26]

So as not to become bogged down in the debate over the Bible, Green moved to higher ground—to the authority of the moral law, those self-evident truths which "are rays from the face of Jehovah." He criticized

Moses Stuart. From the *Dictionary of American Portraits* (New York: Dover Publications, 1967).

Stuart for attempting to search the Bible for "broad statements or blind hints" in support of slavery when self-evident truths declared that every man was entitled to self-government. As if declarative statements were yet too explosive, Green proceeded in rhetorical form:

> And what if we were to discover what we were thus in search of?—something directly or indirectly, expressly or impliedly prejudicial to the principles, which reason, placing us under the authority of, makes self-evident? In what estimation, in that case, should we be constrained to hold the Bible? Could we no longer honor it, as the book of God? The book of God opposed to the authority of REASON! Why, before what tribunal do we dispose of the claims of the sacred volume to divine authority? The tribunal of reason. This every one acknowledges the moment he begins to reason on the subject.[27]

Here Green makes natural religion the test of the truth and authority of revealed religion. His self-evident principles control his interpretation of specific Biblical passages.

Reason, Green asserted, manifests its laws in the treatment of everything according to its nature. Slaves are not tools but human beings impressed with the image of the Creator. Nothing in the New Testament can be found to deny a humanity already given according to natural religion. Green argued that Jesus had honored Reason by making the Golden Rule the test of the truth and authority of revealed religion. In other words, the Gospel was a republication of the maxims of natural theology as derived from the universal human consciousness. Green thus constructed a circular argument, making Reason a mirror of Revelation and vice versa. But in reducing the Gospel to the Golden Rule, he came dangerously close to viewing Jesus as a mere moral teacher. Coleridge's idea of interrelated human consciousness can be seen in Green's view that the Golden Rule is itself an argument for the humanity of the slave. "The natural equality of mankind lies at the very basis of this great precept. It obviously requires every man to acknowledge another self in every other man. With my powers and resources, and in my appropriate circumstances, I am to recognize in any child of Adam who may address me, another self in his appropriate circumstances and with his powers and resources."[28] Here is the ethical basis for Beriah's feelings of being bound in chains with the slaves. It informs his entire controversy with Hodge and Stuart.

The Chattel Principle begins consideration of the standard New Testament passages cited by apologists for slavery only on the forty-fifth of its seventy-one pages. Anticipating modern scholarship, Green ultimately would not concede Moses Stuart's contention that the condition of slaves in the New Testament era was harsher than that of the antebellum slave whose very personality was "swallowed up." He called attention to Paul's instructions (Philemon v. 16) that upon Onesimus' return the runaway was to be received as "raised above a servant to the dignity of a brother beloved, 'BOTH IN THE FLESH AND IN THE LORD.'" With reference to other passages, such as I Timothy 6:1-2, where "servants" are enjoined to render respect and obedience to believing masters, Green took "servants" as a generic term to include both manual laborers and slaves. He argued that having a "believing master" was equivalent to freedom from "the yoke," and that referring to Christians as "servants" was merely a matter of linguistic convenience. Though "emancipated" by common brotherhood with believing masters, they were referred by "the correlative name . . . under which they had been known."[29]

Green's discussion in *The Chattel Principle* of the views of Charles Hodge first takes up Hodge's admission that Christian masters and Christian slaves stood in "perfect religious equality." But the Princeton professor failed to accord the slave any practical rights correlative to "perfect religious equality." Green inferred from I Corinthians 7:20-23 that becoming "the

Lord's freeman" doomed slavery, for the Apostle Paul taught that slaves should use their freedom in Christ to escape from the yoke of slavery. He compared the American system of slavery with Hodge's account of the general requisitions of Christianity in order to convict the Princeton professor with his own words. For example, Hodge asserted that Christianity condemned "all infractions of maternal or parental rights."[30] Green countered that American slavery violated the conjugal and parental rights of the slave. Hodge's version of slavery as a domestic Christian institution had never existed, Green argued, nor could it. To those who claimed that slavery would wither away through gradual Christian enlightenment, as Moses Stuart had, Green responded caustically:

> *"Christianity will ultimately destroy slavery." "ULTIMATELY!" What meaneth that portentous word? To what limit of remotest time, concealed in the darkness of futurity, may it look? Tell us, O watchman, on the hill of Andover. Almost nineteen centuries have rolled over this world of wrong and outrage—and yet we tremble in the presence of a form of slavery whose breath is poison, whose fang is death! If any one of the incidents of slavery should fall, but for a single day, upon the head of the prophet who dipped his pen, in such cold blood, to write that word "ultimately," how, under the sufferings of the first tedious hour, would he break out in the lamentable cry, "How long, O Lord, HOW LONG!"*[31]

We cannot claim that Green's exposition of the New Testament argument against chattel slavery was the first of its kind. George Bourne, the Presbyterian clergyman from Virginia, probably deserves the honor for the earliest and most comprehensive critique of the notion that Southern slavery could be defended on biblical grounds. William Lloyd Garrison gave credit to Bourne's *The Book and Slavery Irreconcilable* (1816) as second in importance only to the Bible in shaping his immediatist views. The Reverend LaRoy Sunderland's *The Testimony of God Against Slavery*, a collection of proof-texts against slavery, had appeared in 1835 and was widely read. Elizur Wright's twelve page pamphlet, *Does the Bible Sanction Slavery?* published in 1832, covered some of the same ground as *The Chattel Principle.*[32]

Despite precedents such as these, Green's essay is of special significance. Because of his thorough knowledge of moral philosophy and expertise in biblical studies, Green was able to meet his opponents on equal terms. Stuart and Hodge represented weighty academic and theological traditions. Once these Northern men, whose reputations as being "sensible" on the controverted question of slavery had gone unchallenged, were flushed from their hiding places and forced to confront slavery as it was and not slavery as they idealized it, their claim that religion and morals had nothing to do with abolitionism was exposed as a sham. The "grave and learned ecclesiastics" were then shown to have been carried along not by love of the truth but by fear of change. Beriah's immediatist colleagues felt that he had dealt a mortal blow to those who had tried to set the Bible against Reason. *The Chattel Principle* was widely distributed and became a staple in abolitionist libraries and bookshops.[33]

In September 1839, with his antislavery New Testament argument nearing completion, Beriah sat down to compose the annual valedictory address for Oneida's graduating seniors. His concern with the interpretation of the New Testament by the apologists for slavery carried over into his valedictory address. In *Education of the Apostles*, Green examined the insidious effects of slavery upon education as a whole and asserted that slavery had greatly injured Northern literary institutions. He alleged that white students from the land of the slaves had been received into Northern colleges "with great deference," while his scholars, coming from poor families, were despised. "It is not to be denied that indolence, and the cord of caste, and the foppery of literature, and the extravagances of science, and the 'dark spirit of slavery,' are all against the admission of the arrangement I plead for, into the system of education."[34] Green always saw the manual and the mental in service to each other, thus his hearty support for the manual labor movement and curriculum reforms. But he saw education as a means to a greater end. Learning, he asserted, was a dead letter no matter the form until the student was "quickened by the spirit of the living world."[35]

To those who charged him with the madness of innovation, Green asked whether or not his scholars were expected to cease being men by becoming students. Most of Oneida's students were "advanced to the age of manhood," as Green put it, older than those found at other American colleges. Many had come from the world of business.[36] Thus they were well-acquainted with the real world and were eager for a practical education which would equip them for reform. Green believed that the combination of manual labor and intellectual pragmatism was essential in view of the "commanding questions" of the 1830s. The mind was a tool, no less than the axe or the hoe. Green firmly believed that education founded on "the apostolic method"—manual labor, free discussion of social and political issues, and study of the Bible as the chief text book for moral reform—was best suited for defeating the monstrous anomaly of slavery.[37]

6

"A TROUBLER OF ISRAEL"

Had Oneida Institute been self-sustaining, Beriah Green would have been spared considerable agony. Responsible for an institution now without either endowments or public financing, he had to cultivate the good will of his school's natural constituency—the churches of Oneida County. This became even more critical to the Institute's survival after the national education societies withdrew support and wealthy benefactors began to redirect their gifts to Oberlin College. When Green was forced to reach out for help, he went first to the churches whose "Presbygational" traditions and values had given birth to Oneida Institute.

Since its founding in 1827, the Institute had been most intimately connected with Whitesboro's Presbyterian Church. The Reverend John Frost, pastor from 1813 to 1833, was one of Gale's coadjutors and a dedicated supporter of the manual labor school until poor health forced his resignation. His successor, the Reverend Ira Pettibone, accepted a call in January 1834, and remained at First Presbyterian until March 1836. Pettibone and several prominent laymen from his congregation served as trustees of Oneida after Green became president. Green, his family, faculty members and their families, and many of the students worshipped at First Presbyterian. Green's wife and the older children became communicant members, though Beriah himself did not, as was the custom among the clergy. Green did participate in meetings of the Whitesboro session, occasionally hosting them at the college or in his home.[1]

Most Whitesboro families were of Yankee origin and heirs of New England's Congregational establishment. As a result of the Plan of Union of 1801, however, they had adopted many of the features of Presbyterian polity and structure. The First Presbyterian congregation began as the United Society of Whitestown in 1794. It belonged to the Presbytery of Oneida under the jurisdiction of the Synod of Utica, which had been created out of the Albany Synod in 1829. The Synods of Utica, Geneva, and Genesee were so influenced by Finney's revivals and "New Measures" that they, along with the Synod of the Western Reserve, were "excinded" by the Presbyterian General Assembly in 1837. Most of the "excinded" ministers and churches in the Burned-over District were sympathetic to social reform, though few approached Green's radicalism on the slavery issue.

The Oneida Presbytery, part of the Synod of Utica, went on record in opposition to slavery as early as 1834. It passed resolutions declaring slavery to be "a flagrant violation of human rights; as contrary to the laws of God; and as a crying sin in our land, admitting of no apology."[2] But the Presbytery made no mention of the abolitionist attack on the colonizationists nor offered any solution other than recommending that churches pray on behalf of the slave. This silence is striking because the Presbytery's resolutions appeared amidst Green's struggle to transform Oneida Institute into an abolitionist school.

Though Green still maintained official connections with the York Association of Congregational clergymen in Maine, where he had been pastor of the church at Kennebunk, he attended Oneida Presbytery meetings and was received as a corresponding member. Lacking documentary evidence, we can but speculate on his reaction to the antislavery resolutions. Though the Oneida Presbytery had not been fully radicalized, Green was certainly within a more congenial religious circle than that of Western Reserve. The revivalist heritage of the Burned-over District doubtless contributed to this. "No other section of the country," Whitney Cross wrote in his classic study of enthusiastic religion in upstate New York, "would throughout the years before the Civil War prove to be so thoroughly and constantly sensitive to antislavery agitations."[3] However, disagreement existed in the Burned-over District as to the *means* by which slavery was to be abolished. Most Presbyterians hoped for a peaceful, divinely wrought solution to the problem.

The session of First Presbyterian, Whitesboro, voiced its own unhappiness with the perpetuation of the "peculiar institution" and took a somewhat stronger stand than the Oneida Presbytery. On December 11, 1835, it passed resolutions condemning slavery as "a sin against God and man" and affirming the right of citizens to freely examine and discuss the subject, a right which had come under attack in the October anti-abolitionist riot in Utica. First Presbyterian's leaders urged the slaveholding states to lose no time in giving freedom to the slaves but held that the slave states alone had the constitutional right to enact their emancipation. This squared with the commonly held abolitionist view of the early 1830s that slavery was a state rather than a federal problem. The session also endorsed moral suasion ("free remonstrance and fervent supplication to God") as the only Christian means of abolishing slavery.[4] Though moderate in tone, the resolutions of the session reflect the heating up of the slavery question in Oneida County in the mid-1830s. The Reverend Ira Pettibone and his congregation seemed to be heading in the right direction.

Pettibone's pastoral relation with Whitesboro Presbyterian ended in February 1836. Session minutes give no cause for his departure, though the Oneida Presbytery official records suggest that certain members of the congregation had quarreled with him regarding who should be allowed access to his pulpit.[5] Pettibone had several times invited Green to preach, a privilege granted him as a clerical colleague. Green used these occasions to spread his brand of abolitionism. In the bitter aftermath of a schism which rent the congregation in 1837, the abolitionists who left to form their own church charged that the wealthier members had forced Pettibone out by refusing to raise his salary because of his antislavery associations.[6] Whatever the case, Pettibone's resignation not only deprived Green of an important supporter but also raised the possibility that someone might be invited to serve the church who would actively oppose the abolitionists.

Green's nemesis came in the person of the Reverend David Ogden. A graduate of Yale who studied theology at Andover Seminary, he was serving a Congregational church in Southington, Connecticut, when the call came in July 1836, from the Presbyterians in Whitesboro. According to Ogden's version of the events, he accepted the call in good faith and with full disclosure. He wrote S. Newton Dexter, a church leader:

> It is well known that Abolitionism, so called, is agitated with great warmth in your region, and common fame does not put Whitesboro behind in this matter. Now I cannot conceal it that I am a friend of the American Colonization Society from deep, conscientious conviction, not without much examination. I am an Abolitionist too of the old school, such as New England men have always been. My question here is, would such a sentiment when generally known as it must be, create difficulty or diminution of my influence?[7]

Dexter, according to Ogden, responded cordially with assurances that even the abolitionists in the congregation wished him to be their pastor: "There are many here deeply attached to Mr. Green, who are exceedingly anxious for you to come here. They know your feelings on this delicate subject—and still they want you to come."[8]

David L. Ogden. Courtesy, the First Presbyterian Church, Whitesboro, New York.

Ogden also inquired whether or not he would be allowed to take up a collection for the American Colonization Society each Fourth of July, as was the custom in New England. Luther Holbrook, one of the confirmed abolitionists, felt that none would object but averred that Ogden would have little success were he to try to proselytize for colonization. Ogden responded that he would not be the pastor of any party but of the whole flock, and that he saw no reason why a man could not be both a colonizationist and an abolitionist.[9] Before accepting the call, he visited Whitesboro and met with Green to discuss their respective views on slavery. "We distinctly understood that we differed," Ogden later wrote. "We parted, however, with mutual expressions of good will."[10] After receiving assurances, so he claimed, from the abolitionists in the church that they would stand by the society though its pastor might be a colonizationist, Ogden began his ministry in November 1836, and served through most of 1844, the year of Oneida Institute's demise. Green had reservations concerning Ogden's election but persuaded himself that with "ever-increasing light" the man might become an advocate of the enslaved. He would later write, "We erred, greatly erred."[11]

Green did not wait for Ogden's installation to attempt to radicalize the congregation even further. On July 17, 1836, he delivered a discourse entitled *Things for Northern Men to Do*, in which he urged his hearers to "act as if you felt that you were bound with those in bonds, as if their cause was all your own, as if every blow that cuts their flesh, lacerated yours." He castigated northern Christians who preferred the "peace of the church" to moral rectitude and argued that the church had "the rusty key" to the dreadful prison in which the slaves, brothers and sisters in Christ, languished. Green spoke eloquently on the moral duty of all professed Christians and warned of divine judgment should the American church fail to remove its "pet-sin." As Oneida Institute's president sounded ever stronger the theme of Northern complicity in the sin of slavery, his Whitesboro audience must have grown uneasy:

> If we would have peace, let us listen to the voice which calls us to duty and to glory. Let us, with sackcloth upon our loins and dust upon our heads, kneeling with broken hearts at the foot of the Christ, call the nation to repentance. With many tears—for we have all sinned—let us lift up a great and lamentable cry. And let us "spare not," till "every yoke is broken!"[12]

Green intended to bring the battle home, beginning with those Presbyterians in the Whitesboro vicinity whose support he desperately needed in order to keep Oneida's doors open.

Ogden initially promised that he would not hinder Oneida's president, but that he himself would not use the pulpit to preach upon slavery. True to his word, Ogden said nothing about the subject on Sabbath mornings for nearly ten months. However, on July 30, 1837, he took to the pulpit with a sermon denouncing the "fanatical abolitionists" and attempted to absolve himself of responsibility for preaching against slavery by noting that no slaveholders sat in the pews before him. "Now I might reason to the day of my death, and whatever theories I might establish, I could not make one of you practically feel that you are guilty of the sin of slaveholding, admitting it to be a sin in every possible case, any more than I could make you confess the guilt of Adam's sin as your own." Ogden pledged that he would have nothing to do "anti or pro" with the subject of slavery, because it did not come "within the bounds of the gospel."[13] Fortunately, Ogden's uncensored private journal, entitled *Thoughts on Men and Things,* has survived.[14] As we shall see, it belies his public claim to neutrality.

Because of his commitment to abolitionism, Green could not tolerate neutrality. Shortly after Ogden's anti-abolitionist sermon, he wrote Gerrit Smith: *"Our* people here are uneasy at Mr. Ogden's course [and] have sent him a letter. Last Sab. he gave them a blast, cold and loud, like the North wind. The parish is in a wretched state! It will be, I expect, til the cause of the poor slave is admitted to its proper place in the pulpit.'"[15] Beriah took the bait and within days of Ogden's sermon responded in a series of eight letters addressed to Ogden and published in the *Friend of Man,* the official organ of the New York Anti-Slavery Society.

In the first letter, Green dismissed Ogden's disclaimer of responsibility for preaching on slavery as so much theological rubbish. Were not Ogden's hearers bound with the whole human family, responsible for the welfare of those most "cruelly deprived of the common blessing of this life and the hopes of salvation?" Were they not also Americans and therefore guilty of the iniquity of slavery perpetuated in the District of Columbia? Were they not citizens of New York, where blacks, fellow citizens, were subjected to "oppressive disabilities?" Green challenged Ogden to examine his members to determine whether or not any of them had ever personally profited from the traffic in human flesh. With typical directness, he concluded with a personal word of warning:

> Let me assure you, that you hazard not a little in thus insinuating, that slavery was a subject foreign from the responsibilities of your people. . . . O, Sir, it is no trifling thing to soothe the wicked in their sins. None are more responsible for the guilt and danger, in which slavery has involved this country than you. Rouse up, I beseech you, and hasten to the rescue of bleeding humanity.[16]

Green penned weekly attacks upon Ogden throughout August, during September, and into early October. He criticized him for attempting to maintain a "deceitful peace" and for robbing the pulpit of its "inspiring and sustaining influence." He employed the premises of intuitionist moral philosophy in telling Ogden that the "immutable fundamental difference between the right and the wrong" is inscribed on the very foundation of human nature. Those who refused to act on self-evident principles were clearly men of no principle. As to Ogden's charge that it was the abolitionists who were breaking up the congregation, Green admitted that the peace of the parish had been disturbed by the discussion of slavery. But he countered that it was those who ignored the oppression of the poor who were guilty of setting one Christian against another. As to Ogden's complaint that Green and his associates were a quarrelsome lot bereft of common courtesy and Christian civility, Green warned that those who fell silent with regard to the wrongs of crushed humanity would one day reckon with their complacency before the divine throne.[17]

In the seventh letter, Green addressed Ogden's complaint that abolitionists were making the plight of the slave their "hobby." Though the accusation bore some truth, at least with regard to the intensity of his abolitionist commitment, Beriah denied any lack of concern for all categories of the poor and suffering. Yet he saw the southern slave as the archetype of the poor and oppressed with whom all Christians were bound, as depicted in the Bible. The slaves best symbolized those whom Jesus had instructed his followers to visit, clothe, and feed. In the last of the eight letters, Green addressed those members of First Presbyterian who thought they could support the ministry of a compromiser and colonizationist. He warned them to resist the blandishments of the "tempter" in their pulpit and to consider what the Divine Judge would have to say to those who refused to plead for the poor slave.[18]

The entries in Ogden's journal following the sermon that fired Green's anger show him to be decidedly less neutral than he publicly claimed. For example, he wrote on August 2, 1837, following the Sabbath on which he declared why he could not preach on slavery, "They [the abolitionists] have a poor general in Pres. Green. Like the devil when he tempts men to sin, he puts them into a scrape, but he does not get them out of it."[19] In another entry, Whitesboro's pastor pledged that just as he had fought Baptists and Universalists in New England for the sake of the church, he would not flee the present danger: "Now I am fighting these spurious Abolitionists—fanatical ones; or rather, defending the church of God against their wicked machinations."[20] Concerning those memorialists who had accused him of preaching "another gospel," and their coadjutors, Ogden wrote:

> In general it may be said that the Abolitionists are the rabble of the church headed by some fiery, rash, ambitious leader. In Whitesboro they are such as do not see through Green, but are imposed upon by his professions of benevolence. If a man is led by Green he must be either an ignorant man, or else one whose blind side is accessible. Green has got around Gerrit Smith by approaching his blind side, and has made him appear ridiculous before the public.[21]

Given this animosity, Ogden's dislike of Oneida Institute comes as no surprise. "The Oneida Institute is the greatest humbug I know of. Lectures on Nigerology, as Mr. Berry called it, are about all they got." He described the students as "a parcel of conceited fools" who under the guise of free discussion intended to revolutionize society. He had heard that due to

Green's influence some began their prayers with "O thou head Abolitionist in Heaven!" In September, as Green's public attack on him intensified in the *Friend of Man*, Ogden's journal entries began linking Green and the Institute with assorted heresies, such as Garrison's anti-clericalism, Fanny Wright's social radicalism, and Locofoco politics in New York State. "Strange that men these days," Ogden wrote, "do not know when to stop the work of reformation."[22]

Ogden concluded that Green and company really intended to ruin society in their efforts to reform it. Where Green saw questions of principle, he saw threats to social order. In September, he attended commencement exercises held in his church, only to be assaulted by student orators decrying (using Green's favorite expressions) the "factitious distinctions and artificial arrangements of society." Ira Pettibone's son declaimed, "Infidels, ecclesiastics, and civil oppressors have united to crush humanity!"[23] Ogden had no stomach for Green's incessant talk of elevating the "colored man on equality with whites." He believed that Oneida Institute, which he described as "upon us and within us and around us," was the font and source of dangerous and newfangled notions. Fundamentally, though, Ogden blamed Green for his troubles: "B. Green the President is bitter against me because I don't pronounce Shibboleth as he does."[24]

Having publicly assumed a neutral position, Ogden could not openly and directly attempt to mute Green or silence his students. He found a surrogate in Charles West, who had been hired to teach chemistry in 1836. West joined the Oneida faculty at the start of the 1837 academic year but resigned in March after only seven weeks. He wrote a letter containing the reasons for his resignation but received no reply from Oneida's trustees. He then decided to place his case before a wider audience and published an attack upon Green and the Institute in the *New York Observer*, an important Presbyterian newspaper. West accused Green of dropping mathematics, bullying students with all the reform fancies of the day, propagating a "leveling system . . . under the banner of abolitionism" which would reduce social classes to the least common denominator, and of urging students to treat disrespectfully ministers who differed with them on their favorite causes.[25]

West's letter, framed as it was by an insider, threw Green into an apoplectic fit. He demanded an emergency meeting of the trustees and would not be put off by Gerrit Smith's tepid counsel to let the matter pass without further bad publicity. "Mr. West's crime is so enormous," Green huffed, "as to be in part protected by its enormity."[26] Green, the trustees, and committees from each of the four classes in the college division rushed detailed rebuttals concerning each of West's charges to the *Friend of Man*. They denied West's allegations but transformed his slur against them for maintaining "a hotbed of sedition" into an accolade. Oneida Institute was indeed a school of the prophets dedicated to breaking "the cord of caste." Among other corrections, they pointed out that West had never attended Green's lectures during the period that he was on the faculty, that certain branches of mathematics, such as algebra, had been dropped only so that more attention might be given to the natural sciences, that what West derided as a "leveling system" was in fact a legitimate concern with the artificial distinctions of social class, and finally, that students had not been disrespectful except where the claims of righteousness were at stake.[27]

Had the West affair been confined to the printed page or been merely an academic controversy, it would not have so severely damaged Oneida Institute. But it became a divisive emotional issue in the Whitesboro community and eventually split First Presbyterian Church, to which the protagonists all belonged. Pelatiah Rawson and Reuben Hough initiated formal ecclesiastical charges against West in November 1837. These allies of Green accused West of subverting Christian ethics by publishing "misrepresentations, slanders, and false statements respecting the Oneida Institute, its President and other Teachers and Students."[28]

The West trial lasted from mid-November through late December. As moderator of the session, Ogden presided. Green served as counsel to Hough and Rawson and testified himself on one occasion. West claimed that he had not meant to accuse Green of attempting to undermine church government. But by a vote of five to three, the session sustained the charges against West and proceeded to suspend him from the privileges of the church. Ogden immediately registered a complaint on behalf of the minority and notified the other elders that he intended to get its action reversed by the Oneida Presbytery. In a breach of his role as moderator, he expressed his opinion that Oneida Institute was all that West had said it was.[29]

When Ogden announced his plans to file a formal protest, Elder David Foster, one of the voting majority, proposed that he, Foster, and fifty-eight other members be given a peaceful dismissal unless Ogden assented to the excommunication of West. Ogden called Foster's hand by accepting most of the names, but he tried to thwart the plan to form a new church on abolitionist principles by denying a peaceful dismissal to Hough and Rawson. Green's wife and two of their eldest children were among those dismissed on December 26th. Hough and Rawson eventually received letters of dismissal. Within a short time, seventy-one communicant members, including most of the elders, joined in the exodus and put themselves under the leadership of Beriah Green. On January 6, 1838, he wrote Gerrit Smith: "Today for the first time, the friends of Humanity in this place have had public worship by themselves. Some 70 perhaps of Mr. Ogden's chh., as the fashion is to speak, have obtained letters of dismission to form themselves, if God will, into a new chh. With these, including 6/9ths of the Session, we of the Institute have united. We hope soon to be organized into a chh."[30]

Green told Smith that he personally hoped to entice Amos Phelps to come to Whitesboro as a professor for the Institute and as pastor of the abolitionist church. Such was not to be. Green, who not incidentally had begun worshiping at New York Mills prior to the schism at First Presbyterian, was (as Ogden had claimed) the principal figure around whom the abolitionists rallied. The fate of their as yet untested bark was in his hands. By the middle of 1838 this band of "comeouters" had organized themselves as an independent Congregational church. Green counseled in favor of the Congregational arrangement as the best means by which his small band might avoid "the superintendence and interference of spiritual courts." He argued that the principal of self-government fostered "sounder character, loftier enterprise, warmer zeal, [and] greater activity."[31] Ogden credited Green with having chosen the congregational form of government "for the sake of having more of a popular cast which would be more acceptable to the poor and the low."[32]

Having won control of First Presbyterian only by default, Ogden and the conservatives sought vindication within the Presbytery. Ogden charged Green's fledgling fellowship with covenant breaking, irregularity in organization, defective ordinances, factionalism, and self-righteousness. He expressed amusement over the excesses which Green's group exhibited in their new freedom, such as substituting water in which raisins had been soaked for wine in the Lord's Supper.[33] Ogden was doubtless partly responsible for the Oneida Presbytery's demand in August 1838, that the Congregational church furnish a formal explanation of its irregular action. In 1839, the Oneida Presbytery determined that the reply of the Congregational Church in Whitesboro did not demonstrate adequate reasons for the separation.[34] Green as author of the reply not surprisingly saw the main issue not as a matter of church discipline but "WHETHER THE PRINCIPLE OF HUMAN EQUALITY SHALL BE CARRIED OUT IN THE ABOLITION OF SLAVERY—OR WHETHER, IN OPPOSITION TO THIS PRINCIPLE, THE FREE SHALL BE ENSLAVED."[35]

Green united with the clergy of several other antislavery congregations to form a comeouter organization known as the Whitesboro Association. Its constitution consisted primarily in "the heady recognition and strenuous assertion of the principle of self-government."[36] Green broke off fraternal relations with the Oneida Presbytery in February 1841. For a time a representative of the Whitesboro Association sat as a corresponding member of the Oneida Presbytery. This privilege ended in June 1841. The Presbytery refused to recognize the Association as a regular ecclesiastical body and denied that the licenses and ordinations of Green and his colleagues had any validity.[37]

The schism within Whitesboro's Presbyterian community left Green and his school with fewer and fewer friends. Beriah no longer had access to most Presbyterian pulpits, and Oneida Institute was barred from soliciting funds from area churches. In 1837, six months before West openly attacked Oneida Institute, the school had 130 students, fifteen more than nearby Hamilton College, the traditional Presbyterian institution. At that time the Oneida Presbytery had officially described Oneida Institute as being "in a flourishing condition, and as deservedly receiving the confidence, and patronage of the community."[38] The schism in First Presbyterian soured church leaders on Green and his school. In the aftermath of his battle with Green, David Ogden wrote, "The Oneida Institute is a vile concern—a conspiracy to the interests of literature and religion."[39] But Green's abolitionist allies, such as Gerrit Smith, readily understood that West's attack upon Oneida Institute was motivated by the school's identification with the "bleeding cause" of the slave.[40]

On March 19, 1839, Green, as was his custom during the midst of controversy, sent Smith a long letter rehearsing his personal trials. In the midst of formulating the reply to the Presbytery, Green wrote, "I now feel strongly inclined to transfer from the bands, which ecclesiastically tie me in any way to those ministers, who find it so hard to distinquish a man from a thing."[41] Green's moral perfectionism on the slavery question would soon carry him into a conventicle of his own making, one unable to hold even his ardent supporters in the controversy with West and Ogden.

From a wider vantage point, the story here recounted of the controversy among Presbyterians in Whitesboro from 1837 to 1841, mirrors that in other Northern churches, especially those in the Burned-over District. Religious comeouterism spread rapidly as abolitionists, frustrated by their inability to reform the religious denominations from within, sought to separate themselves from contaminated churches. Green became active in the Union Church movement, a loose confederation of Christian abolitionists who had been read out of their parent denominations because of their insistence that separation from all those blind to the sin of slavery was necessary. Gerrit Smith, who established the Free Church of Peterboro in 1843, and William Goodell, who set up a Union Church at Honeoye, New York, joined with Green in attempting to further abolitionism on the basis of new nonsectarian congregations. Unlike the anticlerical William Lloyd Garrison, Green, Goodell, and Smith did not abandon hope that one could work through organized religion to advance the cause of abolitionism.

The Union Church movement lost momentum in the late 1840s in part because of the difficulty in creating a harmonious organization around abolitionist sentiments alone. Several comeouter sects, such as the Wesleyan Methodist Connection, organized at Utica in 1843, and the Free Presbyterian Church, established in 1847, tried to remedy this by forming new ecclesiastical bodies along denominational lines. They, as did the Union Churches, protested the failure of the great Northern denominations to cleanse their membership thoroughly of the sin of slavery even after the breakup of the national church bodies along sectional lines in the mid-1840s. The divisions of the national church bodies, made possible because of evangelical voluntarism, or the right of individuals to chose churches which made them feel politically and socially comfortable, had their political counterpart in the doctrine of states rights, that shibboleth of the Southern firebrands.

The controversy which erupted in 1837 within Whitesboro's Presbyterian church should not be isolated from the national debate over slavery and the consequent ecclesiastical divisions. But our examination of the local records suggests that the schism is best understood in terms of the personalities of the main protagonists—Beriah Green and David Ogden. Shortly after Charles West's attack first appeared, Green wrote Gerrit Smith, "Mr. West has done his uttermost to stab especially me in the heart. This is a rare opportunity of setting the claims of the Institute in a true light without at all seeming to intrude ourselves upon public attention. Our enemies furnish the occasion!"[42] Green had invested his entire self in Oneida Institute; an attack upon it was an attack upon him. Ogden ridiculed Green's claim to be a "man of principle." "Green's principle," he groused, "is personal ambition."[43] Green was ambitious, not for himself, but for Oneida Institute and all it stood for.

Ogden opposed Green because he feared Green meant to revolutionize society just as he had Oneida Institute. "I have an unhappy trait of character, partly moral and partly physical," Ogden confided in his journal, "which I should call a disposition to look back with sighing upon the past to the disadvantage of the present."[44] Ogden saw the future in Green's school and did not like it, confessing a "natural repugnance" at seeing white and black students thrown together "at table, studies, and [in] recitation rooms." What could this lead to but "amalgamation!" Ogden believed that Africans had been reduced to slavery because "they had not the talents; they had not the strength of mind" to live in freedom. By its very presence, Oneida Institute challenged Ogden's notion that, as he wrote in 1839, "the Negro race had all along [been] inferior to the white."[45]

Not surprisingly, Ogden privately celebrated the departure of Green's party from First Presbyterian. He believed that this would hasten the day when Oneida Institute would fall upon the refuse heap of failed social experiments. He commented in his journal on August 2, 1839, "It is a matter of no small joy and gratitude to God that the Oneida Institute is evidently on the decline. Green has made the Institute a sort of Ishmael, his hand against every man's, and every man's hand against his."[46]

No one ever accused Beriah Green of being a politician, at least not in the sense of one who trades on principal to achieve practical objectives. Green suffered the prophet's curse: devotion to principle clouded his ability to judge the practical outcome of a given course of action. For example, in February 1837, seven months prior to West's attack, the Oneida Presbytery passed a memorial by a vote of seventeen to seven which condemned slavery in language reminiscent of Green's own sermons. Though opposed by a minority led by Ogden, the memorial specifically rebuked fellow Presbyterians in the South for their complicity in the sin of slavery. In 1840, the Oneida Presbytery also sent a very strong memorial to the General Assembly urging that "no person guilty of the sin of buying or holding human beings as property shall without good evidence of repentance be admitted to communion in our branch of the Church of Christ."[47] Significantly, Ogden registered the only dissent. Green, of course, was not around to witness Ogden's isolation, for he no longer participated in Presbytery affairs.

Had Green been able to forge an alliance with the Oneida Presbytery majority in the wake of West's attack, appealing to their antislavery sentiments and pro-Institute sympathies instead of moving out under the banner of the "self-government principle," Oneida Institute might have faced a different future. In 1839, however, Ogden was moderator of the Oneida Presbytery, and several of his friends were busily arranging for his archenemy's censure. Green also prepared for battle. "I was obliged to take very strong ground," he wrote Smith, "and was regarded as a troubler of Israel."[48] Green seems to have sensed what the controversy had cost him and his school. He informed Smith in early 1839, "I feel that the present is the crisis year with the Institute. . . . I am more and more uneasy at being thrown upon the patronage of those who manifestly do not sympathize very strongly in our design."[49]

Many of Beriah's abolitionist colleagues felt as he did about the orthodox clergy of the North who refused to take a bold stand against slavery. Some of them simply gave up on organized religion. Elizur Wright, Jr., for example, wrote Green in 1838 that he found church services a "fog-land" in which he could barely catch "sight of the most precious beacons of the faith." Wright later wrote his parents that he no longer belonged to any church.[50] Had Green not been burdened with Oneida Institute, he too might have drifted away from organized religion in the bitter aftermath of the West-

Ogden controversy. But he still saw himself as occupying the office of the sacred ministry. Wright had never been ordained. Green felt possessed of a divine call, one which had to be exercised at all costs among his small flock of abolitionist-minded parishioners and, even more importantly, among his students.

7

"GONE, GONE, SOLD & GONE!"

The immediatist generation of American abolitionists failed in part because it did not capture and hold enough schools and churches. Beriah Green's contemporaries organized voluntary societies, conducted abolitionist fairs or bazaars, gave lectures, held rallies, and published a wide variety of antislavery literature. The abolitionist R. G. Williams thought that the press had "probably made seven-eights of all the abolitionists in the country." Williams' observation, as Ronald G. Walters points out, reveals more about the abolitionists' lack of serious thought about tactics then it does about abolitionist realities.[1] With the exception of the ill-fated Liberty Party and several score comeouter churches, the immediatists did not show much interest in institutionalizing abolitionism.

The early immediatists saw themselves principally as teachers, preachers, and prophets who were to rely upon the tactic of moral suasion. Those who tried to establish institutional alternatives to slavery, such as stores which sold nothing made by slave labor, were the exception rather than the rule. Regardless of what we might think of the whole of his argument, Stanley Elkins is correct in observing that slavery in America was as much an institutional problem as an intellectual or moral one.[2] Unfortunately, the professional reformers of the 1830s lacked the tools, such as organized political and ecclesiastical power, with which to effect societal change. Green clung to Oneida Institute long after many of his contemporaries had pronounced its demise, because he understood the necessity of institutionalizing abolition. Stubborn in the face of opposition, unyielding on matters of principle, and blindly confident that Oneida would and must survive, Green managed to keep his school open until early 1844.

Had Oneida not been an extension of himself, Green might have abandoned it as early as 1837. He wrote Gerrit Smith in February of that year that the Institute was in a "healthful state." But by June, he was complaining, "my poverty is almost abject."[3] Then the West controversy broke upon his shoulders amidst the Panic of 1837, from which the country did not begin to recover until 1843. In 1837, Oneida Institute had a total of 140 students, 93 in the college division and 47 in the preparatory.[4] Never before had so many young men enrolled. Collections had to be taken in surrounding congregations so that the poorest of them might remain. To compound Green's troubles, Innes Grant, Professor of Languages, was proposing to leave because of the financial embarrassments of Arthur and Lewis Tappan, the New York City merchants who had been subsidizing his salary. In addition, the New York Anti-Slavery Society owned Oneida Institute more than two thousand dollars for printing the *Friend of Man* and various tracts. Green had already lost the aid of the education societies, and after the West affair he felt that the general public did not "care a fig" for Oneida Institute.[5]

The 1838 academic year opened with an enrollment of 105 students, a decline of nearly thirty young men in the upper division and a half dozen in the preparatory. Innes Grant was still on the faculty, but Green had neither a professor of Chemistry and the Natural Sciences nor a professor of English Literature. The college faculty consisted of Green, Professor of Intellectual and Moral Philosophy, Pelatiah Rawson, Professor of Mathematics and Natural Philosophy, and Innes Grant. Colquhoun Grant served as Principal of the Preparatory Department and Lecturer on Anatomy and Physiology. Green badly needed coadjutors, but he could not promise potential faculty the security of a regular salary. He tried to keep student costs to the minimum. College tuition was $22, laundry, light and fuel $10, and the price of meals in the dining hall, $1.25 a week.[6]

Oneida Institute's fiscal problems had been inherited in large part from the Gale years, for Gale left the school saddled with numerous financial obligations. Reuben Hough struggled to alleviate the school's debts for four years and had made some progress. The Oneida Institute of 1838 was much improved over that of 1833. Buildings and grounds had been expanded, the library augmented, and classroom equipment for the study of science was in more plentiful supply. But the Panic of 1837 brought new "pecuniary embarrassments," far more serious than the earlier debts since the Institute was so dependent on a few wealthy donors. Oneida's enemies, Green understood, could not be expected to help. Should the school fail, he predicted that many ignorant of the facts would raise "the charge of Abolition, or Manual Labor, or the substitution of Hebrew in the room of Latin."[7]

Green considered 1839 to be "the crisis year," though he persisted in saying that his school was "healthful amidst deep poverty."[8] His own salary went unpaid, as it had to be applied against the Institute's debt of nearly ten thousand dollars.[9] Gerrit Smith, himself strained for cash, donated three thousand eight hundred acres of land in Vermont. The Executive Committee of the trustees hoped to raise $7,600 by selling the land for two thousand dollars an acre. In a circular addressed "To the Friends of Learning and Religion," the trustees gave the public details concerning Smith's liberality but acknowledged that a rapid sale and ready payments could not be expected. Because of the general economic decline, Hough was forced to accept promissory notes totaling nearly three thousand dollars from hard-pressed students. Others had to take a leave of absence. Enrollments in both divisions totaled only ninety-one in 1839, fewer than at any time during Green's presidency.[10]

Beriah was now nearly overwhelmed by forces beyond his control. His oldest daughter, Ann, became concerned about his health, writing relatives in Vermont, "Sometimes I am sadly afraid that he will not be able to sustain the pressures of so many and such heavy burdens. . . ."[11] In addition to his campus duties, her father conducted services for Whitesboro's Free Congregationalists and occasionally occupied the pulpits of neighboring independent churches. He cultivated about twenty acres and kept two cows and a horse. As if this were not enough to keep him busy, Green circulated a prospectus for a collection of his writings. As he wrote Wright, "I am as much as ever—perhaps more—a student, manual and mental." Weary of the day-to-day struggle, Green began to think of leaving Oneida Institute in order that someone more adept at soliciting donors might rescue the school from financial bankruptcy. Wright urged him not to leave his post, assuring him that he would not be a "neglected martyr" among friends of the slave, though the whole world might think him a "martyr to negate."[12]

Green's pessimism derived in part from his inability to obtain new faculty with abolitionist principles. In 1839 he appealed to Amos Phelps to accept a professorship in theology and rhetoric. "If I cannot obtain coadjutors this year," he pleaded, "I see not how I can maintain my position."[13] Green argued that a theological department would increase the Institute's influence and attract new patrons. Phelps, however, chose to remain in the security of a Boston parish. Green solicited others, but to no avail. His valedictory address for 1839, delivered to a senior class of only twelve members, was a spirited defense of Oneida Institute, its practical curriculum, manual labor system, and dedication to service rather than mere intellectualizing. He promised to keep the doors of the Institute open as long as humanly possible. To admit defeat would be tantamount to violating the very principles upon which he had staked his sacred vocation.[14] With the opening of a new academic year in February 1840, ninety-two students enrolled, more than Green expected. But the school's treasurer was "very greatly discouraged." Green lashed out at the banks as "carrion-crows; feeding improvidently and voraciously on starved and dog-bitten sheep and lambs."[15]

In June, Elizur Wright wrote from England chastising Green for not attending the General Anti-Slavery Convention then being held in London. Wright urged that Oneida Institute was the "world's School" and should fling itself upon the philanthropy of the world.[16] Sponsored by the British and Foreign Anti-Slavery Society, the convention was the godchild of British and American abolitionists who hoped to join forces. Oberlin, also suffering from the effects of the Panic of 1837, had already sent two representatives in order that its story might "burn and glow" before the British public. The Keep-Dawes Mission raised nearly enough to offset Oberlin's indebtedness. During the proceedings of the General Anti-Slavery Convention, which ran from June 12th through June 23rd, 1840, John Keep presented Oberlin's case most forcibly. He portrayed the Ohio school as the only college in America which had surmounted caste and color distinctions.[17]

Alarmed at reports in the British press concerning Keep's remarks, Amos Phelps, also in attendance at the convention, pleaded with Green to provide him with information to counteract the false impression left with English reformers. He specifically wanted to know how many black students had studied at Oneida. Green responded rather half-heartedly. He complained of being "misunderstood, misrepresented, traduced, opposed, insolently and extensively both in church and state." He begged to be excused, for he felt "poorly qualified to build up, as the phrase is, this, or any institution." Green seemed more concerned about reports that Arthur Tappan was giving money to Oberlin at Oneida's expense. Beriah wrote Smith complaining that a rumor had reached him that Tappan had asserted, "Pres. Green has nothing to say, to set us all astirring. . . . Give the knave a goat." Green viewed Tappan's loyalty to Oberlin as a personal affront. He complained to Phelps, "And so, I must be content to be forgotten; even by my friends."[18]

Green suggested to Phelps that Charles Stuart, then also in England, might render assistance. He described Stuart as "a very cordial friend of friends of the Oneida Institute and a dear friend of mine."[19] Stuart was attending the World Convention as a delegate from Jamaica. Described as exceedingly eccentric and zealous in whatever he did, Stuart was well-known in the Burned-over District. He taught school at Utica in the early 1820s and was the mentor and confidant of Theodore Dwight Weld. In the mid-1830s Stuart lectured against slavery throughout western New York.

Green hosted him on several occasions at "the Old Hive" and introduced him to the faculty and students of the Institute. As a token of esteem, Green named his seventh child, born August 8, 1835, Charles Stuart Green.[20]

Stuart responded positively to Phelps's intercessions on Green's behalf and produced a twenty-page essay on the competing claims of Oneida and Oberlin. The pamphlet describes the unique character of the Institute, its curricular radicalism and its opportunities for manual labor—"a printing press, a work shop for carpentering and cabinet making, a farm for roots, vegetables, and grain, and cows to supply milk for the fine market of Utica, about four miles distant." Stuart quotes liberally from Green's letter to Phelps of July 31, 1840, in which Green summarized his abolitionist career. He praises Green as "bright, grave, generous, fervent, free from self, disdaining the recital of his trials and persecutions in the cause of religion, humanity, and holy freedom." Furthermore, "the productions of his pen, have been of the highest order; his lectures and addresses, are almost numberless, and have been given in season and out of season, spurning toil, and freely hazarding life." Stuart argues that with the exception of Theodore D. Weld, James G. Birney, Elijah P. Lovejoy, and a certain "Dr. D. Nelson," Green and his school had done more for the cause of the slave than any other individual or institution in the United States. As to Oneida's claims over against Oberlin, Stuart concludes, "The writer of this article appeals in its behalf, to the Abolitionists, both of Britain and America, or rather, of the world; and he does so, because Oneida is the oldest and most thorough Anti-Slavery Educational and Literary Institution which exists in the United States."[21]

Stuart's essay gives equal space to the origins of Oberlin and its claims upon philanthropists with antislavery sympathies. But it is careful to note that most of the students who withdrew from Lane Seminary to help found Oberlin in 1834 had once been at the Institute. Of Oberlin's faculty, Stuart says, "Mahan, Morgan and Finney, with the other Professors of Oberlin, in moral beauty and sublimity of mind, could scarcely be surpassed. Beriah Green, of Oneida, fully equals them, and in the Anti-Slavery cause is surpassed by none."[22] When Stuart considered the delicate question of which school deserved the support of the public, he sought the security of the middleway. His pamphlet maintains that as the two institutions were at least five hundred miles apart, no natural competition should exist. Oneida could be said to have "peculiar advantages, as a point of attack upon the common enemy, the *pro-slavery spirit of its country*," because it was situated "in the most flourishing county of the most powerful State in the Union." Nevertheless, Stuart does not dismiss entirely Oberlin's claims upon the purse strings of the British, because Oberlin's faculty and students were beacons of impartial liberty in the Great West. He suggested that any who wished might deposit subscriptions "in behalf of Oneida and Oberlin" with him at Bath or with G. W. Alexander in London.[23]

Elizur Wright remained in England at Dorchester upon the conclusion of the General Anti-Slavery Convention. He also wanted Oneida Institute to be fairly represented before those who had the financial resources to stave off her creditors. He drafted several appeals for the British newspapers and fellow abolitionists. One, entitled "To Those Who Know the Oneida Institute," listed prominent graduates, such as Henry B. Stanton, Theodore Dwight Weld, and Henry Highland Garnet. With hyperbole suitable to the occasion, Wright wrote, "Our country and our race can better afford to lose half a dozen such institutions as Cambridge, Amherst, or Yale than that solitary Oneida Institute."[24] A much longer, but untitled essay by Wright began:

> *With no feeling but good will toward the Oberlin Institute, I should be exceedingly sorry to have British philanthropists taught to regard it as the only institution in our country free from the pestilence of caste. I cannot believe that the agents of Oberlin would intentionally leave such an impression. Were they to be reminded of the Oneida Institute under the Presidency of Rev. Beriah Green, they would not fail to admit the justice of its claim to the first honor in the warfare against the American prejudice of color. It would be difficult to point to any man among American abolitionists who has labored longer or more effectively than President Green in the work of breaking down caste.*[25]

Of the African Americans at Oneida, Wright wrote, "Sure I am that those colored young men who have had the happiness to be the pupils of Pres. Green will testify that prejudice does not live in the atmosphere which he breathes, or if it lives it is but a sulking, dying life." Finally, Wright, in distinction to Stuart, came down firmly on the side of Oneida over against Oberlin. "I sincerely hope," Green's former Western Reserve colleague wrote, "that British and all other philanthropists will be made to understand that the work of opening the fountains of knowledge to the colored man is not done, nor half done, by the endowment of Oberlin. Oneida is the parent of Oberlin."[26]

Wright and Stuart failed to appreciate Green's state of mind. He viewed Oberlin's rising prominence in abolition circles as a threat to Oneida Institute and, to the extent that patrons of reform were financing Oberlin's expansion, as a personal repudiation. By 1840 Oberlin had overcome its reluctance to admit blacks.[27] It fully endorsed the manual labor philosophy and yoked Christian piety with social reform. Yet Green would not admit that it belonged in the same league as his school. His valedictory address to the senior class of 1840, published as *A Right Minded Minority*, summed up what it meant to be an alumnus of the Oneida Institute of Science and Industry:

> *This day dissolves your connection with an institution, which in various respects consigns its members to a small minority. You have been manual labor students; and have done something towards breaking down the barrier which separates the working man from the scholar. The sacred books in the languages, in which they were first written, have had your attention in preference to the pages of pagan antiquity. In your literary labors, you have welcomed to your side companions from a persecuted family. You have here been trained to be, and are understood to be, the fast friends of universal freedom.*

Green warned the graduates that because of their identification with his school, they should expect reproach from the "professed scholars" and "pretended republicans" who claimed to be free from prejudice yet dubbed the Institute "the negro college."[28]

Indeed, one must wonder as to the kind of young men who sought out Oneida Institute during its last few troubled years. If Josiah B. Grinnell, the future missionary to the West and abolitionist who became one of Iowa's most prominent politicians, is a fair example, the students were attracted to Oneida Institute specifically because of its radical reputation. Grinnell left Vermont in 1841 with the intent of entering Yale College. He actually toured the New Haven campus, only to be discouraged by the low and gloomy buildings and antics of the students. He then visited a cousin in Meriden, the ward of the Reverend Erastus Ripley, who was a thorough abolitionist and partisan of the study of the Bible in Greek and Hebrew. Ripley told Grinnell about Reuben Hough (a former native of Meriden), treasurer of the Oneida Institute (to which Ripley had frequently contributed). As Grinnell was an orphan, Ripley offered to pay for his journey to Whitesboro and provided him with a letter of introduction to President Green.[29]

When Grinnell arrived, he found that Oneida's students, despite their precarious financial situation, were thoroughly engaged in the business of reform. They took their recreation in impromptu debates, organized colloquies and lyceums, and went Sunday after Sunday into the outlying churches and Sabbath-schools spreading the gospel of Beriah Green.[30] In addition to getting the *Friend of Man* printed, the students also published their own paper, *The Freshman Gem*, a vehicle for sophomoric essays and poetry as well as social and political commentary. For example, in the issue of May 5, 1840, Daniel Van Alstyne, a young man from a Lutheran abolitionist family, mocked the "time-serving D.D.s" who exclaimed, " 'O if I pray or speak in behalf of the oppressed, I shall be branded as an abolitionist! If I get that name my popularity is gone!' ''[31]

In December 1840, the Executive Committee of the trustees recommended that the Institute suspend operations for a year. Hough would remain to manage the property. Green wrote Smith on New Year's Day, "So here I am with my wife and eight children [Charles, b. 1835, and Ruth, b. 1837, had been added to the family since its move to Whitesboro] on this first day of January without the promise of a salary to any amount."[32] Rumors reached him that the New York Anti-Slavery Society had expressed an interest in purchasing his school. He rejected any such proposal, pointing out that the society's unpaid debts had contributed to the Institute's pecuniary embarrassments. Green also felt that some of the society's leaders, notably Alvan Stewart, had been lukewarm or even hostile toward him all along. He did agree to a suspension of one year.[33] Neither suspension nor sale took place.

In February, the *Friend of Man* announced that the ordinary operations of the Institute would commence on the first day of April. Stanley Hough, son of the school's treasurer and an alumnus of the class of 1836, had been engaged to teach Algebra, Geometry, and Natural Philosophy. A "Prof. Elmer" was assigned to teach Greek and Hebrew. Green planned to offer courses in Intellectual and Moral Philosophy, Political Economy, the Science of Government, and Natural Theology. The trustees hoped to make accommodations and instruction available for twenty-five students. About thirty actually enrolled.[34]

During the summer of 1841 Green occupied himself with his books and garden. Though he kept engagements with his students and congregation, he spent six to seven hours a day at manual labor. A volume of his collected works, printed on the press at Oneida Institute, was selling slowly. It ran to 408 pages and included sermons, addresses, and essays from the New England, Western Reserve, and Oneida County years. Beriah confessed that he was no salesman and attributed the poor market for his writings to his being "in rather ill-odor in all the parties."[35] His 1841 valedictory address, *Faith and Works*, emphasized the ideas with which both he and his school were firmly identified in the public mind—the foundation of ethics in self-evident principles, the evils of "negro-hate," especially as exhibited by the pious and learned, the necessity of joining manual with mental labor, the importance of the study of the Greek and Hebrew Scriptures, and the moral requirement to be of service to the world, even as students.[36]

As soon as classes ended in the fall, Green accompanied Hough on a fourteen-day tour to Rome, Syracuse, Rochester, Penn Yan, and westward hoping to collect at least two hundred dollars from professed friends of the slave, especially those in evangelical circles. A circular describing their mission tells of indigent students cut off from any assistance by the education societies, of faculty who had taught the recently completed academic year "almost gratuitously," and of "earnest efforts and protracted struggles" to reduce the debts of the Institute. Green and Hough closed with an appeal to the antislavery sentiments of their potential contributors:

> *In the cause you are devoted to, Brother, the Institute has in various ways labored long and earnestly. . . . The foes of Freedom have long been intent on crushing it. They have in the use of multiplied expedients been waiting for its downfall. Shall their malignanty be gratified? How they would exult to be able to point to its ruins, as a proof that the cause of Freedom in this country must be hopeless! And how many hearts on the same ground would sink in despondency! In the name of God our Savior and his drooping poor, we beseech you, Brother, help us.*[37]

Though cordially received in most places, Green and Hough managed to garner only $125 above expenses.[38]

Visitors to the grounds of Oneida Institute could now see the effects of four years of cutting corners. Fences went unrepaired, and the rooms had deteriorated. Hough had been forced to sell off most of the cattle and grain raised on the farm. The manual labor shops lacked the busy productivity of earlier years. Donations from the outside had practically dried up. Gerrit Smith, whose own fortunes had suffered loss upon loss, took up a collection in Peterboro and managed to send Green fifty dollars. Green began once again to muse about the virtues of abject poverty. Though reluctant as usual to ask for money, he joined Hough on a foraging trip to New York City, Philadelphia, and New England in January 1842. He returned greatly disappointed, especially in New England's clergy.[39]

Somehow the trustees saw fit to announce the opening of the 1842 academic year. About fifty scholars showed up.[40] By August, Green had become entangled in a controversy over the subscription list to the *Friend of Man*. The Executive Committee of the New York Anti-Slavery Society wanted to transfer it from Oneida Institute to Wesley Bailey. It was then to be published at Utica under the editorship of James C. Jackson. Stanley Hough, husband of Green's daughter Ann and editor since Goodell's departure, attempted in vain to purchase the subscription list. Green was of no mind to have the paper turned into a Liberty Party organ by Bailey merely to support the candidacy of Alvan Stewart, then running for governor. The whole business, Green grumbled, reeked of trickery. He saw the hand of Alvan Stewart behind the effort to wrest control of the *Friend of Man* from

Oneida Institute, ca. 1844. From D. Gordon Rohman, *Here's Whitesboro: An Informal History* (New York: Stratford House, 1949).

the Institute and expressed irritation that the Utica lawyer, a man of comfortable means, had never personally contributed to the Institute. Green's anger was understandable, as Reuben Hough was now having to cover the debts of the Institute out of his own pocket.[41] In November, Beriah delivered an address to the graduating class of 1842 on the theme of the divine significance of work. He urged his hearers to identify with the condition of the slaves and the working poor. Only then could they understand their duty to humanity. On the thin edge of poverty himself, he felt a spiritual kinship with all those who lived by the work of their hands.[42]

Despite the financial plight of his school, Green retreated from none of the positions which had offended so many former supporters. On the contrary, he was moving more and more beyond the boundaries of theological orthodoxy. His *Thoughts On the Atonement* appeared in print during the summer of 1842. Originally a sermon preached to his small band of comeouter Congregationalists, it was published at the request of several of his theological students. The prudent course of action would have been not to disseminate the sermon, as Green depicts Jesus not as the god-man but only as man. "He was incalculably superior to all His fellows. In His endowments, aims, activity, attainments, He towered above the human family into the heavens." Green further claimed that Christians could only benefit from Christ's atonement through service to humanity. Samuel Green tells us that the tract was eagerly seized by ecclesiastics hostile to the Institute as grounds to impeach his father's orthodoxy.[43]

In early January 1843, Benjamin S. Walcott, Ira Pettibone, and Alvan Stewart resigned from the board of trustees. Though Green was able to find replacements, the general sentiment of the board was to suspend operations. Beriah agreed. He wrote Smith in February:

> *Here we are. We have made an experiment. The principles on which we have proceeded are divine. We bow to their authority, gratefully. We have with some degree of honesty tried daily to apply them. The public gives us to understand plainly enough that it "can get along without us." The path of duty is, therefore, plain. We ought, I am persuaded, to suspend operations.*[44]

The inevitable, however, was postponed, and in April the Institute opened on a much modified and contracted scale. Hough and Hiram Elmer, one of the new trustees, looked after the property. Green gave lectures to a handful of students still on the grounds. Though describing himself and his wife as "old people . . . with spectacles at our noses," Beriah found himself a father once again in May with the birth of Clara Foote Green.[45] The Green household now totaled eleven.

In July, Green published a thirty-six page history of his nearly ten-year struggle to build up and then save Oneida Institute.[46] After reviewing the purposes, curricular reforms, manual labor system, and tribulations of his school, Green stressed its lasting significance—the effect it had on the young men who had attended. Students "from the haunts of poverty" but of "attractive character and good promise" had eagerly sought out the educational and moral benefits of the Oneida system. They represented a "variety of complexions." Green wrote with justifiable pride, "The red man's son, the black man's son, and the white man's son have here met together; side by side they have worked, side by side they have eaten, side by side they have studied; and all in love and peace and harmony." He also noted that the "colored students" at the Institute, despite their early disadvantages, had proven themselves in "no wise inferior to their palefaced fellows."[47]

Green carefully reviewed the benefits of Oneida's manual labor system. He felt that it kept his students from displaying the "vicious propensities" so in evidence at other literary institutions, such as "cutting bell-ropes; disfiguring benches; burning outhouses; robbing hen-roosts, gardens, and orchards; annoying cattle; removing gates; [and] insulting and injuring plain and honest laborers." Oneida's graduates could stand in the public eye without embarrassment. They had worked with their hands in honest labor without sacrificing the mental discipline of a truly liberal education. Despite Oneida's financial troubles, the manual labor educational philosophy had been proven effective in producing sound minds in sound bodies.[48]

Green and family awoke about 5 A.M. on a Saturday in late September 1843 to the cries of "FIRE! FIRE!" An addition to the main part of the house was ablaze. Though the greater portion of his furniture, clothing, and books escaped the flames, Green lost many pamphlets, papers, and mementos. The "stereotype plates" of *The Chattel Principle* were destroyed, as well as correspondence between Green and his first wife. The family moved into one of the Institute buildings but found the facilities very inconvenient. Mrs. Green, however, did not want to remove to a house in the village.[49] Thus her husband was to be in residence at Oneida Institute when the end came.

On November 1, 1843, Green walked the short distance from his campus lodgings to the chapel. He was to deliver his last valedictory address. With the prospect of failure so close at hand, he had decided to snatch victory from the ashes by speaking on "Success." His address began with a review of other institutions to which the plaudit "success" had been wrongly applied—to Hamilton College, where the faculty forced a student abolitionist group to disband; to Andover Seminary, where the Bible was interpreted in opposition "to the fundamental principles of the Gospel consistent with a healthful and a sound character," and to Princeton, where "the same Divine book is so explained as to justify the foulest crime, that ever disgraced and afflicted human nature."[50] With an eye to how history would judge his educational experiment, he launched into a grand preoration:

> *We don't deny that we have been traduced, derided, opposed. We confess that we are called onion-grubbers and the negro-school. Fashion has tossed up her pretty nose at us. The grim ecclesiastic, as he "passes by on the other side," exclaims, with a knowing air, "That will never do." Sectarianism, with or without canonicals, whether it prates about the Apostolical [sic] succession, or glories in immersion, or boasts of a perfection as pure as the driest sand, or loudly insists on order, order, always scowls cross-eyedly at us. It can make nothing of us. All who regard the peculiar institution, with its handcuffs, chains and scourges, as a thing to be endured, look on us as a disturbing force among the settled arrangements of society. And among our professed friends, all "who halt between two opinions;" who are inclined to the position of Mr. Facing both-ways, find it exceedingly inconvenient to afford us assistance. And then some of our debtors, and many of our patrons, the Times have pinched, and what we expected from their hands never reached us. And*

how shall we pay our own debts without breaking in upon our arrange-
ments, is a question not so easily answered. If all this implies a failure,
we have doubtless failed. But, if to hold on our way through ten years of
toil and trial; and to maintain the principles on which we set out with an
ever-deepening conviction of their weight and worth; and to do somewhat
towards training up a goodly number of young men, of different complex-
ions, for stations of usefulness; and to find ourselves, amidst our studies
and labors, borne constantly onward to higher degrees of improvement,
inward harmony and self-possession; if in these things the elements of
Success are to be recognized, then have we, under God been successful.
What we have done remains for the benefit of the great cause of Educa-
tion. The future we commit to the wisdom of Heaven.[51]

Green stood aside as others oversaw the denouement of his school.
The *Liberty Press* announced that Oneida Institute would re-open on November 15, 1843, this time with the addition of a female department.[52] No
evidence exists that the plan went into effect. The trustees met in January
1844. Some wanted to make another pecuniary effort, but Green had given
his last valedictory. He was for attending to "the main business" of dispos-
ing of the property.[53]

In February, Hough offered the buildings and grounds (only six acres
remained) to representatives of Clinton Seminary. A Free Will Baptist
school founded in 1841 by antislavery Baptists from Vermont, the Seminary
had outgrown its facilities in the Village of Clinton, home of Hamilton College. The Baptists intended to expand their school by offering theological
courses and negotiated with Hough for the sale of the Whitesboro site. The
Seminary, according to the *Liberty Press*, emphasized manual labor and was
"free from the odious system of *caste.*" Alvan Stewart had visited it in
January 1843 and reported that there were seven black students enrolled,
male and female, and that they were treated "with perfect kindness and
equality."[54] Hiram Wilson, a white alumnus of Oneida Institute who had long
been active in educational work among the fugitive slaves in Canada, also
gave his blessing to the Free Will Baptist venture:

The school will be open to candidates for the ministry of all denomina-
tions and of ALL COLORS free of a slaveocratic cast. Here young men
looking forward to the work of the ministry, can study theology without
having the font out of which they drink polluted with a slaveholding spirit.
Whitestown Seminary is the only school of a high order in this state, that
is conducted upon the anti-slavery principle.[55]

Green surely noted the irony in all of this. Some of those who should have been his allies in trying to save Oneida Institute salved their consciences by embracing Whitestown Seminary. Several of Green's former students enrolled in the transplanted Baptist institution. He was allowed to stay on the property until May, when he took up residence at the "Bartlett place," a small farm on the outskirts of Whitesboro. The Free Will Baptists moved into their new facilities during the summer. Whitestown Seminary, coeducational and open to blacks, continued in some ways the traditions of Oneida Institute. Reuben Hough stayed on for a time as financial manager. According to its partisans, Whitestown Seminary, after being chartered in 1845, grew rapidly, in direct correlation to the dissipation of the odious reputation of Green and his school.[56] The Baptist institution lasted until 1884. Thereafter, the buildings were modified to accommodate a textile factory.

Something of the fighting spirit went out of Beriah with the loss of his school. He wrote Smith, "I am less and less disposed to dispute with any body. People must try their own experiments." His school, his institutional axe, was, as he informed Amos Phelps on May 22, 1844, "Gone, Gone, Sold and Gone!"[57] In June, Green's daughter Ann, always a great comfort to her father, died. Married just over a year to Stanley Hough, son of Reuben Hough, she left a young child to be taken into the Green household. Her father was heartbroken. Of his nine children, Beriah felt that Ann understood best the principles he avowed, the objectives he pursued, and the trains of thought, which as a teacher, he employed.[58] To honor Ann and mitigate his sorrow, Green wrote and published a forty-page memorial in which he quoted liberally from his daughter's diary. One quote, from March 24, 1840, reveals much about father and daughter when Beriah Green was yet President of Oneida Institute:

> *And there are grey hairs there, and deep furrows—the once smooth cheek and brow are marked, yet more by thought than time—and the straight form is bowed—and thou art forty-five! Full many a fleeting year hath rolled its course, since thou wast my father—for I am now sixteen—and on this thy natal day my full heart would bless thee in its dearest core. . . . The poor and perishing—the outcast and the wanderer, the down-trodden and oppressed, the victims of a foul prejudice, accursed in the sight of God, and hateful to good men and true—these all shall bless thee! I count it far richer to be thine own, than any other earthly good. What though dark, gloomy eyes have scowled upon thee, and falsely-speaking lips have uttered ill of thee? For God is on thy side—Truth thy motto, Truth thy shield, and everlasting Truth shall be thy blest reward.*

And there is no lie there; an every-during [sic] *firmest basis is thine. For thou has nobly stood, in firm defense of what thou deemest Right, amid the world's contumely, and a church's scorn. Long be thy sojourn with us—a prophet art thou, that with far-seeing eye foretells of future years; and on thy grave it shall be written, with many tears, yet with holy joy, a* good man *has gone home!*[59]

8

THE AXE AND THE POLITICAL SCEPTER

With the closing of his school, Green now 49, was thrown back upon personal resources and forced to reevaluate the role he was to play in the ever-changing abolitionist drama. There was a new antislavery spirit in the North, rooted in fear of the extension of the political power of the South rather than in dedication to the erection of an egalitarian social order or the abolition of the "peculiar institution" where it existed. The revivals which had generated the moral suasion impulse had burnt out, even in central New York, homeland of the Great Revival. Contrary to the expectations of the earlier abolitionists, America had not become a country in which Christian principles prevailed.

Having found moral suasion ineffective, some abolitionists began to look to politics. Delegates to the fourth anniversary meeting of the American Anti-Slavery Society in May 1837 had advised against organizing a distinct political party but did urge abolitionists to work against pro-slavery candidates at the polls. Immediatists in Oneida County began to question candidates regarding their positions on issues such as the annexation of Texas, the petition gag law, slavery in the District of Columbia, and the elective franchise for blacks. The *Friend of Man* editorialized that the ballot box was "an element of reformation which God has put into the hands of abolitionists."[1] Green was strongly in favor of expressing moral principles through politics. He wrote Smith in October 1838, "I am well convinced that God, the God of the Oppressed, calls us into the field of Politics; and we must obey. I enter without any very great reluctance; as I am clear on the point of duty. And Politics is with us a Sacred Concern."[2]

The tactic of questioning Whig and Democrat candidates did not prove fruitful. Thus Green put his signature to a pledge circulated in

Oneida County in 1838 which went a step further. Abolitionists were to stay at home or give a "scattering" or write-in vote if neither the Whigs or Democrats put forth suitable aspirants.[3] To those who complained that a write-in vote for someone not approved by the major parties was an empty gesture, Green replied, "Count them anything but lost. Scattered they may be; but lost they cannot [be]. . . . They will point you out as standard bearers in the sacramental host of God's elect."[4]

Some central New York abolitionists, judging that the scattering tactic was tantamount to self-disfranchisement, put together a "Freeman's ticket" composed of independent nominations. This too brought nothing but frustration. Green thought he knew why. He wrote Smith in November, "How much have we done for the ten years past to elevate politics to their proper place? . . . We have treated politics too much as a smutty concern, with which our clean hands had nothing to do." Having themselves considered the political system too tainted by "every sort of wrestling and scuffling," the abolitionists were ill-prepared to use it for the benefit of the slave. "The Science of Civil Government," Green acknowledged, "is ill-understood."[5]

Talk in the Executive Committee of the New York State Anti-Slavery Society now turned on how to be more effective at the polls. At a January 1839 meeting, Alvan Stewart suggested the formation of a new party.[6] Myron Holly, an abolitionist from Rochester, joined Stewart in the call for a third party in an address given on July 4th at Perry, New York. He maintained that religious convictions should be institutionalized "in the civil government, in legislation, in the administration of justice, in the ballot box, as well as in the temple of God." A veteran of the anti-Masonic movement and a former New York congressman, Holly urged friends of the slave to venture into Bible politics. "Abolitionists," he proposed, "should . . . purify political life, at present the most potent source of social control."[7]

William Lloyd Garrison dispatched one of his Boston lieutenants, Henry C. Wright, to western New York to stem the rising interest in political organization. Wright wanted to know how a third party could expect "to make an anti-slavery Congress out of pro-slavery materials?"[8] Like Garrison, he argued that civil government was just another form of coercion, no different in principle from slavery. The Garrisonian nonresistants abjured partisan politics, instead upholding the ideal of harmonious self-government, wherein the individual voluntarily observes the moral laws of God in all spheres of life. Garrison's opponents dubbed his nonresistance ideas the "no-human-government theory."

Green had always been suspicious of the perfectionism implicit in the philosophy of non-resistance to evil, for it tended to give slavery merely metaphorical significance. According to Garrison's disciples, slavery was to

MADISON COUNTY
and the adjoining Counties!
AWAKE!

The friends of Freedom and of righteous Government — the enemies of land-monopoly and tariffs, and secret societies — are invited to come by thousands to the Meeting, which is to be held in Peterboro, Wednesday 1st day of September next, and which is to begin at precisely 9 o'clock A. M.

Beriah Green, William Goodell, John Thomas, and other distinguished speakers from abroad, are expected to address the Meeting.— Such an opportunity to hear great truths, eloquently spoken, seldom occurs. Let all, who can, improve it.

The Inn-keeper, Mr. Hyde, will have dinner ready at 1-2 past 12.

August 12, 1847.

be endured, like all sin, until the millennial transformation of all earthly relationships. In the meantime, the North was to break off from the South and purify itself. Dis-unionism, Green rightly understood, would leave the slaves to the mercy of their masters, and he did not care to be identified with the dogmatic pacifists. Green wrote Gerrit Smith in 1837, "Bro. H. C. Wright's doctrines on these subjects I would be very sorry to have my children embrace."[9] Green's first priority was ridding the nation of slavery, for in it all the country's ills were congested. He saw politics in the light of moral issues and adopted a pragmatic approach.

Green tried to put a positive face upon the divisions among the friends of humanity over the legitimacy of using political means. He wrote Theodore Dwight Weld in April 1839:

> *How quarrelsome our brother Abolitionists are growing! I am more pained with their differences, than alarmed. Dead men never quarrel. So many men of intelligence, independence, and decision of character—all and each alive to the responsibilities, which so heavily press upon them; sharp strife now and then must be expected and put up with. We must be willing to quarrel for the slave and endure the quarrelling of others. God grant, we may be saved from contending for ourselves and against the slave! "Oppression maketh a wise man mad." A little of the inconveniency of madness must be expected and borne with. We are so formed, moreover, and so affected often, that we too easily slide into the temper and conduct, which we most condemn in others. Hence, we sometimes invade right in defending rights!*[10]

Green had good cause for being alarmed, for the rift between the Garrisonians and non-Garrisonians had widened.

Several leaders of the New York Anti-Slavery Society wanted to purge the Garrisonian ideologues from the American Anti-Slavery Society. The state society, headquartered at Utica, was rapidly growing more independent of the national body by assuming many of its functions and maintaining tighter control over fund raising. With the American Anti-Slavery Society close to breaking apart, the New York abolitionists pushed the third party idea all the more. An antislavery convention held at Warsaw, New York, in November 1839 nominated James Birney for president and Francis J. Le-Moyne of Pennsylvania for vice-president, but both men declined. Alvan Stewart, however, pressed forward with the third party alternative, arguing in a letter to the *Emancipator* in January 1840, "An independent abolition political party is the only hope for the redemption of the slave!"[11] The following month, Gerrit Smith proposed to William Goodell that the new organization be named "the Liberty Party."[12]

When Stewart first suggested that abolitionists organize a single-issue party, Green had written Smith, "I must oppose such a movement, promptly and decisively."[13] He was obviously still ambivalent about becoming involved with a third party in the spring of 1840. He confessed to Smith: "How to maintain in the common form a Human Rights party without involving ourselves in the same evils, as now stare so frightfully upon us from the ranks of the existing parties—that is a problem, which demands for its solution more wisdom than most men are gifted with"[14] Had Alvan Stewart not been one of the principle advocates of a third party, Green might have embraced the idea much earlier than he did.

The non-Garrisonians went ahead with the attempt to create a new political organization free from moral compromise by organizing the Liberty Party on April 1, 1840, at a convention held in Albany. They nominated Birney for president and Thomas Earle for vice-president but did not give the new organization a formal structure. Thus the stage was set for a showdown in May 1840, when delegates to the seventh annual meeting of the national society gathered in New York City. The Garrisonians gained control of the convention and elected Abby Kelly to the previously all-male business committee. Arthur and Lewis Tappan, James Birney, Amos Phelps, Henry Stanton, and the other conservatives who retained more faith than Garrison in the country's basic institutions, took this as an excuse to bolt the meeting. In addition to the "woman question," the conservatives also differed with Garrison over his aversion to politics and attacks upon the orthodox clergy. Unable to outvote the Garrisonians, Lewis Tappan and his allies organized the American and Foreign Anti-Slavery Society.

Green shared the conservatives' attitudes regarding female participation. At the constituting convention of the American Anti-Slavery Society in 1833, he had broken precedent by inviting Lucretia Mott to speak, telling her, "Go on mam, go on; we shall be glad to hear you."[15] But by the mid-1840s he was arguing that "the rights of woman, as woman, are naturally modified by her characteristic powers and capacities." He warned of a veritable Babel of confusion were women to step out of the place assigned to them by the divine "division of labor" as the moral guardians of the domestic sphere. "The doctrine of Equality," Green told Smith, a proponent of female suffrage, "alters not the nature of things."[16]

Despite Green's affinity for the positions of Lewis Tappan and the other conservatives, he did not abandon all respect for Garrison. He had written Birney prior to the break-up of the American Anti-Slavery Society, "I cannot think that Bro. Garrison and his co-adjutors are the men to blame. . . . We might as well ascribe the excesses and terrors of the French revolution to . . . such as Danton and Robespierre." Green thought responsibility for the discord within abolitionist circles should be placed where it had been in the case of the French debacle: "The Clergy and the Court; the Throne and the Church;—they were the hateful, guilty authors. . . ."[17] He wrote Smith shortly after the divisions of May 1840: "You know how little sympathy I have with the extravagances of Mr. Garrison. But in my mind he stands Heaven-high above those ministers who early in the controversy threw themselves in the way of Truth and Righteousness. No extravagance is so bad as their inhumanity."[18] Smith shared Green's reluctance to endorse fully the American and Foreign Anti-Slavery Society. Both men focused their attention upon the Liberty Party Birney-Earle ticket for the national elections of 1840.

Central New York abolitionists served important functions in the Liberty Party campaign of 1840. Green sat on the central corresponding committee for Oneida county, the purpose of which was to get out a large vote for Birney and Earle. The Executive Committee of the New York Anti-Slavery Society endorsed the Liberty Party, and the *Friend of Man* published an extra edition in July comparing the positions of Birney, Martin Van Buren (the Democratic nominee), and William Henry Harrison (candidate of the Whigs). It charged Van Buren with "obsequious subservience to the wishes of the slaveholders" and reminded its readers that Harrison had told Virginia Whigs in 1836 to say that he was "sound to the core" on the subject of slavery.[19] The Libertymen, however, did not enjoy an exclusive claim to righteousness in the 1840 campaign. The Whigs successfully portrayed *themselves* as the party of moral rectitude and Christian influence in politics over against the Democrats, whom they depicted as irreligious and morally repugnant.

The Birney-Earle ticket did miserably at the polls. The Liberty Party candidates won about seven thousand votes out of the millions cast across the nation, less than one per cent of the total. New York provided about twenty-eight hundred of these.[20] Single-issue politics, no matter how much the voters might abhor slavery, had not drawn much interest. Antislavery voters were anxious to know where a candidate stood on the other issues which had troubled the country since the Panic of 1837, such matters as banking, tariffs, and public land policy. The Liberty Party had been built on the "One Idea" platform. Its early supporters thought of it as a temporary party which would disband once the slaves were liberated. But in the wake of the 1840 elections, some members began to urge a broader platform. Green saw adopting positions on issues not related to slavery as a matter of moral duty. "I abhor the notion of making Abolition exclusively a matter of chattel principle slavery," he wrote Smith in 1841.[21] Others saw a broad platform as a way to woo potential evangelical supporters away from the Whigs or even the regular Democrats.

The political abolitionists now began to debate among themselves over the wisdom of expanding their objectives. Smith attempted to restore harmony by calling for a convention at Albany in 1842. Garrison and some of his allies showed up, creating more confusion. Green protested to Smith:

> *I cannot persuade myself, that our meetings are rendered at all more useful by enlisting the assistance—shall I call it?—of such men as Mr. Garrison. Think of your Albany meeting. The impression on the general mind of such things as occurred there is any thing but happy. And it was rather too much of your good-nature, patience and magnanimity—the self-seeking and officious boisterousness of the Boston gentlemen. For my own part, I am heartily sick of such things. I can find no pleasure in seeing a wanton hand throw addle eggs at my mother. Besides, the way is opened by such ill-advised come-togethers for strife and contention.*[22]

Green's resentment may have been sparked by an experience he had in New England a month or so prior to the Albany gathering. In May 1842 he spoke before the Connecticut Anti-Slavery Convention. Young men, led by an Irish law student from Yale, expressed displeasure at his remarks. "They were exceedingly vulgar and impudent," Green recalled, "hissing, striking the floor with their walking-sticks, etc. I regard this as a fair expression of the general sentiment of New Haven."[23]

As the 1843 elections approached, the Liberty Party had difficulty in finding candidates to field for state and local offices. Green did not support Alvan Stewart as the gubernatorial nominee for New York. He could not

Gerrit Smith (arms outstretched) and Frederick Douglass (seated to his left) at the Great Cazenovia Fugitive Slave Law Convention, August 22, 1851. An extremely rare early daguerreotype. Courtesy of the Madison County Historical Society.

forgive Stewart for failing to champion the Institute or for being so miserly with his own wealth. "Can we not have a name," Green pleaded with Smith, "whose sound shall be a little more musical. Honesty and magnanimity! They are worth something; let the 'supreme quack' say what he will. Our first business here is to acquire and maintain character." As Stewart's influence grew within the Liberty Party, Green became more and more embittered. He accused Smith of treating the Utica lawyer with too much "easy charity" as he propelled himself to center stage in the New York State Anti-Slavery Society.[24] Despite Green's objections, Stewart had led the state Liberty Party ticket in the 1842 elections. He received over seven thousand votes, about three times more than the Birney-Earle ticket had garnered in 1840, but went down to defeat. Green's quarrel with Stewart came to a head at the January 1843 meeting of Oneida Institute's trustees. Stewart resigned from the board.

The Libertymen announced plans for another national convention to be held in Buffalo on August 30-31, 1843. Green excused himself on the grounds that he could not afford to travel far from Whitesboro. Those who did attend again nominated Birney, after being unable to convince William H. Seward to bear their standard. The delegates, much to Beriah's pleasure, resolved that the Liberty Party would promote the "paramount authority of God" over all human compacts, laws, and constitutions.[25] Green was less pleased with the results of the state Liberty Party convention which met in Canastota in September. Stewart was again chosen to head up the state ticket.

William Chaplin and James C. Jackson, Liberty Party leaders, asked Green to write a biography of Birney for the 1844 campaign. He wrote Birney in April requesting primary sources and declaring that his purpose was to "lay hold of the characteristic features of *the man*." Green was already impressed with Birney: "I have indeed for my own benefit a most grateful and refreshing impression of your design. It is my privilege to regard you with love and confidence and a respect, bordering upon, if it does indeed involve, veneration."[26] The project afforded Green some relief from the depression he felt at the closing of Oneida Institute. He finished the 119 page volume, largely a compilation of Birney's writings, by July. Green reminded potential voters that the former Kentucky slaveholder had voluntarily and at his own expense raised all his father's slaves to the dignity of freemen, a laudable example of demonstrating in practice what one held in principle.[27] The *Liberty Press*, the party newspaper, declared that every voter in the land should read Birney's biography before the election.[28]

Green attended the national Liberty Party convention at Albany in early December 1844. Despite earlier misgivings about making the fight against chattel slavery the only goal of the Liberty Party, he now urged the delegates to adopt the "GRAND ONE IDEA as the professed friends of freedom, and wear it as our insignia." The Whig candidate, Henry Clay, drew Green's censure for being "a great duelist, Sabbath-breaker, profane swearer, gambler, and SLAVE-HOLDER." The Democratic standard-bearer, James K. Polk, was just "another great slave holder." Green wanted to name a "WISE AND VIRTUOUS MAN." "Show the man you vote for," Green demanded of the delegates, "and I will tell you the precepts you cherish."[29] The Libertymen had little to show for their efforts when Birney garnered only 62,197 votes, about 2.3 percent of the national total.

The Liberty Party did better in New York State in 1844 than in 1842, rolling up almost sixteen thousand votes as compared with seven thousand. Most Liberty voters were from the small Yankee farming communities of the Burned-over District. As Alan M. Kraut has argued, the rank-and-file, New York's "bone and muscle," saw their interests at stake in the fight against a system of labor that threatened to undercut their opportunities as free laborers.[30] Though the Liberty Party vote was only three per cent of New York's presidential vote, it robbed Clay and the Whigs of enough votes to give the state's electoral ballots and the national victory to Polk and the Democrats. Green was bitterly disappointed, for he considered Polk, who was committed to the annexation of Texas as a new slave territory, as the least acceptable of the two major candidates.

Gerrit Smith attempted to woo William H. Seward, the recently defeated Whig Governor of New York, into the Liberty Party as a potential candidate for the next presidential election. Green strongly opposed such overtures, noting that Seward had supported Clay in the campaign of 1844. He burned with indignation at the prospect of Seward as the standard-bearer of the Liberty Party: "No man especially of high intelligence and commanding influence, ever yet pursued the object and employed the expedient, which characterizes the Whig party, who, in doing so, was not as wicked as he was mischievous." Smith responded, "Have patience with him and the thousands of Whigs, who sincerely believed that they were aiding the cause of the slaves, when they were casting their votes for Henry Clay."[31]

Except for a few local elections, the Liberty Party had not been able to mount successful campaigns on a single issue. During the state convention at Port Byron in June 1845, William Goodell urged that the Libertymen go beyond "One-Ideaism" and take stands on all reform issues. They were to purge themselves of all expedient considerations and prepare to govern the nation. Green now allied himself with Goodell, Jackson, Chaplin, and Birney in calls for a broader platform. He wrote Smith in the fall of 1846, "If the L. Party is too ignorant to understand the duties of Am. citizens, it is unworthy of the name and influence of a national party." He now wanted to transform the Liberty Party into a model party, one with correct reform views on a wide variety of issues. "If the shabby one-idea-ism," Green fairly shouted, "which is made so much of in various quarters is all it has to boast, it is poor indeed."[32] Abandonment of the One Idea was dangerous in two respects. First, political-action abolitionists might be tempted to dilute their abolitionism in order to widen their appeal. Second, widening the platform was potentially divisive, for it would set abolitionist against abolitionist and bring in either Whigs or Democrats who did not share the radical principles of the founders of the Liberty Party.

Oneida County abolitionists began to quarrel among themselves over abandoning the concept of a single-issue, temporary party. Green, quite predictably, found himself at odds with Alvan Stewart. He gave a lengthy account of their differences in a letter to Birney, dated September 23, 1846:

> *I cannot put the same construction as Alvan and his friends on the phrase; The One Idea of the A. S. Enterprise. They confine themselves in explaining and applying it exclusively to the abolition of slavery. This, they affirm, is the great object, to which in the sphere of Politics we should direct thought—on which we should expend our energies. For my own part, I maintain, that our platform should be wide enough, to give free scope to all our powers in discharging our duties as American citizens. Otherwise, we are not—cannot be—a National Party. Under any such character, we are manifestly bound to occupy just the ground, we would have the Government occupy. For I insist upon it, that we are now an essential part of the Government;—have just the same responsibilities in Kind to honor, as if the visible scepter were placed in our hands.*[33]

Green's dispute with Stewart, whom he derisively called "the oracle of the Liberty Party," doubtless played into his decision to move beyond the original aims of political abolitionism. He wrote Smith, "Better to hold fellowship with bears and owls than hold to such a party." He would have said the same to Stewart's face, but the lawyer, according to Green, turned "another part" of his anatomy toward him.[34] Beriah's thorn-in-the-flesh fell ill in 1846 and moved to New York City, where he died in 1849.

Now fifty-one, Green began to lament the physical effects of aging. He resorted to the cold-water cure and his axe as stratagems to counteract weakness of body and despondency in spirit. Whatever the immediate cause, mental or physical, he exhibited more and more a trait of personality that even his closest friends found tiresome. He became increasingly irritable, suspicious, and contentious. He had always been combative, a man of principle who brooked no compromise, but his verbal pugilisms had been directed primarily at the enemies of Oneida Institute. Now he began to find fault with friends and colleagues who could not follow him down an ideological path that eventually led him far astray from the evangelical circles in which he had once been welcome.

Green's break with the American Board of Commissioners for Foreign Missions severed one of the few remaining ties he had with the national benevolent agencies. Amos Phelps, corresponding secretary of the American and Foreign Anti-Slavery Society, led a petition drive charging the commissioners with tolerating slaveholders in the congregations established among the western Indian tribes. The abolitionists also criticized the American Board for failing to establish missions in Africa among the Mendians of Nigeria who had been freed by the Supreme Court in 1841 after the Amistad incident. Beriah and his brother Jonathan supported the abolitionist Union Missionary Society and later the American Missionary Association, organized in 1846.[35] In the late-1840s, Green became more and more concerned with smaller and smaller circles of influence. It was as if there were a direct correlation between the dissipation of his sense of relatedness to the benevolent empire of interlocking reform agencies and his attacks on those closest to him.

Green had been identified most intimately with the circle of abolitionists in the Burned-over District which centered on Gerrit Smith. These evangelical immediatists included, in addition to Green, William Chaplin, William Goodell, Alvan Stewart, and Myron Holly. The Smith circle broke up in the late 1840s, sooner than either that of William Lloyd Garrison in Boston or that of the Tappans in New York City. Beriah's disputes with members of the Smith circle arose to a large extent from his discovery of a new ideological friend at a time when he was nearly despondent over the difficulties of saving Oneida Institute and embroiled in the controversy with West and Ogden at First Presbyterian. In August 1838, he informed Smith, "Since I saw you, I have made a new acquaintance, who exerts a powerful influence upon me. Thomas Carlyle is his name. He seems to be an Englishman. Have you seen his French Revolution?" Of Theodore Dwight Weld, Green inquired, "Have you read Thomas Carlyle's French Revolution? Or his Hero-worship? Or his Chartism? Pray read some of these." Green digested Carlyle's life of Cromwell and recommended it to Smith as "a great book." He corresponded with Carlyle, invoked Carlyle's name and ideas in letters to Smith and others, and, finally, was carried away by Carlyle's notion of "God-sent rulers." Though Beriah had hinted even before 1838 that he was dissatisfied with democracy as a form of civil government, since it failed to deal adequately with the great evil of slavery, his enthusiasm for Carlyle opened up a chasm between him and others in Smith's circle which could not be bridged.[36]

Elizur Wright actually visited Carlyle in 1846. Though intrigued by the Scottish historian, essayist, and moralist, he came away from a half-hour interview with the conclusion that Carlyle knew little of the everyday world and of the prejudice against blacks in his own land. Wright believed that Carlyle lived in a "mesmeric state." He published his impressions in the *Weekly Chronotype*, the reform paper which he had started in Boston. Green saw Wright's columns and rose to the defense of Carlyle's views on civil government and human nature. William Goodell soon joined in the debate, siding with Wright against Green, and the whole matter was aired in the *Albany Patriot*.[37] Copies of the *Patriot* apparently reached Carlyle, for he wrote Ralph Waldo Emerson on July 17, 1846, "Do you know Beriah Green? A body of Albany Newspapers represent to me the people quarrelling in my name, in a very vague manner, as to the propriety of being 'governed'; and Beriah's is the only rational voice among them." Carlyle seems to have been more amused than seriously interested in the debate, for he had written his wife two days earlier, "Nothing of the Letter Kind; only another Yankee Newspaper with further dreary controversy about the character of Carlyle,—which I have already disposed of."[38]

Green had long harbored reservations about the elective franchise. When he examined the character of those elected to public office in Jacksonian America, he found them wanting, so he faulted the democratic system itself. In a letter written to James Birney in September 1846, he complained, "Alas to a frightful extent our poor country-men cannot—at any rate do not, distinguish between a conspiracy and government."[39] About a year later, Green again wrote Birney, this time with obvious reference to Carlyle's views: "A greater delusion was never hatched from any cockatrice's egg, than what is commonly boasted of as the Democratic principle. The thing has neither Truth nor Decency. We must insist upon the control of Wisdom. The wisest and the strongest we must seek out and welcome to their proper places."[40]

Green wanted to put the scepter of civil government into the hands of a Moses or a Jesus and argued that "the *throne of God* is the only Model on which a government can possibly be formed and maintained." "The wisest, strongest man in any community is its King," he told Birney, "and Earth and Hell can by no means deprive him of the scepter." He offered little advice as to how such men were to be identified and put into office, except to say that "true rulers can only be trained for their places in the School of Obedience."[41]

Birney shared Green's disapproval of representative democracy or popularly elected government. William Goodell did not. Busy writing a two-volume reconstruction of democracy on the basis of Christianity, Goodell tried to convince readers of the *Albany Patriot* that Green's views, while understandable in that they were born of frustration with the persistence of slavery, were fundamentally inimical to the abolitionist cause. Convinced that all of mature age who were not criminals were entitled to vote, Goodell could not accept the proposition that the masses must be governed by a gifted minority in a perpetual apprenticeship. Green argued to the contrary. He demanded that those who approached the ballot-box be possessed of "Integrity, Wisdom, Magnanimity [and] Heroism." Those lacking these moral credentials were unfit to exercise the elective franchise. Green wondered whether or not Goodell was prepared to extend the principle of equal entitlement to all areas of life. He inquired, "Now does William Goodell believe that all men are equally entitled to shoe his horse, or pull a defective tooth, or print the *Investigator?*"[42]

While Green labored to convince his colleagues that access to the ballot box should be dependent upon character, Goodell, Jackson, and several others in Smith's circle attempted to form a pressure group to ensure that the Liberty Party would not choose popularity over purity of principle. Goodell wrote a declaration of sentiments that set forth a philosophy of civil government which vested authority, under God, not in a select few but in the "mass of the people." Green authored a series of long essays for the *Albany Patriot* in which he criticized Goodell, Jackson, and the other signers of the "Declaration" for their defense of democracy but approved of their efforts both to purify the Liberty Party and to address a wide range of issues.[43]

The seceders from the Liberty Party met at Macedon Lock in June 1847 and founded the Liberty League. Its constitution took a position on a wide variety of social problems in addition to chattel slavery. It specifically protested "the withholding of suffrage from permanent resident citizens on the ground of birth, parentage, race, color, or avocation." Among the platform's list of nearly twenty reforms were calls for the repeal of all tariffs, the end of the Mexican war, cheap postage, abolition of the army and the navy, and limitations on the amount of land that could be held by individuals and corporations.[44] As William Wiecek has observed, "Where the moderates were simultaneously trying to dilute the Liberty program in order to broaden its appeal, the radicals [who went into the Liberty League] sought to extend it to embrace all reform issues."[45]

Green was not willing to embrace either faction. He wrote Birney in August:

> *The Liberty Party lacks, it seems to me, the vitalizing presence and sustaining power, of Principle. It is a party. The League is better. But I cannot give it my confidence. If my fellows, whoever they be, will not demand Government, I must. I rather go alone in the right path than with a number of companions in the wrong. The throne of God is the only Model on which a government can possibly be formed and*

maintained. . . . The wisest, strongest man in a community is its King,
and Earth and Hell can by no means deprive him of the scepter.[46]

Here was Carlyle's heroic man. Green had consigned the elective franchise
to the rubbish heap of failed experiments. It had produced a conspiracy, one
that fostered slavery and not righteous government. Green preferred divine
authority: "How much better to be alone with Justice, Mercy, Fidelity,
Consistency, Magnanimity—with God, than in the midst of applauding multi-
tudes in the infliction of Injustice—the perpetuation of Folly—the spread of
Misery!"[47]

The Liberty Leaguers tried to persuade the remaining Libertymen to
expand beyond single-issue politics and sought to prevent a coalition of
antislavery forces with the "conscience" or antislavery Whigs and moderate Democrats. The Libertymen met at Buffalo, October 20–21, 1847, with
the Liberty Leaguers or universal reformers representing about one-third of
the convention. The Leaguers came away having failed to convince the
majority to declare slavery unconstitutional in the states as well as in the
territories and to broaden the Liberty Party platform. Green had not
attended, as he was once again suffering from nervous exhaustion and felt
that the requisite manual labor exertions which were his salvation could only
be done at home. But he followed the proceedings in Goodell's paper, the
Christian Investigator, and concluded that Joshua Leavitt, Henry Stanton,
Lewis Tappan, and the other leaders of the Buffalo majority deserved "little
confidence" for having rebuffed the Leaguers.[48]

Gerrit Smith, leader of a rump faction of the Liberty Party, called for
another convention to be held in Buffalo in June 1848. Smith's band hoped
to nominate candidates true to Liberty Party principles. The Leaguers, led
by Goodell, met about two weeks prior to the Buffalo assembly and, further
confusing matters, nominated Smith for the national presidency. The one
hundred four delegates of Smith's rump convention then convened under
the banner of the National Liberty Party. Green was there, representing
Libertymen in Oneida County. The delegates voted to oppose not only
slavery but also "wars, tariffs, the traffic in intoxicating drinks, land monop-
olies, and secret societies, and whatever else is opposed to that comprehensive, great and glorious One Idea." They condemned the war with
Mexico and castigated General Zachary Taylor, the Whig nominee, for being
"an enslaver of men, and a butcher of men."[49] They assailed the Democratic hopeful, Lewis Cass, as nothing but a demagogue. Upon the motion
of Green, they too nominated Smith as their presidential candidate.

Green gave a speech on "Civil government and the mutual relations
which bind rulers and subjects together." In his view, many of the Libertymen and Leaguers were still laboring under the false assumption that

human government could aspire to the heights of the divine "Law of Rectitude." He noted that the slaveholders appealed to human government in
defense of their right to own other human beings. He argued that slavery
made a mockery of the very idea of moral law, since the slave, having been
reduced to a thing, could not be held accountable to any moral standard.
Should the slaves kill their masters, they would not fairly be liable, for
chattels could not logically be tried, convicted, and punished. A conflict
between masters and slaves would simply be "a fight among mere
animals—one herd rushing wildly upon another."[50]

Green next turned to the prerequisites of a civil government capable
of fostering justice. He argued that "heaven-anointed rulers"—that is, individuals distinguished not by popular election but by their righteous character, integrity, wisdom, magnanimity, and ability to give and afford
protection—were essential. He repeated his objections to universal suffrage, arguing that "no man can have a right to do what he is not qualified to
accomplish." Having dispensed with representative democracy, Green proposed a theocratic alternative: "God is the only Potentate. Civil Government must be a reflection of His Throne." Green wanted "Heaven-
anointed" rulers empowered by "Nature, character, necessity. . . . As they
are not indebted to the popular voice for the high qualities for which they
are distinguished, so the popular voice cannot degrade them from the high
position, where they stand."[51] Green's hatred of slavery had led him to the
court of last resort—a theocracy or, more accurately, a divinely instructed
oligarchy.

A coalition of antislavery Whigs, Liberty Party men such as Joshua
Leavitt and Henry Stanton, and disgruntled Democrats from New York
known as the Barnburners, met in Buffalo during early August 1848. They
organized the Free Soil Party around the slogan, "Free Soil, Free Speech,
Free labor, and Free Men." Green termed the new party "wholesale apostasy!"[52] Since its goal was primarily to keep slavery out of the western
territories in order to preserve homesteads for whites, the Free Soil Party
reduced antislavery to its lowest common denominator. Sensing this, Green
worked with Gerrit Smith to keep the Liberty Party alive. Smith attempted
to revive it through a series of conferences and by backing the *Liberty Party
Paper*, a weekly edited and published by John Thomas in Syracuse. Green
published an essay, dated September 1848, in which he urged surviving
members of the Liberty Party forthrightly to condemn the candidate (Martin Van Buren, "the Northerner with southern principles") and the platform
of the Free Soilers. He was incensed that Joshua Leavitt and the other
Liberty Party defectors should subscribe to the heresy that the federal
government did not have the power and responsibility to end slavery in the
states.[53]

The Liberty Party was by now badly split between those who favored universal reform and those who were willing to join the Free Soil coalition. The Leaguers, having been rebuffed at the Buffalo Free Soil Convention, reorganized themselves as the True Liberty Party and ran Smith as an abolitionist alternative to the Free Soil Van Buren–Adams ticket but managed to garner only 2,500 votes in the election of 1848. The Liberty Party majority merged with the Free Soilers and went out of existence in 1848. Joshua Leavitt, a Liberty Party leader from Massachusetts, asserted that the Liberty Party was not dead but merely "translated." Green felt that the Liberty Party had been "sold, spirit, soul, body and name, or rather FLUNG AWAY!"[54]

With the Liberty Party moribund and a handful of radicals still vainly trying the third-party route, Green began to drift more and more toward the notion of the moral government of God as the only ideologically pure position. He had inherited concepts of the sovereignty and millennial reign of God from his Calvinist mentors in New England, had seen them flourish in "New School" revivalism, and had tried to relate them to society in the academic discipline known as "political economy." But as a result of the failure of Bible politics, he concluded that the American populace did not have the requisite virtue and intelligence to conform voluntarily to the divine model of righteousness. The country was no nearer to restoring the sovereignty of God in 1848 than it had been when the immediatists first sounded the call to abandon the sin of slavery in the early 1830s. The instrument of moral suasion had been blunted and broken upon the rock of slavery. Democracy had failed to conform to the moral government of God.

Though Green had been critical of the Garrisonian philosophy of nonresistance, he was now coming around to a similar view of the relationship of divine government to civil government. Garrison's critics wrote in scorn of his "anarchism," as if he was promoting lawlessness. But as Lewis Perry has argued, "Garrison understood . . . that the only irrefutable argument against slavery is a denial of any man's right over the liberty of another under any conditions whatsoever."[55] The opposite of anarchy was slavery, not lawlessness. When earthly interlopers, such as the masters of slaves, were destroyed, then God's rule would begin. Slavery was an extended metaphor for all forms of coercion and sin. Any civil government which made the individual respect the rights of his neighbor by threats of punishment was an evil conspiracy. Garrison asserted that all human governments were coercive and therefore wrong, but he left the ideal of republican government to the realm of imagination.

Green, however, attempted to make the practical transition from the ideal to the real by interjecting subalterns between God and the common

James Gillespie Birney. From the *Dictionary of American Portraits* (New York: Dover Publications, 1967).

man. He urged, *"Put true Rulers at the helm, and all is well."* These rulers were to be distinguished for their godlike qualities; they were "Heaven-anointed" and could not be created or destroyed by the whim of the majority.[56] He gave no examples of leaders who fit such stringent criteria, though he had applauded James Birney in 1846 as an example of "genuine heroism."[57] Having lost interest in the ballot box, Green was left with, as historian Lewis Perry aptly puts it, "a mysterious operation of influence by which men sift themselves, some becoming leaders and some followers, without any trace of coercion."[58]

If there is a fundamental reason for Green's drift toward government by the elite, a kind of oligarchy of the wise or perhaps even a monarchy, it is rooted in his lifelong search for a basis upon which to ground moral behavior. The evangelicals appealed to the conscience, informed by reason and, when pressed, to the "naked will" of God as revealed in Scripture. Green had subsumed Scripture to the self-evident principles of reason. Then he discovered by bitter experience that his enemies both appealed to Scripture over against reason and refused to live by the self-evident principles of reason. He then turned away from republicanism to "the politics of saint-hood."[59]

Yet rule by the saints, as Roger Williams discovered in colonial Massachusetts and Michael Servetus did in Calvin's Geneva, involves coercion. Many a free spirit has fled the constraints of rule by moral absolutes or been made to suffer the consequences. Green's model of civil government entailed rule by an elite. In principle it was not hierocratic, for he was not proposing to give ultimate power to the clergy. But so intense were his convictions that leaders should be men who were themselves obedient to the sovereignty of God, that he opted for rule by agents of God rather than representatives of the people.

9

"A VOICE IN THE WILDERNESS"

The fusion of many immediatists in 1848 with the Free Soilers and later with the Know-Nothing and Republican parties gradually drew down the curtain on the evangelical holy enterprise to rid America of slavery and racism. Abolitionism gave way to her weaker sister—antislavery, which sought to contain slavery rather than eliminate it.

The antislavery era was not particularly kind to Beriah Green. He struggled to keep the abolitionist ship afloat in the turbulent sea of sectionalism and felt as if he were a solitary figure in an ocean of moral indifference. The public at large offered no home port, and his former abolitionist colleagues found him irascible and intractable. Green's importance in the 1850s derives not from his popularity with any group but from the persistence with which he pursued the original course of immediatism when others were tacking to suit the changing winds.

Green acknowledged that his anti-democratic views had not brought popular acclaim in the reform circles with which he had been associated. Samuel Green began a small newspaper called the *Model Worker* and published it in Utica to serve as a vehicle for his father's increasingly idiosyncratic political philosophy. The first issue contains an essay with the title "A Voice in the Wilderness." Green signed it with "Thus saith the Misanthrope."[1] Though some critics had described him as a hater of mankind, he wore the label proudly, for he thought of himself an enemy of the species, universally, which degraded human nature into a merely animal existence. He scorned democracy precisely because the voters had consistently failed to rid America of the demon of slavery. Samuel admitted that there was but "a little band" in sympathy with his father's dour views on human or civil government, as distinct from self or divine government.[2]

During the 1850s, Green's old colleagues solicited his advice, tolerated his increasing obstreperousness, and where possible, sought to draw him back into reform circles of one kind or another. Some expressed concern over his obstinance, even over his mental health. But those who knew the Beriah Green of the early abolitionist controversies and of the Oneida Institute years, respected him for what he had been and were willing to put up with what he had become. In many ways, Green's last twenty-five years testify to the failure of white America to respond to the abolitionist vision of a truly egalitarian, prejudice free, society. Black abolitionists such as Henry Highland Garnet and Martin Delany sought refuge in Africa, while others emigrated to Canada. Green came to feel like an alien in his own country and escaped into an ideological conventicle that left him at odds with most of his former abolitionist colleagues.

Perhaps the most painful separation was that which ruptured fraternal ties with Gerrit Smith. The Green-Smith relationship went beyond that of reformers yoked in common cause. Their households were interconnected in many ways. Smith had honored Green by naming a newborn son after him: "Green Smith was born 1/2 past 2 P.M. this day [April 4, 1842]. Who is Green Smith?, you will ask. He is my only son, named after my beloved brother Beriah Green."[3] Over the years, Green and Smith had counseled each other in domestic matters and shared advice on diet and personal health. More than two hundred letters survive from Green's voluminous correspondence with Smith. Green had always treasured Smith's friendship, because the Peterboro reformer recognized that Oneida's president was sincerely interested in open and honest ideological debate, but differences over the nature of civil government soon strained their relationship.

Smith reluctantly began a public debate with Green on the nature of civil government in a printed circular that appeared on April 4, 1849, addressed to "President Green, Whitesboro." He argued that just as impiety did not cancel the right or obligation of prayer, so a failure to honor the claims of justice did not rob one of the right or obligation to vote. "I would just as soon say," Smith affirmed, "that a man must stay away from the mercy-seat, as from the ballot box." He labeled Green's notion of God-appointed rulers "impracticable" and "perilous"—"Does not the history of the world and of the human heart teach us, that the theory of the God-sent ruler is the very one that the Devil-sent usurper always stands ready to avail himself of?—and that, wherever it prevails, the people are vexed and cursed with tyrants?"[4] Smith accurately identified the root cause of the controversy with his old friend:

*You have none, while I have the utmost confidence in the capabilities of
the masses to care for themselves. Hence, these wide differences. When*

Gerrit Smith. From *Harper's Weekly*, January 16, 1875, from a photograph by Kurz.

Carlyle makes the masses cry out: "Govern us"—"Govern us": this cry, which is so humiliating and disgusting in my ears, is delightful music in yours. . . . You would, in short, have government present in all the departments of conduct, and in all the relations of life. . . . To protect is the only duty and province of Government—and happy for its subjects were it to protect them, and to have nothing more to do with them.[5]

Smith sent multiple copies of the circular to Green. Angry at being held up to public reproach, Beriah wrote back, "my personality, whatever it may be, lies off at an infinite distance from the poor scarecrow, which your circular intends—and in an opposite direction."[6] Adding insult to injury, Smith also sent the circular to the *Liberty Press* and other papers and to a segment of Green's congregation in Whitesboro. Though the congregation had finally obtained a permanent home in 1848, it was becoming increasingly troubled by its pastor's ever more radical views. Several families, including that of Reuben Hough, resigned. Green blamed Smith for fueling the fires of his critics. Smith attempted to pass over their differences with the excuse that he was no philosopher: "Well, this is the first time I have appeared in the character of a Metaphysician. May it be the last! I always felt that I could not understand metaphysics. The feeling is now confirmed."[7]

As in the months following the closing of Oneida Institute, Green turned his thoughts toward leaving Whitesboro. He again contemplated purchasing land in Ohio or Michigan, where he could draw up his daily bread from "the sacred soil." But with little capital, he could not find a way to move a large family and resigned himself to cultivating a small farm near Whitesboro. Smith asked him to recommend landless blacks who might be given farms on thousands of acres Smith owned in Franklin and Essex Counties, in the Adirondacks. It was not an easy task. Green found too few who had the requisite moral character and accused Smith of giving away land to some who were "lazy, shiftless, [and] gluttonous."[8] Smith countered that need alone, not character, made one eligible for the "God-given right" of a homestead. Green's reservations about Smith's scheme were borne out by experience. Few of the blacks who settled on Smith's lands stayed very long. The lands were marginal anyway, and most of the black recipients could not cope with subsistence farming in the harsh climate of northern New York. In 1856, John Brown, later of Harper's Ferry, bought a farm just south of Lake Placid and settled among the few remaining black recipients of Smith's land grants.

In December 1849, Green wrote Smith: "For a long time, I have been silent in my relations to prominent members of the Liberty Party—to yourself as well as to others. It seems to be next to impossible for me to say a word, which they admit to be at all intelligible. They represent me as an amazing novelty—a very monster, to be classed with nobody knows whom or what." After a long discourse on why additional efforts to clarify his views on civil government would be useless, Green told Smith:

> *Dear Brother, I can myself be in your eyes nothing less than an amazing novelty. I am, indeed, radically unlike those, by whom I am surrounded—those even, with whom in the A.S. enterprise, I was formerly connected. So it is, and I cannot even wish to help the matter. All genuine friendships—all true cooperation seem to me have their vitalizing basis in principle . . . where this is sacrificed, they vanish.*[9]

The Smith House in Peterboro, Madison County. It burned in 1936, just prior to being declared a state historical site. From Octavius Brooks Frothingham, *Gerrit Smith* (G.P. Putnam's Sons, 1878).

As if to close the book on fraternal relationships with Smith, Green wrote that he no longer cared to accept invitations to preach in Smith's Peterboro congregation.

Smith attempted to mollify his old abolitionist colleague during the following months. As to Green's feeling that it had become impossible for them to work cooperatively while they disagreed over the nature of civil government, Smith wrote, "You may cast me off, but I shall never cast you off."[10] He tried to draw Green out of his self-imposed isolation by inviting him to abolition meetings, but Green refused on the grounds that he felt as if he were occupying another world than that of his former associates. Further explanation of his views would be as unintelligible as "Choctaw and Sanskrit." Green even confessed that he had lost confidence in Carlyle after reading of Carlyle's approval of the suppression of the rights of East Indians by the British.[11] In August 1850, Smith wrote Green to acknowledge what had become painfully clear. "From your not replying to my last letter, I inferred that you did not wish to continue a correspondence with me, and that you did wish me to understand, that you no longer recognized me in your circle of friends."[12]

Green now began a hermit sort of existence. Except for one letter concerning the difficulties of finding suitable candidates for Smith's land donations, Green apparently did not write him for nearly three years. He did correspond with James Birney in April 1852, concerning a forthcoming National Liberty Party convention called by remnants of the Liberty League. "How I should rejoice to see you, and, communicate with a living voice, my convictions and persuasions on the subject!" he told Birney. "I know of no name, from whom I should expect a more patient and candid hearing." Green complained of rheumatic attacks and described efforts to find relief via open air walks and hydropathic or "Watercure" appliances. In language as vitriolic and bitter as he once used against slaveholders, Green condemned the "monkey-chatter" about "Universal Suffrage" with its "brimstone smell." He described those who would "offer office or accept office on any other ground and for any other purpose, than to furnish a true medium, thro' which the throne of the Messiah may be reflected" as committing high treason and worshiping the Devil. He wished no party, including the National Liberty Party, any success as long as it affirmed "that bad men, while they continue as such, have—can have any right to share in the prerogatives of government." He labeled human government "hoghaunted" and "an atrocious conspiracy" to whom one was no more obligated to submit than to the "demands of a band of robbers."[13]

Beriah's missionary brother Jonathan had not seen him since leaving for the Sandwich Islands in 1827. Yet he had watched approvingly as his brother fought against the colonizationists, slaveholders, and conservative Northern ecclesiastics. Jonathan sent abolitionist essays to the American press and established a comeouter church of his own in Hawaii, but he could not understand nor approve of his brother's anti-democratic views. Smith received a letter from the Sandwich Islands written during November 1852, in which Jonathan inquired concerning his brother, "Please tell me, if you can, what ails him." Smith's response, entitled "My Explanation of Beriah Green's state of mind," was not very helpful, for he had not seen his old friend in more than four years. Beriah's "strange state of mind," one that viewed the world as "evil and devilish," perplexed Smith. The Peterboro reformer could only admit that Beriah seemed "to have lost his confidence in all men. He, once, loved my wife and me. But I fear he does not now. We love him however and his dear wife also—and shall be very glad to visit them, if invited to do so."[14]

Indicative of his confidence in the political process, Smith successfully represented the twenty-second congressional district on an independent ticket, with support from antislavery Whigs, Democrats, Free Democrats, and voting abolitionists in 1852. He resigned his seat in the House of Representatives in August 1854, citing the pressures of private business. Green had criticized Smith for going to the Sodom that was the nation's capital in the first place. Upon hearing of Smith's resignation, he wrote a long letter congratulating him for abandoning "the kennel of hell-dogs" that had enacted such foul monstrosities as the Kansas-Nebraska Act. Green was especially upset over rumors that some of the slaveholding legislators had spoken favorably of Smith's "sumptuous dinners" and "name and deeds" during his Washington years.[15]

In theology as in politics, Green was staking out positions which caused consternation among his former associates. Nothing from his pen had appeared in print since his 1848 address at the Buffalo Liberty Party convention, in which he proclaimed his novel views on civil government. In 1853 Samuel Green published *Faith and Infidelity*, which his father had preached at Whitesboro. "Infidelity" Green argued, was a "mad-dog cry" raised by his opponents "in the sphere ecclesiastic." Green confounded justification by faith with the demonstration of that faith:

> *It is not essential to his welfare, that a child of Adam should be able to spell the name or read the history of Jesus Christ; it is essential to his welfare, absolutely, exclusively, eternally, that he should loyally bow to the supremacy of the principles which are the soul and substance, the life and power of the Messiah and the Messiahship. Thus the assurance, that "he who believeth on the Son hath life," and the declaration, "He that feareth God and worketh righteousness is accepted" of heaven, have one and the same meaning—are to be applied to the same names for the same purposes.*[16]

Having defined faith as the evidence of things seen, Green gave an equally empirical definition of infidelity. Anyone who tolerated the "cord of caste" and "the negro-pew" violated the essentials of the Christian faith. In a sermon on "Redemption" Green acknowledged that by stressing works he was laying himself open to "the gravest suspicions" in evangelical circles where salvation by grace alone was taught. But he was unwillingly to sacrifice compassion on the altar of correct doctrine.[17]

Green regarded the denominational arguments over the person of Jesus Christ as the "gambling tools of God-forsaken sharpers" who preferred orthodoxy to justice, mercy, fidelity, and character. He had no stomach for ecclesiastics who talked incessantly about the atonement but who failed to identify themselves "amidst the practical arrangements of life with the great Sufferer." Concerning the divinity of Christ, he wrote:

> *As to the two-fold nature and double personality of our Savior, I am*

neither with the Unitarians nor the Trinitarians. Both the one and the other, I regard as rash and arrogant—as attempting to comprehend what infinitely exceeds their capacities and to define what they are entirely unable to understand. It is enough for me, that I find in Jesus Christ our Human Nature divinely perfect—sublimely God-like—an all-glorious Model—worthy of the deepest complacency—the thorough confidence—the most fervent worship.[18]

Samuel caught the spirit of his father's views concerning the deity of Christ in a brief memorial written in 1875:

He knew that in whatever direction he pushed, Jesus was ahead; towering so far above him that he could not transcend or see beyond him; and to him the perfections of the Christ were infinite. He could draw no line where Humanity was passed and Deity begun; he himself was not great enough for that. But the character and mission of Christ were wholly natural, and His influence in its great volume exerted by exactly the same laws and in precisely the same manner as the influence of any man, however feeble.[19]

Green's apostasy did not derive from mere rationalism or skepticism. Nor did his heresies spring from the critical study of the Scriptures, at which he was adept. "The historical records, in which the advent, the objects, the career—the words, the deeds and the sufferings of Jesus are recorded," he acknowledged, "are worthy of the fullest confidence."[20] "His intensest scorn," Samuel rightly understood, "burned into the forehead of an 'orthodoxy' that hid neglect, contempt, and oppression of men behind its dogma of total depravity, and that of a Unitarianism which, in spite of the 'dignity of human nature' in its creed, could tolerate the degradation of that nature."[21] Had orthodoxy demonstrated fervent respect for the slave and the outcast, Green would have hoisted its flag.

The road from evangelical or modified Calvinism to the religion of humanity was well-traveled. James Birney, Elizur Wright, Theodore Dwight Weld, and Gerrit Smith, to mention only some of Green's abolitionist colleagues, each in their own way abandoned denominational dogma for a faith which emphasized showing mercy and doing justice. Having found the churches to be, in Birney's words, "the bulwark of slavery," they made reform rather than correct doctrine the test of faith. Samuel Green eventually became a Unitarian, but however closely his theological views might mirror the advanced wing of the Unitarian or Universalist denominations, Beriah could not make the transition. Like the conservative Presbyterians, these liberal churches balked at taking a clear and public stand against slavery.

By the 1850s, most Americans accepted a divorce between piety and moralism. The clergy no longer stressed connections between a Christian's personal relationship to God and his or her duties as a citizen. This practice of separating the devotional and public dimensions of Christianity was a reaction to the intensity of religious activism and public chaos of the 1830s and 1840s. Green had begun his reform career on premises derived from the theocentric communalism of the traditional New England order, in which the rules of conduct in the public sphere as well as the requirements of individual piety were derived from a single source—the moral government or sovereignty of God. But the clergy of the 1850s spoke to social issues with less assurance than did the evangelicals of the Second Great Awakening or the Puritan preachers. "Though condemning slavery and calling for its eventual end," historian Donald Scott writes, "organized Christian antislavery opinion contained neither a program nor a direct strategy for abolishing slavery in the South. In addition, while they denounced slavery as a moral evil, few churchmen of the New England strain tied antislavery opinion to the problem of one's personal standing with God."[22]

Green could not adjust to any abandonment of the prophetic role. He was still the agitator of old, operating out of a philosophy of the organic connection between piety and public duty, between devotion and citizenship. Like the breadwinner who loses his job and turns in anger on those closest to him, Green reacted to the public's indifference by quarreling with colleagues and kin. Depressed and hurt, feeling that his vocation was at an end, he lashed out at his brother Jonathan. The dispute ostensibly began when Jonathan got the impression that his elder brother had pronounced their mother's religion a "sham." Jonathan also informed Smith that Beriah had made it a condition of fraternal intercourse between them that Jonathan hate Oberlin. When Smith tried to mediate the dispute, Green wrote him, "Both you and my brother go very, very wide of the mark. . . . I am used to misconstruction and misrepresentations, what is the use of complaining." The brothers went their separate ways. Because Beriah felt that Smith had sided with Jonathan, he once again took up his argument with Smith over the circular of 1849 and the question of civil government: "When I am essentially and especially myself you represent me as occupied with 'the strange,' 'the novel,' 'the startlin',' 'the astonishing!' "[23]

When the winter snows gave way to spring, Green's spirits lifted and he busied himself with improvements on his small farm. He even offered to preach at Smith's church in Peterboro. His own congregation had suffered numerous defections, so that he occupied the pulpit in Whitesboro only on alternate Sabbaths. Upon returning from a visit with Smith in May 1853, he wrote, "Your friendly faces and friendly words haunt us. I hope that as a result a higher and more substantial than a temporary exposition will follow."[24] Green was rereading William Goodell's *Slavery and Anti-slavery* and confessed to a renewed interest in studying the bearings of his own political views on national events. Did this portend a change of temperament, a willingness to agree to disagree among friends? Green had not heard from some of them, such as Elizur Wright, for a long time. Though he confessed to being "quite at home" with his scythe and axe, he felt the urge to write and study so as to benefit others with his thoughts.[25]

In November, Green received an invitation from William Goodell to deliver his essay *Personality and Property* in any county of the state. He had written it to combat the notion that the constitution had nothing to do with slavery, or worse, was a pro-slavery document. He denied that the framers of the Constitution either by intent or by some secret understanding meant to exclude slaves from the inalienable rights of justice, freedom, and the general welfare so eloquently proclaimed in the preamble. Though not blind to the "inconsistencies" and "absurdities" which the drafters of the Constitution included, he resisted a literal reading. He argued that just as the framers were men both enabled and limited by the light of reason available to them, so men of reason in the 1850s needed to reinterpret the specifics of the Constitution in light of its general principles and objectives.

> *Clearly, there is only one way of honoring the claims of the Constitution; and that must be by wisely and resolutely promoting the objects to which it is avowedly devoted. Thus, and thus only, submit to its authority. If any incidental feature can be detected in it in conflict with the sublime objects which it avows, that feature must have been admitted UNCONSTITU-TIONALLY.*[26]

Green's interpretation was certainly not unique, for in the mid-1840s, Alvan Stewart, William Goodell, Lysander Spooner, and James Birney had worked out the basic premises of radical antislavery constitutionalism. They did so by appealing to the natural law principles embodied in the Declaration of Independence, over against the detailed provisions of the constitution. Legal historian William Wiecek has perceptively argued that while this line of argument was a failure in the short run, it did contribute to modern libertarian constitutional thought as found in the ideas of substantive due process, equal protection of the laws, paramount national citizenship, and the privileges and immunities of that citizenship.[27] Green's evolutionary understanding of the constitution, so contrary to strict constructionism, presaged the post-Civil War recognition that each generation must interpret the

Constitution for itself. As Green put it, "Every man is to receive the Constitution for himself. As the Indian chief, when King George held out his hand for him to kiss, said, 'No! Me king too!' so, even at the graves of our fathers, we interpret, as living men, the Constitution for ourselves."[28]

Shortly after his fifty-ninth birthday, Green fell into a more introspective mood. He wrote cryptically of the "hastening" hour when all personal and societal problems would be solved "clearly and definitely." He described the changes wrought by advancing age: "My hair is becoming white rather rapidly, my face is strongly indented, my teeth are sadly dilapidated and I begin to present the old man's mouth. It seems but yesterday that I was a flaxen haired boy—full of impulse, curiosity, impatience—restless and inquisitive and hopeful enough." Green depicted his wife as also showing signs of aging, yet after thirty years of marriage, she still possessed in his eyes the "enterprising, quick of foot, resolute, diligent, provident, most trustworthy" character which first attracted him to her. "She has been to me," Green confided to Smith, "an unspeakable blessing; and never appeared so beautiful and attractive to my thoughts and affections as now."[29]

Green and his wife were concerned about making plans for their old age. Beriah gave Smith an accounting of the family's assets: a house and lot in the village of Whitesboro, worth perhaps one thousand dollars; three acres on the Mohawk flats worth about one thousand dollars; and sixteen acres on "the Hill," about three-fourths of a mile from the village, for which Green was in debt to the amount of approximately one hundred and eight dollars. As a hedge against the insecurities of old age, he planned to fence in the rural acreage, drain it, start an orchard, plant a garden, obtain some chickens, and construct a house and the necessary outbuildings. In typically blunt fashion, Green laid claim on Smith's charity.

1. We have for many years stood together on the footing of friendship.

2. You are very rich.

3. You furnish a great deal of money for the benefit of those, whom you, perhaps, hardly love more warmly than you love me.

4. My name by arrangements originating in you is very often repeated in your Family; and must be, while your son retains a place in your affections. You would be unwilling to have Green see me a poverty-stricken and tempest-torn old man, with means as scanty as my Friends must be few.

5. If I could now be aided in some such way as this letter indicates, I might hope to stand erect among my fellows. . . .

6. My usefulness would be greatly increased. If I could maintain the Divine Authority in rural affairs in the midst of my atheistic fellows, a deep and happy impression would be made upon their minds. Whenever I might proclaim the name of God from the Pulpit, my acres, impressed with His image, would be sure to offer a distinct and emphatic response.[30]

A marginal note in Smith's handwriting on one of Green's letters refers to a gift of one hundred dollars. Smith may have donated more, but in the end it was not enough to permit Green to set up his rural experiment on divine principles.

When many former abolitionists were in transit to the Republican party and the Garrisonians were advocating disunion, Gerrit Smith, Lewis and Arthur Tappan, William Goodell, Frederick Douglass, and S. S. Jocelyn, among others, organized the American Abolition Society in 1855. The Society advocated the doctrine of the unconstitutionality of slavery and ran Smith as its presidential candidate in 1856. Green looked with favor on what Goodell's *Radical Abolitionist* called a "revival of primitive abolition."[31] He participated in several of the early conventions but in 1857 declined to stand for public office. Green explained in a letter to the *Liberator* that he wanted nothing to do with a government that was a "stupid, grim, malignant conspiracy."[32] He also ignored his nomination by a remnant of the Liberty Party for the position of Judge of the Court of Appeals. In short, he could not be party to efforts by diehard immediatists to use political means to achieve moral ends when government itself seemed to be the problem.

Obsessed with righteousness, Green was not of much help in the late 1850s beyond that "transcendental" plane of which his brother complained. However, he did have quite specific prejudices concerning the activities of his former abolitionist colleagues. His quarrel with Charles Stuart arose primarily out of differences over the English treatment of the people of India. Green wrote Smith in 1857, "I loathe the whole thing and all who give it their countenance and support,—Can that mean our dear Charles Stuart among the rest of loyal Englishmen, I seem to hear Mrs. Smith exclaim? I mean, my sister, every man, woman and child who regards such a bloody conspiracy with any complacency."[33] Smith must have come to Stuart's defense, for a week later Green sent an impassioned letter in which he argued that Stuart's hands were bloodied by association. Stuart, no matter how much he pitied the people of India, was, after all, "Major Stuart of the English Military!" Green went on, "I hold any man, Charles Stuart or Gerrit Smith, responsible for the crimes of the wretches, with whom under the name of the government! the one or the other identifies himself with." After a long discourse on the evils of government, Green closed with, "Remember me affectionately—I can't help it if you call it a kind of meat-axe affection; I think it is a genial tender affection—to your cherished Circle. Your Brother, B. Green."[34]

Clearly, Green's friends were loosing patience with him in proportion to his retreat into despair. When he showed up at conventions, they shifted uncomfortably in their chairs while he went on and on haranguing them. Lewis Tappan once hustled Green off the podium with remarks to the effect that someone more congenial was next on the agenda. At one meeting, Charles Stuart responded to Green's query, "How do you do, today?" with "None the better for you, Beriah!"[35] Green had found more on which to disagree with Smith. He disliked Smith's sermon on the "Religion of Reason," though at first glance it would appear both occupied similar positions. Smith's liberal, optimistic faith, however, did not square with his pessimistic views of human potential. Beriah had none of Smith's faith in the democratic experiment nor hope that the Union might yet be preserved. He vowed loyalty to only one tribunal—the right of private judgment. He would not suspend that right before any authority, be it the majority of his fellow citizens, some high council, the Pope, or a Judge of the Supreme Court. He denounced the suffocating falsehoods of the Dred Scott decision as judicial lies proceedings from the "bloodless" lips of Roger B. Taney and swore himself to be obedient only to his own conscience.[36]

History was now to be Green's final judge. He decided in 1859 to publish a second volume of his sermons and speeches and wrote Ralph Waldo Emerson asking for an endorsement, since Emerson had once commented favorably on his essay *Success*. Green admitted that raising subscriptions for the proposed volume would be difficult: "I am in a very high degree unpopular—regarded by the sects with suspicion or aversion. . . ."[37] *Sermons and Other Discourses with Brief Biographical Hints* appeared in 1860. It ran to 556 pages, mostly material written since the publication of *Miscellaneous Writings* in 1841. A second edition came out in 1861 and a third in 1872. Samuel, who had finally established himself as a printer in Brooklyn, published all three editions.[38]

Green made contact with another New Englander after John Brown's 1859 raid at Harper's Ferry and subsequent martyrdom. Wendell Phillips had conducted a memorial service at North Elba, New York, in Brown's honor. "From my obscure corner," Green wrote, "I cannot well help joining the myriad host in the heart bursting exclamation, Servant of God, well done! . . . you have identified yourself with a great soul—a true Hero—a genuine Son of Humanity."[39] Though the Buchanan administration considered Brown an outlaw, Green did not. The government was nothing but a conspiracy, an outlaw itself, against which "John Brown nor any other Name *could* [not] commit a crime." "I regard myself," Green told Phillips, "as among a mob of outlaws." He was willing to venerate Brown's name as a hero and a martyr, though he did not approve of Brown's violent methods. Unlike Smith, Green probably had no direct or indirect foreknowledge of Brown's plans. He was, however, acquainted with the ex-slave Harriet Tubman, whom he described as "one of John Brown's Captains," and may have been visited by Tubman prior to the raid on Harper's Ferry."[40]

John Brown served as a surrogate for impulses long dormant in many immediatists. Green saw Brown as the instrument of God who had acted out of a sense of righteous indignation. His endorsement of Brown's raid was the final indication that he had given up on the political process. Consequently, Green looked with disdain on the elections of 1860. He was by no means enamored with the prospects of Abraham Lincoln becoming the chief executive of the nation. He wrote Elizur Wright expressing outrage that Wright should even consider Lincoln suitable to occupy "the tallest chair in the nation."

> *He who goes for the Fugitive slave bill of '50! Hasn't made up his mind that the interstate slave trade should be abolished! Is against negro equality! A man is not to be classified with men! . . . Is against the abolition of slavery in the District except on conditions which none but a damned cross between a knave and a fool could either impose or endure!*[41]

Contrary to the Lincoln administration, Green could not abide the notion that preserving the Union was of a higher priority than abolishing slavery everywhere and in all its forms.

Wright responded in October 1860, expressing puzzlement over Green's harsh words. He wondered as to the origin of the differences Green alleged existed between them and only partially jested, "Is it that you were baked harder in the old theological oven than I?" Wright confessed to having lost the fear of the "God of books." He was for facts, and the facts made it clear that his vote would not make Green, Smith, or Goodell president. "I do know too," he chided his friend, "that by adapting a certain definition you may make both Lincoln and Douglas knaves, liars, craven wretches, etc." But Wright felt that any realistically-minded abolitionist would rather see them in office than the pro-slavery candidates. "I think it my duty," Wright wrote, "to commit the country rather to the humane rather than the inhumane lives."[42] Green replied that "he had a right to be righteous" and that he knew full well that he was "essentially other" than he once was—than the majority around him were.[43]

Why did Beriah Green persist as a "voice in the wilderness" in the 1850s? He wrestled personally with the question, for he acknowledged that the profligate majority of his fellow citizens did not understand nor care for his sacred vocation. He felt kinship only with "the loyal souls sparsely scattered over a wide surface—here one and there another—in retired nooks and obscure corners," known by those around them as strangers and pilgrims, open to suspicion and aversion because they attempted to apply morality to public issues.⁴⁴ He viewed politics as belonging to ethics and therefore part of "the kingdom of God." As a Christian he felt duty-bound to come to the rescue of Humanity in the name of the Messiah. Therein Beriah saw his own salvation. He hoped to be found acceptable before the Lord by being faithful to the organic principles of "the Kingdom of God" as discovered in his inner being. Thus he struggled on while many about him were willing to accept compromise in the fight against slavery. Well into his sixties, Green was under a heavier burden than most of those who opposed slavery, for he faced the prospect of going to the grave with his vision of an egalitarian society unfulfilled while others prepared for a bloody sectional conflict.

10

STAYED ON RIGHTEOUSNESS

L
incoln's election in November 1860 led to the secession of seven
Southern states by the time of his inaugural in the spring of 1861.
Green was predictably upset by Lincoln's vow to oppose the rebellion of the South but not to interfere with slavery where it existed.
"I regard my native Land," he wrote Gerrit Smith in March 1861,
"as doomed and damned." Green had no confidence in the Republicans who now held the reigns of civil government and was especially angry
that William Seward, a fellow upstater whom the Libertymen once considered friendly to their cause, should serve as Lincoln's Secretary of State.
"I regard Benedict Arnold's name," Green grumbled, "with less abhorrence than his."[1] As he watched the nation move closer to civil war, he
predicted a great conflagration in which victory by neither the North or the
South offered any consolation.

The attack upon Fort Sumter caused many abolitionists to reassess
their attitudes toward the Union. Some were motivated by patriotic sentiment to side with the federal government in its attempt to preserve national
unity. Others adopted a wait-and-see attitude, for if the war effort could be
transformed into a fight against slavery, then good might come from evil.
Green adopted an anti-Unionist position, on the grounds that Lincoln's government was as treasonous as that of the Confederate states. He expressed
his views in a letter that Garrison's *Liberator* published on April 19, 1861,
alongside announcements that the Civil War had begun, Fort Sumter captured, troops mustered, and "The North United At Last." "Traitor throt-
tles traitor," Green wrote Garrison. Perhaps the "Potsherds of the earth
striving with each other" would "blindly clear the way for something essentially other than now obtrudes its ghastliness upon our loathing thoughts."

These sentiments were so disturbing that Garrison felt it necessary to add a personal codicil. He described Green an esteemed friend but disassociated himself from the attack upon Lincoln, around whom he urged all the friends of freedom to coalesce. Garrison called for a clean break with the South: "Let 'the covenant with death and the agreement with hell' be . . . annulled."[2]

The galvanizing effect of the opening of hostilities between North and South made Green more of a curiosity than ever before. He complained to Smith that he could not find any of the "Friends of Humanity" who would agree that the federal government was "no government." They were too troubled by the South's rebellion against the Union. "What are ten thousand Fort Sumters to one poor Baby reduced to chattelship?" Green asked. Such anti-Unionist views cost him whatever support he still had in the few remaining churches open to him. Though pressured to support the Union, Green held firm to the opinion that the Union had always been "the chief prop of slavery." Lincoln was but "the presiding blood hound of the nation." Smith urged him to set aside his differences with the Republicans until the rebellion had been put down. Beriah countered, "I am not a war-man" and once pointedly demonstrated it by refusing to "get up" an audience for a Union rally speaker.[3]

Green's displeasure with the Lincoln administration waxed more vehement as the war progressed. He called the Republicans a set of "sworn kidnappers" and "common pirates" and wished the government "bad luck" in its efforts to subdue the rebellion.[4] Essentially, Abolition's Axe saw the Civil War as an American apocalypse in which God was, in the words of Julia Ward Howe's famous hymn, "Trampling out the vintage where the grapes of wrath are stored." He could only hope that some phoenix would rise from the ashes of Armageddon to usher in the millennial age. The Emancipation Proclamation was not a sign that the Lincoln administration was any closer to understanding the true mission of civil government. It was merely a "fulcrum" to pry the Confederates back into the Union. Green looked with horror upon the prospect of having to live under a government which reunited at the expense of his enslaved brothers and sister. Had he been able to change his few acres into cash, he would have taken his family into asylum among the fugitive slaves who had settled in Canada West.[5]

Green's personal situation worsened during the Civil War. Except for an opportunity to preach once a month in Utica, he was denied access to any of the pulpits which once welcomed President Green of the Oneida Institute. He blamed this on the "apostasy of the Friends of Humanity." The Whitesboro comeouter church had largely disbanded. Its building was sold, moved, and turned into a blacksmith shop. A small band of Green's most loyal members met for a while in his home, but even they became disheartened, he acknowledged, as his "misanthropy" intensified. Poverty, "stark poverty," Green wrote, stalked the family. Daughter Marcia, a widow, had to leave the "Old Hive" and work as a seamstress in Utica, leaving her two small children in the care of their grandparents.[6]

Green approached the seventh decade of his life as the Civil War came to a close. His post-war correspondence has little to say about the Northern victory or even the freeing of the slaves. No letters, if written, survive from Green to Smith for the years 1863-66. Smith was in poor health. Perhaps Green refrained from badgering him on that account. More likely, he had little to say in the closing months of the war and during the euphoria over the Union victory. President Andrew Johnson's reconstruction plan, which permitted southern legislatures to pass Black Codes restricting the newly freed slaves, drew Green's fire.[7] Here was proof that no human government could be trusted to exercise justice and mercy. Though chattel slavery was at an end, Green saw little prospect of a social order structured on the egalitarian principles operative at Oneida Institute. What could an old man offer? The post-Civil War generation would have to work out its own salvation.

Green's last letters are replete with musings about old age, reminiscences of his youth, and family affairs. Longevity was a hallmark of the Green family line. In 1865, he described his father, who was still living in Twinsburg, Summit County, Ohio, as active, bright, and jovial at ninety.[8] With his seventy-second birthday just ahead, Green took stock of his library, which in many respects chronicled his life. He wrote Elizur Wright of the joy of rediscovering several of the textbooks from his schoolboy days, but Webster's blueback speller, one of his favorites, had disappeared.[9] Green's hair had turned nearly white, but his wife, about two year's his junior, had "hair as black and sleek as a girl's, with only here and there a thread of white in condescension to, and sympathy with my gray locks."[10] Though Beriah complained that his legs wearied from the mile-long, twice-daily walks out to his acreage to milk the cow, he generally felt in good health. True to the habits of a lifetime, he mixed mental and physical exercise. He was worried about his daughter Marcia, whose emotional extravagances led one doctor to judge her insane and to advise that she be placed in the Utica asylum. Though Marcia was not institutionalized, her father anguished over her emotional well-being the rest of his days.[11]

In 1871, Green, now seventy-six, wrote Gerrit Smith (one year Green's senior) to share advice on a regimen for one's declining years. "I begin," he informed Smith, "by plunging my head into a pail of water, set in the bath tub, a poor man's bath tub, which I have used so many years. I take very great pains with the towel in 'rubbing off,' rubbing the surface from head to heel, very thoroughly." He then engaged in manual labor from four to eight hours. Before retiring, he went through another session of applying friction, using his fists from head to toe. He then threw water over his body, rubbed himself with a towel, put on a night shirt and "plunged" into bed. Should nightmares or bad dreams awaken him, Green again went through the cold water and friction ritual. He recalled for Smith the time about 1820 at Andover when as a student he was nearly prostrated by nervous exhaustion. Since then, he had employed "water appliances, exercise in the open air, rubbing and kneading, and strict temperance" in an effort to maintain a healthy body and a healthy mind.[12]

In the last existing letter written to Smith, Green reminisced about the time he spent on the east end of Long Island in 1822. With the vivid preciseness of the elderly, he recalled seeing windmills, how the parsonage door swung outward, and a man who wore a checkered shirt to Sabbath meetings. "I feel a special interest in hoary heads," Green told Smith. "We are nearing the goal."[13] Green reached his first, some nine months before Smith, who died December 28, 1874, while spending the Christmas holidays with a nephew in New York.

On the morning of May 4, 1874, Green walked the three blocks or so from his residence on Main and Brainard in Whitesboro east down Main to the Town Hall. At the request of and in concert with a group of temperance advocates, he intended to admonish the Board of Excise not to grant any new liquor licenses. With his hands upon his cane, his white head bent forward, Green began to address the board. "Suddenly without a moment's warning," according to an obituary notice, "he fell backwards upon the floor, and expired almost instantly, breathing but once or twice afterwards."[14] A physician was summoned to no avail. Green's body was carried to the "Old Hive" and afterwards laid to rest in Grand View Cemetery overlooking the Mohawk Flats upon which Oneida Institute once stood. Inscribed today on his gravestone is the text Green used the day before he died in addressing a tiny congregation in his house: "He that doeth righteousness is righteous, even as He is righteous."[15]

When news of Green's death reached John Greenleaf Whittier, the Quaker post and veteran abolitionist sat down and penned a memorial to his fallen comrade: "I am pained to learn of the death of that noble man, Beriah Green. How thick the Cypress shadows fall, and how few are left of those whom I met at the anti-slavery convention in 1833." With considerable accuracy, Whittier wrote, "The world never knew Beriah Green. He was a great man morally and intellectually." Noting that Green collapsed while

"I present the old man's mouth." The last known picture of Beriah Green, ca. 1870. From the Library of the Hawaiian Mission Children's Society.

giving a temperance speech, Whittier observed, "He has died as he would have wished to die, lifting up his voice for God and humanity.[16]

"The world never knew Beriah Green"—such a judgment says as much about the world in which Green lived as it does about the man. The "great swilling world" beyond the environs of Oneida Institute generally did not know or care about Beriah Green and the burden of his message. Most of his abolitionist colleagues came to consider him something of an oddity, and not a few allowed him to drift into self-imposed isolation during the 1850s.

This history of Beriah Green and the Oneida Institute, to which he dedicated his private and public self, has not attempted to deny that he eventually occupied a lonely rampart in the abolitionist crusade. Nor has it sought to hide or explain away the unpopular ideas and contentious personality which Green presented to friend and foe alike. By being who he was, without apology and without embarrassment, Beriah Green helped to define the outermost boundaries of American abolitionism. By coming to know him, we have better understood the strengths and weaknesses of nineteenth-century American reform.

In the summer of 1848, Elizur Wright, then situated in Boston and engaged in various actuarial calculations which earned him the title, "father of American life insurance," traveled to Oneida County. He visited at the "Old Hive" in Whitesboro and reported his impressions of its owner for the readers of his weekly paper, the *Chronotype*, in a column entitled "Finding a Man."

> *Beriah Green is a man of not more than middling stature, earnestly stooping forward as a man of progress should, purity, magnanimity and benevolence beaming from his strongly marked, nervous, decided face. You know him at once for a man in whom high affections and deep thought hold the mastery over all that is animal in him. There is not one atom more than fat enough in him to provide against the injuries of friction. There is sternness in him, no mawkish pity for pain, but an ineffable contempt for injustice and falsehood. His likes and dislikes are expressed without much reserve, not any in regard to consequences, but only in regard to justice. He worships God with deep reverence, and sees in him all that is good, but has marvellously little room for theological subtleties and empty forms of religion. Indeed with hypocrites he passes for an infidel. But such preaching of the Gospel by an infidel!*[17]

Wright described his "find" as "altogether earnest and unartificial," a user of "strong and appropriate language," whose only fault was in assuming that his readers and hearers had thought as much or as well as he did concerning an issue.

Indeed, Green had thought so much that he was far in advance of his fellows. "Beriah Green," Wright argued, "is one of those far-seeing men who content themselves with the actual government of generations unborn." He thought of his old friend as an intense hater of "sham, humbug, and deception" who saw the slave not in "some black man a thousand miles off" but in "any man, woman, or child, far and near, and especially near, who is restrained from his rights no matter by what form of selfish tyranny it may be." Wright admitted that few had or could understand Green's political thought and that library shelves did not "groan with Beriah Green's works—bound in cloth, sheep or calf." No, one had to study Abolition's Axe by those living volumes, black and white, who could be seen "perambulating this broad land, instinct [*sic*] with undying impulses received from his great head and heart." Wright concluded, "Of the great unseen influences which are governing our age for good, I know not one so potent as Beriah Green. Therefore am I persuaded that in finding him I have found the most indisputable live man."[18]

Wright hit the mark in pointing us to Beriah Green's true legacy. The world may have forgotten the president of Oneida Institute, but his students—his living epistles—did not. Those African Americans who came under his influence sang hymns of thanksgiving in his honor. William G. Allen spoke for them when he described Green as one of the chosen few whose true greatness derived from a combination of wisdom and virtue. "To the strength and vigor of a man," Allen wrote in 1853, "he adds the gentleness and tenderness of a woman. He has never taken an active part in the world of stir and politics, but in the line of his proper profession [Beriah Green] has immeasurably advanced the cause of human progress."[19] As a victim of the cord of caste, Allen fully understood that Green's abolitionism, as Elizur Wright put it, "began at home."

Green affirmed the humanity of both the slave and the free black in word and deed. Most abolitionists, especially the more cautious and comfortable, many of them Green's friends and neighbors, preferred to love blacks at a distance. Though they talked of freeing the slaves, they displayed antipathy toward a truly biracial society in which blacks might enjoy the same rights as whites. Wright once said that Green's parishioners were not so shocked by what they heard in his sermons as they were by what they witnessed in his living: "They are not particularly dissatisfied with his preaching but can not bear that he should mean so much by it, as he evidently does, by living up to it himself."[20]

Green surely took the more difficult of forks in the immediatist road of the 1830s and 1840s. While some abolitionists were content to engage in polemics with Southern partisans, he began the work of reform at home among the Northern whites whose class and cultural prejudices separated them from free blacks as much as it did from the slaves. Green's sermon "Iniquity and a Meeting" was typical of his attacks upon racism within the circles of intimacy he shared. The Christians of Whitesboro had flocked to a "protracted meeting" in the winter of 1841. As some members of his Congregational church were tempted to cooperate in furthering the revival, Green felt compelled to raise his voice in warning and protest. He chastised all who allied themselves in meeting-holding, psalm-singing, and prayer-making under the pretense of a regard for human salvation while they disregarded human rights. He pointed to iniquity within the meeting houses of those who loudly called for spiritual revival despite their toleration or "the negro-pew"—

> *that hateful offspring of murderous prejudice, as mean as it is wicked—that consecrated monument of respect of persons—that cage of scorpions stinging souls to death; you must not expose the absurdity and sin in which it had its origin. Though it is a toad breathing venom into the ear of piety, you must not touch it with Ithuriel-spear. The devil thus incarnate must not be exposed, because, forsooth, he had obtruded himself upon the ground of Paradise! The negro-pew is one of the conditions on which alone well-bred souls can consent to be saved; and so, cunning, noisy quacks, in dispensing their balm of Gilead, give the negro-pew a place among their pious frauds.*[21]

Such denunciatory language, reminiscent of the Old Testament prophets who condemned the children of Israel for whoring after foreign gods, or of Jesus cursing the barren fig tree in the Gospel of Mark, did not endear Beriah Green to the religious establishment.

Josiah B. Grinnell, one of a score or more white graduates of Oneida Institute who went on to abolitionist and reform careers of their own, remembered the college as a living monument to its president. Grinnell lionized Green:

> *A striking, pleasant face, and vivacious manners, were in happy association with the scholar, in deep sympathy with the spirit of Goethe, the philosophy of Coleridge, also that of an ardent friend and correspondent of the English rugged Carlyle. His protest against the ethics of the "tall ecclesiastics" was more than verbal—even a close personal alliance with great reform, disregarding obloquy and sacrifice. A spirit genial as the summer sun, proven integrity, varied learning, and eloquence reaching sublimity, would have made him a striking character in the best circles of citizens and reformers.*[22]

Green's welcome did not last long "in the best circles of citizens and reformers." The mature Grinnell judged that his mentor come out "separate" too early, when the church and nation were still asleep.

William Lloyd Garrison, of course, had come out early. Yet he managed to draw around him a circle of intimates who viewed him, despite his severity and impulsive personality, as a "fatherlike messiah." Lawrence J. Friedman employs Max Weber's depiction of an effective group leader to explain Garrison's ability to hold the Boston clique together. Like a brilliant mad scientist, who "had near-magical qualities but did not seem quite balanced," Garrison attracted faithful colleagues who were united by their appreciation of his genius. They felt he had been chosen to lead the nation from the sin of slaveholding despite his extremist temperament and disorderliness.[23] Garrison's anti-institutionalism both fostered the creation of a community of like-minded free spirits and spared him the bitter disappointments of a Beriah Green. Garrison essentially worked to goad the ecclesiastical, educational, and political establishments from the outside. Green tried to work within. The American educational system, churches, and political institutions all failed him. With heart grown bitter, he despaired of his fellows and became a self-professed "misanthrope" among those who shared his passion but not his vision and approved of his ends but not his means.

After Green's death, a spokesman for the Whitestown Seminary lauded Oneida Institute's former president as "made for a great man, and a great leader." Nothing stood in Green's way, the Reverend Dr. Morris said at the semi-centennial of the Seminary, "but his tenacity of purpose, the ardor of his convictions, his unflinching procedure from premise to conclusion, and that violent surging which, under the influence of the social and civil agitation of the period, at last broke the hold of the supernatural and written revelation upon him, and left him to drift over into extremes of rationalism."[24] This is a fair assessment of the process by which Green broke rank with the orthodoxy of the Presbyterians no less than with the liberalism of the Unitarians. As Green told Garrison, the sum and substance of his theology had little to do with disputes over the divine origin of Jesus but everything to do with the dignity of Human Nature.[25] "Election, Decrees, Effectual Calling, Justification, Adoption, Sanctification, in their usual meanings," Samuel wrote concerning his father, "he passed contemptuously by, while he wrought mightily to bring himself and his fellows into true relations, and urged every man for himself to seize and secure his birthright laid up for him from the foundation of the world—in the constitution of things."[26]

Green's feelings of being bound with those who suffered oppression because of the "cord of caste" derived from an elemental Christian piety that informed and shaped both his daily life and his theology. Like the Quaker abolitionist John Woolman, he spared not his own for the sake of the slave. For the cause of Humanity, he wrote Weld in 1841, wealth, reputation, respectability, even the sympathy of the circles one moved in, must be sacrificed. When any of these became the master of the reformer, to that extent the reformer was guilty of apostasy and treachery to the Gospel of Christ.[27]

Beriah Green, heir to the evangelical awakening of the early nineteenth-century, fashioned a theology of salvation by works ever so powerful as the theology of free grace. Duty, obedience to the Law of God which Reason laid upon the human conscience, this was his salvation. The revivalists of the Burned-over District had looked for signs of grace among those at the inquiry meetings and on the anxious benches. Individuals who repented, testified to being "born again" and demonstrated a moral reformation could be credited with having been caught up in the Holy Spirit. The revivalists not only cleansed their own houses but sought to purify the national temple of everything from intemperance to slavery by transforming the country into a holy commonwealth. Green measured individuals not by their professions of faith, though such conversions might cause them to enlist in the army of saints, but by their demonstrations of compassion for the least, the last, and the lost.

The strict or so-called Old Calvinists, who held to the doctrine of total depravity, were pessimistic about human progress, but they had cause for some comfort. Very little can surprise someone who is theologically ingrained to expect evil at every turn. To the extent that Beriah Green believed in the human capacity to obey the promptings of a correctly informed conscience, he opened himself to disillusionment. He early adopted the axiom that to know one's Christian duty was to do it. He soon discovered empirical proof of that characteristic of human nature which the Old Calvinists sought to capture in their doctrine of original sin or human depravity. Then he could neither worship at the shrine of democracy nor stump for the elective franchise. He lost faith with the American public, especially Northern Christians who smothered their compassion for the slave with their piety and who shunned social intercourse with free blacks. His fascination with Carlyle was directly proportional to his loss of faith in humanity, not the Christian model of redeemed humanity enunciated in his many sermons and essays, but the flesh and blood humanity to which he had to appeal in the struggle to keep Oneida Institute open.

Eager for support from any quarter, the American immediatists initially latched onto the writings of Thomas Carlyle in high hopes that he would aid their cause. Whittier, for example, found in Carlyle's earlier writings "evidence of a warm and generous sympathy with the poor and the wronged, a desire to ameliorate human suffering." Whittier lost faith in the Scottish essayist in December 1849, when he read Carlyle's racist diatribe, "Occasional Discourse on the Nigger question." He enthusiastically reviewed Elizur Wright's essay, *Perforations in the Latter Day Pamphlets by One of the Eighteen Millions of Bores*, which exposed Carlyle's monarchical notions of government, hostility to universal suffrage, and maintenance of the divine right of certain unknown, wise, and heroic individuals to take the reins of absolute power.[28] In 1850, Green had voiced disillusionment with Carlyle after reading of his endorsement of British oppression in India. Thereafter, Green no longer invoked Carlyle's name in defense of his views of human government, but he persisted in promulgating a political philosophy inimical to democracy which set him at odds with his abolitionist colleagues.

Green's friends often felt that they had been blind-sided when he broke fellowship with them. William Goodell, for example, found himself flailing defensively at Green in the *Liberty Leaguer* because of attacks made upon him by Green and son Samuel in the *Albany Patriot* and the *Model Worker*. Goodell expressed frustration at the impenetrable dogmatism of his old friend and colleague:

> *For eight or ten years I heard Pres. Green promulgate his doctrine of kingship in our antislavery conventions, and when did I ever demur against it, or assail either him or his pupils, till they threw down their gauntlet before me, in challenge? Why did they select me, in challenge? Why did they select me for an opponent if they thought me an "undesirable" one?*[29]

The Greens had criticized Goodell for setting himself up as an "oracle." He responded in kind: "A singular charge coming from one who vindicates kingship and maintains that a good man's aim should be to become a Messiah!" Goodell felt that he should at least be allowed oracle-status among the "king-worshipers."[30]

What were Green's abolitionist coadjutors to do? Weld, who by the 1850s had retired from abolition circles, might have recalled Green's letter of 1839. With reference to the growing factionalism within the American Anti-Slavery Society, Beriah had then observed: "Oppression maketh a wise man mad." "A little of the inconveniency of madness," he told Weld, "must be borne with. We are so formed, moreover, and so affected often, that we too easily slide into the temper and conduct, which we must condemn in others. Hence, we sometimes invade rights in defending rights!"[31]

Green surely demonstrated the validity of these remarks in his own reform career. "Dead men never quarrel," he had written in 1839. One is tempted to believe that Green quarreled so as to affirm to himself and to others that he was still capable of the "wakeful industry" drilled into him as a youth. Dead men, that is, men dead to morality, do not argue matters of principle.

Elizur Wright probably knew Beriah Green as well as anyone. He too had a falling out with him over the question of civil government. But he didn't let it trouble him much, for he loved his old friend despite their differences. In 1860, the year his son John wed Green's daughter Mary, Wright wrote:

> *It seems that you and I must conclude either that truth is omnipotent or that we have missed it entirely for we don't convince each other at all. As for me, I no longer write expecting to convince any body—only to let off steam. Perhaps we sympathize a little in that respect. When you pitch into the antirepublican Republican Party and blow up its sneaking, lily livered, pharisaical, humbug platform, I feel like holding the bolt and sponge.*[32]

Wright shared Green's skepticism concerning the war policies of Lincoln and the Republicans. He too was angry that the President wasn't "wise enough to see that giving [blacks] all the rights of man must benefit all parties." Contrary to Green, Wright felt that something good due the black man would come out of the struggles of "white men for their own precious white sake." But Wright backed off; he wanted no further quarrels with Green. "So much to let off steam. Never mind—burn it [the letter]. We are mutually unconvertable in politics and metaphysics."[33] All those who were the recipients of Green's "meat-axe affection," as Gerrit Smith put it, could have spared themselves considerable frustration had they come to a similar conclusion.

Many a moral absolutist whose conscience has been outraged by the evils of the world has mistaken his neighbor's sins for his neighbor and concluded that society cannot redeem itself. It needs a righteous leader or, as in Henry David Thoreau's case, a visionary hero. "Thoreau, in Walden," R.W.B. Lewis has written, "is a man who has come back down into the cave to tell the residents there that they are really in chains, suffering fantastic punishments they have imposed on themselves, seeing by a light that is reflected and derivative." The visionary hero, Lewis argues, feels that he "must put his experience to work for the benefit of others."[34] Green had his own Walden, not in nature but in the mind. Elizur Wright said of his friend's world:

> *Happy is the man who has a world of thoughts to live in, a world where he is at home. He may not be well understood or well known now, but he*

lives in truth and shall ever live. The world where Beriah Green lives is a glorious one as this world itself will know when in the course of planetary revolutions it gets up there.[35]

Frederick Douglass wrote in 1855 that there were three kinds of abolitionists—the Garrisonians, the Free Soilers or Republican Party, and the Radical Abolitionists. "Radical Abolitionism," he said, "lays the axe at the root of the tree. It proposes not only to hew down the Upas Tree, but to tear it up root and branch."[36] Beriah Green wielded the sharpest axe of all. In so doing the head often slipped from the helve and injured those about him who were fighting the same battle against the root cause of America's problems. His temperament was such that he was not a gentle humanitarian, such as Samuel Joseph May, the Unitarian abolitionist of Syracuse whom historians have described as "the most universally beloved of the abolitionists." May was apolitical and a peacemaker by nature. "He did not," Jane and William Pease write, "so much wish to remake society and its institutions as to lead the individual to self-realization and fulfillment."[37] Green's frustration and anger derived, in part, from having more radical goals.

Beriah Green began his abolitionist career at Western Reserve by appealing to the conscience of the individual. He then attempted to establish a model of what American society ought to be at Oneida Institute. After its demise, he joined in attempts to fuse righteousness and politics in the Liberty Party and its successors. Here too he was to be disappointed. As the nation drifted towards a fratricidal war, Green opted for the "transcendental" world of government by the wise and became an anachronism among those who saw the preservation of the Union as their first order of business.

We have not sought an explanation of Green's radical abolitionism in some private torment of his own unrelated to the object against which he wielded the axe of righteousness. Indeed, the nature of slavery itself should be sufficient explanation of the passion with which he dedicated his life towards its eradication. Given the tenacity of racism even in contemporary America, we should not be surprised that Green pronounced himself an enemy of all that oppressed suffering humanity in his day. To the extent that he sublimated his whole self in abolitionism, he exposed himself to inevitable disappointment. For the liberation of the slaves came not through the power of individuals obedient to the self-evident principles of reason and moral suasion, but at the point of the sword. Frederick Douglass understood this well. He wrote, "Liberty came to the freedmen . . . not in mercy, but in wrath, not by moral choice, but by military necessity, not by the generous action of the people among whom they were to live, . . . but by strangers, foreigners, invaders, trespassers, aliens and enemies."[38] The preservation of the Union did not avert the tragedy of Reconstruction or do away with the legacy of antiblack sentiment.

W. E. B. Du Bois customarily referred to the National Association for the Advancement of Colored People, founded in 1908, as the "New Abolition Movement." Historian James M. McPherson has appropriately described the neoabolitionists of the NAACP as attempting to revive the immediatism and agitation of the abolitionists of the 1830s. Oswald Garrison Villard, William Lloyd Garrison's grandson, observed in 1912 that the neoabolitionists were bound to be accused of fanaticism. But he was proud to wear the label: "No one who has ever made an impress in a reform movement has ever done so without being called a fanatic, a lunatic, a firebrand, etc. If in this case of human rights I do not win at least a portion of the epithets hurled at my grandfather in his battle, I shall not feel that I am doing effective work."[39]

Given the need for passionate liberators in antebellum America, Beriah Green's place in the annals of American reform is secure. He fought for the goals of primitive abolitionism, no matter the cost to personal fame or fortune. Perhaps the nation itself will one day "in the course of planetary revolutions," as Elizur Wright expressed it, come to embody Green's vision of radical humanitarianism.

NOTES

INTRODUCTION

1. Carl Carmer, *Dark Trees to the Wind* (New York: William Sloane Associates, 1949), p. 7.

2. In addition to Green, the most prominent abolitionist leaders in New York include Gerrit Smith, James G. Birney, Alvan Stewart, and William Goodell. See Gerald Sorin, *The New York Abolitionists: A Case Study in Political Radicalism* (Westport, Conn.: Greenwood Publishing Company, 1971), chapters 1 and 2.

3. W.E.B. Du Bois, *The Souls of Black Folk* (1903, republished New York: Fawcet Publications, Inc., 1961), chapter 12.

4. Ronald G. Walters, *The Antislavery Appeal* (Baltimore: Johns Hopkins University Press, 1978), xii.

5. While I generally will not cite secondary sources in the footnotes, except for direct quotes, Mary P. Ryan's fascinating study of the transitions in family and community life in Oneida County and environs both prior to and during Green's tenure as president of the Institute deserves special mention. See her *Cradle of the Middle Class: The Family in Oneida County, New York, 1790-1865* (Cambridge: Cambridge University Press, 1981).

6. Elizur Wright, Jr., "To Those Who Know the Oneida Institute," manuscript dated August 1840, Vol. 6, Elizur Wright, Jr., Papers, Library of Congress, Washington, D.C.

7. *Colored American* (New York City), May 6, 1837.

8. Henry B. Stanton, *Random Recollections* (2nd ed., New York: MacGowan and Slipper, 1886), p. 39.

9. Lee Benson, *The Concept of Jacksonian Democracy: New York as a Test Case* (Princeton: Princeton University Press, 1961), p. 211.

10. Beriah Green to Gerrit Smith, December 26, 1848, Smith Papers, George Arents Research Library, Syracuse University. Unless otherwise noted, all future citations in chapter footnotes to the Smith Papers pertain to this invaluable collection. See the bibliography for notes on the use and documentation of primary sources, published and unpublished, as well as secondary studies.

11. Whitney R. Cross, *The Burned-over District: The Social and Intellectual History of*

157

Enthusiastic Religion in Western New York, 1800-1850 (Ithaca, N.Y.: Cornell University Press, 1950), p. 278.

1—FORGED IN NEW ENGLAND

1. Beriah Green, *Sermons and Other Discourses with Brief Biographical Hints* (New York: S. W. Green, 1861), p. 5.

2. By a set of fortuitous circumstances too complex to relate here, I discovered several contemporary descendants of Beriah and Jonathan Green late in my research. They provided helpful genealogical information as well as letters passed down among various family members. I wish to acknowledge the generous contributions of Betsy H. Woodman, Newburyport, Massachusetts; William D. Green, Washington, D.C.; and Newell Green, Ascutny, Vermont, all descendants of Beriah Green. Walter P. Green, Providence, Rhode Island, a descendant of Jonathan S. Green, graciously shared the fruits of painstaking research into the mysteries of Green family history in New England.

3. Beriah Green to Anne Lander Green, March 3, 1865, courtesy of William D. Green. *Connecticut Gazette*, June 11, 1795. For existing examples of Beriah's father's handiwork, see Mary Mahler and Frederick Mahler, "Beriah Green, Chair and Cabinetmaker," *Spinning Wheel* (March 1978), 32-34.

4. Green to Gerrit Smith, March 22, 1867, Smith Papers.

5. Green, *Sermons and Discourses*, p. 5.

6. Green's mature views on the evangelical understanding of the nature and nurture of children are expressed in *The Savior's Arms Open to Little Children. A Discourse, Delivered Sabbath Evening, Nov. 8, 1835, in the Broad Street Church, Utica, Before the Association of Sabbath School Teachers* (Utica, New York: Press of Bennett and Bright, 1835).

7. Green, *Sermons and Discourses*, p. 5.

8. Ibid.

9. Stephen A. Marini, *Radical Sects of Revolutionary New England* (Cambridge: Harvard University Press, 1982), p. 39.

10. J. Sessions, Green's roommate, gave the *Proposita* to his daughter, wife of one of the early missionaries to the Sandwich Islands. Mary Jane Knight, Librarian of the Hawaiian Mission Children's Society, Honolulu, provided me with the original Latin manuscript.

11. Green, *Sermons and Discourses*, p. 5.

12. *General Catalogue of Middlebury College*, compiled by Duane L. Robinson (Middlebury: Middlebury College, 1950), p. 41. Robinson also credits Green with an M.A., though I've been unable to determine when it was awarded.

13. Green, letter on manual labor, in (Theodore Dwight Weld), *First Annual Report of the Society for Promoting Manual Labor in Literary Institutions; Including the Report of Their General Agent, January 28, 1833* (New York: S. W. Benedict, 1833), pp. 111-12.

14. Ibid.

15. Green to Samuel W. Green, May 22, 1873. Letter courtesy of William S. Green.

16. Green, in (Weld), *Report*, p. 112.

17. Green to Samuel W. Green, May 22, 1873.

18. John Hough, *A Sermon, Preached April 16, 1823, at the Ordination of Rev. Beriah Green, Pastor of the Congregational Church, Brandon, by John Hough, Professor of Divinity in Middlebury College* (Middlebury, Vt.: J. Copeland, 1823), pp. 19-20.

19. Donald M. Scott, *From Office to Profession: The New England Ministry 1750-1850* (Philadelphia: University of Pennsylvania Press, 1978), chapter 4.

20. Green, "Leaves of A Minister's Journal," *Vermont Chronicle* (1828), in *The Miscellaneous Writings of Beriah Green* (Whitesboro, N.Y.: Oneida Institute, 1841), pp. 49-51. Green, "Dogmatism of Boasted Ignorance—Remarks on Judge Hopkinson's Letter," *Spirit of the Pilgrims*, III (June 1830), 294-301. Green, "Hume and the Puritans," in *Miscellaneous Writings*, pp. 39-40, 44. Green, "Review of the Memoir of the Life, Times, and Writings of Thomas Boston," *Quarterly Christian Spectator*, I (December 1829), 585-92.

21. Green, Letter in (Weld), *Report*, p. 112. Green, "A Fragment," in *Miscellaneous Writings*, p. 41.

22. Green, "Review of Ware's 'Hints on Extemporaneous Preaching,' " *Boston Telegraph* (1824), in *Miscellaneous Writings*, pp. 1-17, *passim*.

23. Green, "On Using Saxon English in Giving Public Religious Instruction," *Vermont Chronicle* (1828), in *Miscellaneous Writings*, pp. 61, 63.

24. Green, "The Taste of the Times," *Vermont Chronicle* (1828), in *Miscellaneous Writings*, p. 55.

25. Green, "Extemporaneous Preaching," p. 8.

26. Green to Hannah Deming and Althea Deming, March 21, 1826. Letter courtesy of Newell Green.

27. Green, *A Sermon Preached in Poultney, June 29, 1826, at the First Annual Meeting of the Rutland County Foreign Missionary Society* (Castleton, Vt.: Published by Order of the Society, 1826), p. 14. See also Green's "Consecration to Christ," presented at the second annual meeting of the Rutland Society, June 28, 1827, in *Miscellaneous Writings*, pp. 24-34. Green, *Duty to the Heathen* (n.p.: T. R. Marvin, 1827), p. 2.

28. Green, "Review of Letters on Missions by William Swan, Missionary to Siberia," *Quarterly Christian Spectator*, II (December 1830), 632-46.

29. Green, *A Sermon Preached in Poultney, Vermont, October 3, 1827, at the Ordination of the Rev. Messers Jonathan S. Green and Ephraim W. Clark, as Missionaries to the Sandwich Islands* (Middlebury: J. W. Copeland, 1827), pp. 3-4, 14-15.

30. Jonathan Green died on January 5, 1878, having spent nearly fifty years in Hawaii. *Missionary Album: Portraits and Biographical Sketches of the American Protestant Missionaries to the Hawaiian Islands*, enlarged from the 1937 edition (Honolulu: Hawaiian Mission Children's Society, 1969), pp. 104-05. Hawaiian Mission Children's Society, *Jubilee Celebration of the Arrival of the Missionary Reinforcement of 1837* (Honolulu: Daily Bulletin Steam Print, 1887), pp. 42-46. "Letters from Rev. J. S. Green," *American Missionary*, I (March 1847), 33-34.

31. Green, "Letter on Agencies," *Vermont Chronicle* (1828), in *Miscellaneous Writings*, p. 45.

32. Green, "Address of the Rev. Beriah Green of Vermont," *Home Missionary and American Pastor's Journal*, II (July 1829), 41-43. Green, "Address of the Rev. Beriah Green, of Brandon, Vermont," *Twelfth Annual Report of the American Education Society* (1828), 27-28.

33. Green, "Evangelical Truths Offensive to the Unrenewed, but Joyous to the Believer," *National Preacher*, III (February 1829), 135-44. Green, "The Long Forbearance of God toward Sinners," *National Preacher*, III (February 1829), 129-135.

34. Quoted in H. P. Smith and W. S. Rann, eds. *History of Rutland County, Vermont* (Syracuse: D. Mason & Co., 1866), p. 506. See also *Centennial Celebration of the Brandon Congregational Church, Brandon, Vt., Rev. Walter Rice, Pastor* (Rutland, Vt.: Tuttle, 1885), p. 10.

35. Green, *Sermons and Discourses*, p. 6.

36. Ibid.

37. Green, "Monthly Concert for Prayer," 43.

38. Ronald Walters, "The Erotic South: Civilization and Sexuality in American Abolitionism," *American Quarterly*, 25 (Winter 1973), 200.

39. Wyatt-Brown, "Conscience and Career: Young Abolitionists and Missionaries," in *Anti-slavery, Religion and Reform*, ed. by Christian Bolt and Seymour Drescher (Folkestone, Kent, England: Wm. Dawson & sons, 1980), p. 194.

40. Green, *An Oration, Pronounced at Middlebury, Before the Associated Alumni of the College, on the Evening of Commencement. August 16th, 1826* (Castleton, Vt: Ovid Miner, 1826), pp. 12-13, 17, 31.

41. Green, in (Weld), *Report*, p. 112.

2—AXE-HONING ON THE WESTERN RESERVE

1. Quoted in C. H. Cramer, *Case Western Reserve: A History of the University, 1826-1976* (Boston: Little, Brown, and Company, 1976), p. 10.

2. *Observer and Telegraph*, September 2, 1830. See also, Minutes, August 26, 1830, Records of the Trustees of Western Reserve College, Hudson, Ohio, Case Western Reserve University Archives, Cleveland.

3. *Observer and Telegraph*, October 14, 1830.

4. *Observer and Telegraph*, September 2, 1830.

5. Quoted in Carroll Cutler, *A History of Western Reserve* (Cleveland: Crocker Publishing House, 1876), p. 24. Cutler served as college president from 1871-86 and as Western Reserve's first historian. He claimed to have obtained information from Bigelow himself and from Loomis Chandler of the class of 1840. See letter, Chandler to Cutler, November 1, 1876, Carroll Cutler Papers, Case Western Reserve Archives.

6. Charles B. Storrs, *An Address, Delivered at the Western Reserve College, Hudson, Ohio, February 9, 1831* (Boston: Pierce and Parker, 1831), p. 10.

7. *Observer and Telegraph*, July 12, 1832. Wright to Cutler, December 5, 1875, Cutler Papers.

8. Caleb Pitkin and Rufus Nutting to Ralph R. Gurley, March 27, 1832, American Colonization Society Papers, Library of Congress, Washington, D. C. A. P. Hawley to Carroll Cutler, November 18, 1875, Cutler Papers.

9. A letter on manual labor by Weld appeared in the *Observer and Telegraph*, October 19, 1835. In crediting Green, Wright, and Storrs for Weld's conversion to immediatism, I share the interpretation of Robert H. Abzug, *Passionate Liberator: Theodore Dwight Weld and the Dilemma of Reform* (New York: Oxford University Press, 1980), pp. 60, 87, 318, n.49. Weld (1803-95), born in Connecticut, was the son of a Presbyterian clergyman who retired in 1824 and moved to a farm in Fabius township, forty miles southwest of Utica. Theodore attended but did not officially enroll in Hamilton College and spent considerable time in Utica, where he came under the influence of Charles Finney in 1826 and was converted. In May 1827, he joined the first class of Oneida Academy, the school founded by George Gale in Whitesboro on manual labor principles. Weld left Oneida in 1833 for Lane Theological Seminary, attended Oberlin College, and became an energetic and widely traveled abolitionist lecturer. He married Angelina Grimké in 1838, wrote *Slavery as It Is*, an important abolitionist tract, and worked full-time in the New York office of the American Anti-Slavery Society in the early 1840s. After a brief period in Washington helping antislavery members of Congress, Weld retired from the abolitionist campaign. Abzug's biography deftly analyzes the reasons for Weld's withdrawal and

provides additional information on his student days, promotion of the manual labor movement, and abolitionist activities.

10. Horace Taylor and David O. Hudson to Ralph R. Gurley, October 29, 1832, American Colonization Society Papers.

11. Ibid.

12. Beriah Green, *Four Sermons, Preached in the Chapel of the Western Reserve College, On Lord's Days, November 18th and 25th and December 2nd and 9th, 1832* (Cleveland: Printed at the Office of the Herald, 1833), p. 3.

13. Ibid.

14. For Green's temperance lectures, see the *Cleveland Herald*, January 12 and February 9, 1832. His other reform, missionary, and manual labor interests can be examined in the following publications: "Christian Obligations," *National Preacher*, VI (April 1832), 353-62; "Review of *Letters on Missions*, by William Swan, Missionary to Siberia," *Quarterly Christian Spectator* II (December 1830), 632-46; "Review of the Fifth Report of the American Home Missionary Society," *Quarterly Christian Spectator* (1831); "Claims of the Prison Discipline Society to the Support of Christians," *National Preacher*, VI (April 1832), 363-68; and "Letter" on manual labor in (Timothy Dwight Weld), *First Annual Report of the Society for Promoting Manual Labor in Literary Institutions, Including the Report of Their General Agent, Theodore D. Weld, January 28, 1833* (New York: S. W. Benedict, 1833), pp. 111-13.

15. Green, *Four Sermons*, p. 3.

16. " 'Light in the West,' Extracts in a letter addressed to the Rev. S. S. Jocelyn, New Haven, Conn., by Beriah Green, dated November 5, 1832," *Abolitionist*, I (February 1833), 29.

17. Recollections differ as to the racial identity of another student, a certain John Fayette from New York City, member of the freshman class of 1832. Oliver Chapin described him as "a native of Hindustan, a fullblooded Hindoo." (Chapin to Carroll Cutler, February 29, 1876) However, another Western Reserve alumnus claimed that "those in 1832 who professed to know . . . alleged she [Fayette's mother] was a West Indian Negress." (Edward Brown to Cutler, November 25, 1875) Both letters are among the Cutler Papers, Case Western Reserve.

18. Green, *Four Sermons*, pp. 7, 11-12.

19. Ibid., pp. 12-15.

20. Green, *The Miscellaneous Writings of Beriah Green* (New York: S. W. Green, 1860), p. 326. Green, *Four Sermons*, pp. 20-29.

21. Green, *Four Sermons*, pp. 32-40.

22. Ibid., pp. 41, 45.

23, Wright to Garrison, letter dated December 15, 1832, *Liberator*, January 5, 1833.

24. Wright to Weld, December 7, 1832, in *Letters of Theodore Dwight Weld, Angelina Grimké Weld and Sarah Grimké, 1822-1844*, ed. by Gilbert H. Barnes and Dwight L. Dumond (New York: D. Appleton-Century Company, 1934), I, 94-97.

25. Ibid., p. 96.

26. Wright and Green to Weld, February 1, 1833, in *Weld-Grimké Letters*, I, 101-109.

27. Wright to Carroll Cutler, December 5, 1875, Carroll Cutler Papers. Philip G. Wright and Elizabeth A. Wright, *Elizur Wright: The Father of Life Insurance* (Chicago: University of Chicago Press, 1937), pp. 55-56.

28. Prudential Committee Report, manuscript copy, Case Western Reserve Archives.

29. Cited in Storrs diary, February 9, 1833, Charles B. Storrs Papers, Case Western Reserve Archives.

30. Ibid., January 16, 1833.

31. David Hudson, Caleb Pitkin, and Harvey Coe, Trustees of Western Reserve College, to *Observer and Telegraph*, February 4, 1833.

32. Green to *Observer and Telegraph*, February 4, 1833. *Liberator*, March 16, 1833.

33. *Liberator*, January 5, 1833.

34. Green to Garrison, March 8, 1833, *Liberator*, March 23, 1833. The original is in the Garrison Papers, Boston Public Library, and contains material not in the published version.

35. Green to "Brother Cummings," April 12, 1833, *Liberator*, August 17, 1833.

36. Elizur Wright, Jr., to wife Susan, April 12, 1833, Elizur Wright Jr. Papers, Library of Congress.

37. Green to Wright, April 22, May 3, 1833, Wright Papers, Library of Congress.

38. *Liberator*, November 30, 1833.

39. Wright to Green, June 7, 1833, quoted by David Charles French, "The Conversion of an American Radical: Elizur Wright, Jr., and the Abolitionist Commitment" (Ph.D. dissertation, Case Western Reserve University, 1970), p. 158.

40. Cited in a letter, James Mason to Carroll Cutler, February 2, 1876, Cutler Papers. Mason was a student at Western Reserve College in 1833.

41. Wright to Weld, September 5, 1833, *Weld-Grimké Letters*, I, 116. After leaving Hudson, Wright (1804-85) moved to New York where he became corresponding secretary of the New York City Anti-Slavery Society. He participated in the formation of the American Anti-Slavery Society in December 1833 and was elected secretary of domestic correspondence. He edited the *Quarterly Anti-Slavery Magazine* from 1835-38, in addition to managing the daily operations of the national society until its breakup. Due to the wrangling between the Garrisonians and non-Garrisonians, the indifference of the churches to abolition, and personal financial problems, Wright gradually withdrew from organized abolition. He settled in Boston, started his own reform paper called the *Chronotype*, tried vainly to market his translation of La Fontaine's *Fables*, and, in the 1850s, became involved in insurance reform. He pioneered in the actuarial field, a return, as it were, to his mathematical interests while a professor at Western Reserve College.

42. Elizur Wright, Sr., to Elizur Wright, Jr., November 7, 1833, Elizur Wright, Jr., Papers, Western Reserve Historical Society, Cleveland, Ohio.

43. *Observer and Telegraph*, January 3, 1832.

44. Donald M. Scott, "Abolition as a Sacred Vocation," in *Antislavery Reconsidered*, ed. by Lewis Perry and Michael Fellman (Baton Rouge: Louisiana State University Press, 1979), p. 72.

3—HEWING ONEIDA INSTITUTE

1. Details concerning the move from Hudson to Whitesboro are given in a letter from Samuel W. Green to Hannah Deming, September 17, 1833. Courtesy of Newell Green. The children Jonathan (b. 1831) and Mary (b. 1833) had arrived during the family's years in Hudson.

2. *First Report of the Trustees of Oneida Academy, March 1828* (Utica, N.Y.: Hastings and Tracy, 1828). George Gale, *Autobiography (to 1834) of George Washington Gale (1789-1861)* (New York: n. p., 1964), pp. 276-90. This printed version is derived from an original manuscript transcribed by Gale's daughter, Margaret Gale Hitchcock. It stops in mid-sentence as Gale is giving a walking tour of the Oneida Institute campus as it appeared in 1834. Charles G. Finney, *Charles G. Finney, An Autobiography* (Old Tappan, N.J.: Fleming H. Revel Company, 1876), pp. 7-24.

3. (George Gale), "Oneida Institute," *Quarterly of the American Education Society* (November 1829), 112-15. On Weld's experiences at Oneida Institute, see Lyman Beecher, *The Autobiography of Lyman Beecher,* ed. by Barbara M. Cross (New York: Cambridge University Press, 1961), II, 234, and Robert H. Abzug, *Passionate Liberator: Theodore Dwight Weld and the Dilemma of Reform* (New York: Oxford University Press, 1980), pp. 61-70.

4. Understanding the history of institutions like the Whitesboro school is complicated by the confusing nature of American education in the Jacksonian era. Gale's enterprise was first known as Oneida Academy. In colonial America, the sons of aristocratic families attended Latin grammar schools in preparation for college. But after the Revolution, due to private energy and benevolence, large numbers of academies were established. The academies took pupils who had completed an English education in the common or elementary schools and offered them a wider curriculum with emphasis on literature and the sciences in addition to the Latin and Green classics. High schools, as we know them, were not normative and in short supply, the first being established in Boston in 1824. When Gale and the trustees applied for a charter from the Regents of the University of New York in 1829, they stressed that the Oneida Institute of Science and Industry was to be dedicated to the "pursuit of literature and science" and suitable for preparing students for "what are called professional studies," such as found in a theological seminary. The Institute had a Juvenile Department, where the course of study was similar to that of the common Latin school. Boys, usually younger than fifteen, prepared for entrance into the Institute, and worked only two hours a day at manual labor. By placing their school under the "fostering care" of the Regents of the University, the trustees of the Institute could take advantage of appropriations from the State Literature Fund, which had been established to encourage the development of academies and colleges. Thus Oneida Institute had a semi-public character at its chartering, despite its religious orientation and ties to Presbyterianism. The trustees had to make annual reports to the state Regents, though the success or failure of the Institute was entirely in their hands. When Gale resigned as principal and Green became president of the Institute in 1833, the school underwent another change. Green added two additional years to the curriculum of the older students and introduced advanced courses similar to those at the traditional colleges. He and his supporters understood the Institute to be a full-fledged college, similar to Oberlin in Ohio and the older New England institutions.

5. *Second Report of the Trustees of the Oneida Institute of Science and Industry, Whitesboro, March 20, 1830* (Utica: William Williams, 1830), pp. 3-6, 16-19. Gale, "Oneida Institute," 112-15. *Western Recorder,* December 28, 1830. *Proceedings of a Meeting Held at the Masonic Hall on the subject of Manual Labor in Connexion with Literary Institutions, June 15, 1831. Together with some Particulars Respecting the Oneida Institute at Whitesboro, N. Y.* (New York: L. Booth, 1831), pp. 5-9.

6. *Third Report of the Trustees of the Oneida Institute of Science and Industry, Whitestown, January, 1831* (Utica: William Williams, 1831), pp. 3-5, 11. Gale to Charles G. Finney, October 20, 1832, Finney Papers, Oberlin College.

7. Gale to Finney, December 3, 1830, Finney Papers.

8. Gale to Finney, December 16, 1830; October 20, 1832, Finney papers. N. S. S. Beman to Theodore Dwight Weld, November 30, 1832, in *Letters of Theodore Dwight Weld, Angelina Grimké Weld, and Sarah Grimké, 1822-1844,* ed. by Dwight L. Dumond (New York: d. Appleton-Century Co., 1936), I, 91-92.

9. Aiken to Finney, March 17, 1832, Finney Papers.

10. Gale to Rev. H. Norton, September 1, 1832, *New York Evangelist,* October 13, 1832.

11. C(harles) Stuart Renshaw and two other students to Finney, July 15, 1833; Asa A. Stone to Finney, July 22, 1833, Finney Papers.

12. Gale, *Autobiography*, p. 305. Gale (1789-1861) had given up most of his teaching responsibilities prior to Green's arrival in late summer 1833 in order to concentrate on the Institute's business affairs. He stayed on until spring 1834 but left Whitesboro in 1835 with about thirty families who were intent upon organizing a colony in the vast military tract of the West. They settled in Illinois, founded Galesburg, and established Knox College on the manual labor plan. Gale later participated in anti-slavery activity in Illinois and supported the Liberty Party. For Gale's story subsequent to his departure from Whitesboro and more about the Oneida Institute-Knox College parallels, see Hermann R. Muelder, *Fighters for Freedom: The History of Anti-Slavery Activities of Men and Women Associated with Knox College* (New York: Columbia University Press, 1959).

13. *Emancipator*, August 3, 1833. *African Repository*, IX (September 1833), 215.

14. *Circular of the Executive Committee of the Whitestown and Oneida Institute Anti-Slavery Societies* (1833), May Anti-Slavery Collection, Olin Library, Cornell University.

15. Green, *An Address, Delivered at Whitesborough, N. Y., September 5, 1833* (Utica: William Williams, 1833), pp. 5-6, 16-18.

16. "V.R.V." to William Goodell, November 1833, *Emancipator*, December 21, 1833.

17. "Speech of Rev. Samuel J. May," *Proceedings of the American Anti-Slavery Society, at its Second Decade, Held in the City of Philadelphia, Dec. 3rd, 4th, and 5th, 1853* (New York: American Anti-Slavery Society, 1863), p. 27.

18. John G. Whittier, "The Anti-slavery Convention of 1833" (1874). From *The Writings of John Greenleaf Whittier in Seven Volumes* (Riverside edition; Boston: Houghton, Mifflin and Company, 1889), VII, 174-75. See also, "Speech of J. Miller McKim," *Thirtieth Anniversary of the American Anti-Slavery Society* (New York: American Anti-Slavery Society, 1863), p. 27.

19. Cited in "Speech of Rev. Samuel J. May," p. 30.

20. *First Annual Report of the American Anti-Slavery Society* (New York: Dorr and Butterfield, 1834), pp. 15, 42-43.

21. Denison to Garrison, January 14, 1834, William Lloyd Garrison Papers, Boston Public Library.

22. Wright to Green. February 7, 1834, Elizur Wright, Jr., Papers, Library of Congress, Washington, D. C.

23. Wright to Garrison, June 30, 1834, Anti-Slavery Papers, Boston Public Library.

24. *Utica Weekly Herald*, January 3, 14, 1834. *Utica Sentinel and Gazette*, January 21, 1834.

25. (Beriah Green), *A Sketch of the Condition and Prospects of the Oneida Institute* (Utica: Bennet and Bright, 1834), pp. 16-19. Green estimated that the school could accommodate one hundred students.

26. Green, *Condition and Prospects of Oneida Institute*, pp. 13-15.

27. Cited in Beriah Green, *The Miscellaneous Writings of Beriah Green* (Whitesboro: Oneida Institute, 1841), p. 266. Green responded with nine letters, later published as "Claims of the Greek and Roman Classics to a Place in a Course of Liberal Study" in *Miscellaneous Writings*, pp. 267-320.

28. Cited in Green, *The American Student: A Valedictory Address to the Senior Class of the Oneida Institute, Delivered September 12, 1838* (Whitesboro: Oneida Institute, 1838), p. 30.

29. Green, *Miscellaneous Writings*, p. 30.

30. Mary S. Bull, "Gerrit Smith," *Good Company*, VI (November 1880), 241.

31. "Diogenes, Jr." (Elizur Wright, Jr.), "Finding a Man," *Model Worker*, August 11, 1848.

32. A(nn) W. Weston to M. Weston, May 16, 1839, Anti-Slavery Papers, Boston Public Library.

33. Smith to the editors of *Freedom's Journal*, March 31, 1827, Letter Copybook, Smith Papers. Smith to Bacon, March 31, 1834, Smith Papers. For a description of the Peterboro Manual Labor School, see *African Repository*, X (December 1834), 312-13.

34. Green to Smith, March 25, 1834, Smith Papers.

35. Smith to Leonard Bacon, March 31, 1834, Smith Papers.

36. Smith, *Journal*, July 12, 1834, quoted by Octavius Brooks Frothingham, *Gerrit Smith* (New York: G. P. Putnam's Sons 1878), pp. 163-64.

37. Wright to Amos G. Phelps, October 27, 1834, Elizur Wright, Jr., Papers, Library of Congress.

38. Green to Smith, August 19, 1835, Smith Papers.

39. Quoted in Howard Alexander Morrison, "Gentlemen of Proper Understanding: A Closer Look At Utica's Anti-Abolitionist Mob," *New York History*, 62 (January 1981), 61.

40. Ibid.

41. Smith, *Journal*, October 25, 1835, quoted in Frothingham, *Gerrit Smith*, p. 166.

42. "Speech of Mr. Gerrit Smith," *Proceedings of the New York Anti-Slavery Convention, Held at Utica, October 21, and at Peterboro, October 22, 1835* (Utica: Standard and Democrat, 1835), p. 21.

43. Smith to Cox, November 12, 1835, *Emancipator*, November, 1835.

44. Smith to Gurley, November 24, 1835, Smith Papers. Also in *African Repository*, XII (January 1836), 36.

45. Green to Smith, December 11, 1835, Smith Papers.

46. Green to Smith, December 24, 1835, Smith Papers.

47. Smith to Green, August 14, 1837, Letter Copybook, Smith Papers.

48. Samuel W. Green to Althea and Hannah Deming, May 26, 1835. Letter courtesy of Newell Green.

49. *The Friend of Man*, a weekly, first appeared on June 23, 1836. It succeeded the Utica-based *Standard and Democrat*. Though published at Utica under the editorship of Goodell, it actually came off the printing press at the Institute. Stanley Hough, son of Oneida's superintendent and treasurer Reuben Hough, took over the editorship in 1839. The paper folded in January 1842 but was, to some extent, replaced by *The Liberty Press* (1843–49).

50. Green, "A Review—The Principles of Reform, Art. X On Political and Ecclesiastical Reform of Wood's *Literary and Theological Review*," No. VI in *Quarterly Anti-Slavery Magazine*, I (October 1835), 41-45, 46, 48, 67.

51. Green, "Radicalism—In Reply to the *Literary and Theological Review*," *Quarterly Anti-slavery Magazine*, I (January 1836), 160, 169, 171.

52. Green, "The Church Carried along, or the Opinions of a Doctor of Divinity on American Slavery," *Quarterly Anti-Slavery Magazine*, II (October 1836), 42, 44, 51, 56. Green quoted liberally from Rice's article in the *Christian Spectator*.

53. Green, "Letter to a Minister of the Gospel," *Quarterly Anti-Slavery Magazine*, I (July 1836), 337. Also published in *Emancipator*, July 1836.

54. Green, *Things for Northern Men to Do: A Discourse Delivered Lord's Day Evening, July 17, 1836, in the Presbyterian Church, Whitesboro, N. Y.* (New York: Published by Request, 1836), pp. 20-21.

55. Samuel M. Green to Althea and Hannah Deming, May 26, 1835. Letter courtesy of Newell Green.

56. *Catalogue of the Officers and Students of the Oneida Institute, 1836* (Whitesboro: Oneida Institute Typographical Association, 1836), pp. 4-7.

57. For Wager's motion, see the *Journal of the Senate of the State of New York, At Their Fifty-Ninth Session* (Albany: E. Crosswell, 1836), p. 216. The printed circular calling for the Utica rally, which includes Green's penned notations, is on the back of a letter from Green to

Smith, March 21, 1836, Smith Papers.

    58. *Emancipator*, May 5, 12, 1836.

    59. Green to A. B. Johnson, January 17, 1834, A. B. Johnson Papers, Hamilton College, Clinton, New York.

4—"TO CUT THE CORD OF CASTE"

    1. W. E. B. Du Bois, *The Souls of Black Folk* (1903; New York: Fawcett Publications, Inc., 1961), pp. 158-59.

    2. Crummell's description of Green is from a letter directed to Bishop Benjamin T. Onderdonk, and originally published about December 1839 in *The Churchman*, copy in the Amos G. Beman Scrapbook II, Yale University, New Haven, Connecticut. Crummell's recollections of Oneida Institute are in his "Eulogium on Henry Highland Garnet, D.D." (1882), in *Africa and America: Addresses and Discourses* (Springfield, Mass,: Wiley and Co., 1891), p. 281.

    3. *Freedom's Journal*, February 15, 1828.

    4. *Freedom's Journal*, March 23, 1827.

    5. Daniel Alexander Payne, *Recollections of Seventy Years* (Nashville: African Methodist Episcopal Sunday School Union, 1888), p. 20.

    6. Tudor E. Grant to Gerrit Smith, October 21, 1826, Smith Papers, Library of Congress, Washington, D. C.

    7. *Proceedings of the New England Anti-Slavery Convention, Held in Boston, May 24, 25, 26, 1836*, quoted in Benjamin Quarles, *Black Abolitionists* (New York: Oxford University Press, 1969), p. 112.

    8. These are: *A Sketch of the Condition and Prospects of the Oneida Institute* (Utica, N. Y.: Bennett and Bright, 1834); *Catalogue of the Officers & Students of the Oneida Institute for 1835*, partial copy in Smith Papers, Syracuse University; *Catalogue of the Officers and Students of the Oneida Institute, 1836* (Whitesboro: Oneida Institute Typographical Association, 1836); *Catalogue of the Trustees, Faculty and Students of the Oneida Institute* (Whitesboro, New York: n.p., 1837). Additional catalogues may have been published, as Green makes mention of attempting to find the one for 1839 to send to Amos Phelps. Green to Phelps, July 21, 1839, Phelps Papers, Boston Public Library.

    9. Green to Amos Phelps, July 21, 1840, Phelps Papers.

    10. "Colleges," *Western Monthly Magazine*, (April 1836), 224. Beriah Green, "Ten Years in Oneida Institute," in *Sermons and Other Discourses* (New York: S. W. Green, 1860), pp. 190-91.

    11. Josiah B. Grinnell, *Men and Events of Forty Years* (Boston: D. Lothrop Company, 1891), p. 30. Grinnell writes (p. 31) that he graduated without a diploma because the State Regents denied Oneida's Board of Trustees the power to confer degrees as punishment for the school's radical innovations.

    12. Wright to Garrison, June 30, 1834, Garrison Papers, Boston Public Library.

    13. Green to Amos Phelps, September 4, 1834, Phelps Papers.

    14. Full citations for the student rosters, from which some information on the Afro-Americans at Oneida Institute has been gleaned, are given above at note number eight. They will not be footnoted hereafter. *Colored American*, August 25, 1838.

    15. Undated note from Beriah Green, Amos Beman Scrapbook I, Yale University.

    16. Note dated October 27, 1835 from Pelatiah Rawson and Innes Grant, Beman Scrapbook I, Yale University.

17. Letter, Freeman to Beman, June, 1841, in Beman Scrapbook I, Yale University. The ordination "Order of Exercises" and additional information on Freeman is scattered throughout Beman Scrapbook II. See also the remark on Freeman in F. T. Ray and H. C. Ray, *Sketch of the Life of Rev. Charles B. Ray* (New York: J. J. Little, 1887), p. 62.

18. Crummell, "Eulogium," pp. 280-81.

19. Du Bois, *Souls of Black Folk*, p. 218.

20. Crummell to Wright, June 22, 1837, Elizur Wright, Jr., Papers, Library of Congress, Washington, D. C.

21. *Colored American*, September 28, 1839.

22. *Washington Bee*, April 9, 1892. Crummell's reasons for wanting an advanced education are revealed in his letter to John Jay, August 9, 1848, republished in *The British Isles, 1830-1865*, Vol. I of *The Black Abolitionist Papers*, ed. by C. Peter Ripley (Chapel Hill: University of North Carolina Press, 1985), pp. 142-48.

23. Cited by Joel Schor, *Henry Highland Garnet* (Westport, Ct.: Greenwood Press, 1977), p. 12.

24. Crummell, "Eulogium," p. 283.

25. Quoted by Crummell, Ibid., p. 287.

26. *Walker's Appeal, with a Brief Sketch of His Life. Also Garnet's Address to the Slaves of America* (New York: J. H. Tobitt, 1848), p. 96.

27. Quoted by Crummell, "Eulogium," p. 279.

28. *Colored American*, June 16, November 2, 1839.

29. See the citations in James de T. Abajian, ed., *Blacks in Selected Newspapers, Censuses, and Other Sources, an Index to Names and Subjects* (Boston: G. K. Hall, 1977), p. 351.

30. Letter, Washington to Theodore S. Wright, January 15, 1846, Beman Scrapbook II, Yale University.

31. *Friend of Man*, August 21, 1839.

32. Clipping in Beman Scrapbook II, Yale University.

33. William J. Wilson to Henry Stiles, ca. December 1862, Henry J. Stiles Papers, Long Island Historical Society.

34. Gallaudet to Smith, December 2, 1834, Smith Papers, Syracuse University.

35. *New York Weekly Anglo-African*, May 11, 1861.

36. Rogers, "Alcohol Personified Written for the Anniversary of the Temperance Convention at Hudson, N.Y. July 8, 1845," Beman Scrapbook II, Yale University. William Wells Brown, *The Black Man, His Antecedents, His Genius and His Achievement* (Boston: R. F. Wallcut, 1863), pp. 273-74.

37. (Jermain W. Loguen), *The Rev. J. W. Loguen, as a Freeman* (1859); rpt., New York: Negro Universities Press, 1968), pp. 351-52 and *passim*. *Colored American*, March 13, 1841.

38. *Frederick Douglass' Paper*, October 9, 1851. *Liberator*, October 10, 1851.

39. Hall to Smith, October 16, 1839, Smith Papers.

40. Allen to Smith, May 15, 1840, Green to Smith, December 10, 1840, Smith Papers.

41. Allen, *The American Prejudice Against Color. An Authentic Narrative, Showing how Easily the Nation Got into an Uproar. By W. G. Allen, a Refugee from American Despotism* (London: W. and F. G. Cash, 1853), pp. 13-14. See also Allen's, *A Short Personal Narrative* (London: R. Chapman, 1860).

42. Wm. C. Nell, *The Colored Patriots of the American Revolution* (Boston: Robert F. Wallcut, 1855), pp. 316-18.

43. *Catalogue of the Officers and Students of the Biblical School and Whitestown Seminary, at Whitestown, N. Y.* (Utica, N.Y.: H. H. Curtiss, 1846), p. 4.

44. Certificate of ordination for Jacob A. Prime, dated October 15, 1849, Beman Scrapbook III, Yale University. For an account of the convention and ordination, see Samuel R. Ward's paper, *Impartial Citizen* (Syracuse, N.Y.), October 24, 1849.

45. Ward, *Autobiography of a Fugitive Negro* (London: John Snow, 1855), p. 58.

46. Green to Smith, March 17, 1835, Smith Papers.

47. Wright to Green, July 8, 1842, Wright Papers, Library of Congress.

48. Wright to Green, August 14, 1841, Wright Papers, Library of Congress.

49. Green, "Ten Years in Oneida Institute," p. 172.

50. Ibid., pp. 190-91.

5—WEAPONS OF THE MIND

1. Letter, Crummell to Benjamin T. Onderdonk, ca. December 1839, from *The Churchman*, copy in Amos B. Beman Scrapbook II, Yale University. Grinnell, *Men and Events of Forty Years*, (Boston: D. Lothrop Company, 1891), p. 30. *Colored American*, December 16, 1837. Smith to Judge Jones, February 27, 1843, Letter Copybook, Smith Papers. The Birney quote is from his diary, July 15, 1852, cited by Dwight L. Dumond, ed., *Letters of James Gillespie Birney* (New York: D. Appleton-Century, 1938), I, 252, n. 4.

2. Charles Stewart Renshaw to Charles G. Finney, July 15, 1833, Finney Papers, Oberlin College, Oberlin, Ohio.

3. Green's views on educational reform are best summarized in *The Education of the Apostles: A Valedictory Address, to the Senior Class of the Oneida Institute: Delivered Sept. 10, 1839* (Whitesboro: Oneida Institute, 1839).

4. Quoted in D. H. Meyer, *The Instructed Conscience: The Shaping of a National Ethic* (Philadelphia: University of Pennsylvania Press, 1972), vii.

5. Green, *Sketch of the Conditions and Prospects of the Oneida Institute . . . (Utica: Bennett and Bright, 1834),* p. 9.

6. See the bibliography of Green's published writings for the valedictory addresses. Green served as the presiding officer of the American Seventh Commandment Society, a reform group which supported the work of the Reverend John R. McDowall among the prostitutes of New York City. See *Friend of Man*, January 23, July 14, 1836. Oneida's students had their own peace and temperance societies. Green rejected all forms of social drinking and eventually came out against the use of wine even in the Lord's Supper. See his letter to Edward C. Delavan in the *Enquirer*, 1 (January 1841), 27-28.

7. Meyer, *Instructed Conscience*, p. 24.

8. Francis Wayland, *The Elements of Moral Science*, ed. by Joseph L. Blau (Cambridge: Belknap Press of Harvard University, 1963), pp. 182, 188-198.

9. Francis Wayland, *The Limitations of Human Responsibility* (2nd ed., New York: D. Appleton and Co., 1838), pp. 163, 173.

10. Green, *The Basis of a Sound Reputation: A Valedictory Address to the Senior Class of the Oneida Institute, Delivered September 13, 1837* (Whitesboro: Press of The Friend of Man, 1837), p. 5.

11. Green, " 'The Church Carried Along,' or the Opinions of a Doctor of Divinity on American Slavery," *Quarterly Anti-Slavery Magazine*, II (October 1836), 46. Green, *Things for Northern Men to Do; A Discourse Delivered Lord's Day Evening, July 17, 1836, in the Presbyterian Church, Whitesboro, N. Y.* (New York: Published by Request, 1836), p. 11.

12. Quoted by J. Robert Barth, *Coleridge and Christian Doctrine* (Cambridge: Harvard University Press, 1969), p. 27.

13. Green was especially fond of this passage from Coleridge's *The Friend*: "Still, however, here are truths so self-evident, or so immediately and palpably deduced from those that are, or are acknowledged for such, that they are at once intelligible to all men, who possess the common advantages of the social state; although by sophistry, by evil habits, by the neglect, false persuasions, and impostures of an ANTI-CHRISTIAN PRIESTHOOD, JOINED IN ONE CONSPIRACY WITH THE VIOLENCE OF TYRANNICAL GOVERNORS, the understandings of men may become so darkened, and their consciences so lethargic, that there may arise a necessity for the republication of these truths, and this too with a voice of LOUD AND IMPASSIONED WARNING. Such were the doctrines proclaimed by the first Christians to the Pagan world—such were the lightnings flashed by Wickliffe, Huss, Luther, Calvin, Zuinglius [*sic*], Latimer, etc., across the papal darkness; and such in our own times— the agitating truths, with which Thomas Clarkson and his excellent confederates—the Quakers fought and conquered the LEGALIZED BANDITTI OF MEN-STEALERS, the numerous and powerful perpetrators of rapine, murder, and (OF BLACKER GUILT THAN EITHER) slavery." Cited in Green, "A Review—The Principles of Reform, Art. X, On Political and Ecclesiastical Reform, of Wood's *Literary and Theological Review*," *Quarterly Anti-Slavery Magazine*, I (October 1835), 52.

14. Green, *Basis of a Sound Reputation*, p. 5.

15. According to one report, Noyes' paper *The Perfectionist* spread "like lightening" among Oneida's students in 1834. See *Religious Experience of John Humphrey Noyes*, ed. by George Wallingford Noyes (New York: The Macmillan Company, 1923), p. 188. Green held a low opinion of Noyes' Oneida Community and all perfectionists. Elizur Wright, Jr., to Green, October 17, 1837, Elizur Wright, Jr., Papers, Library of Congress. Green to Amos Phelps, March 29, 1838, Phelps Papers, Boston Public Library.

16. Green, "No Principle at Strife with Principle, or, Ciphers in Battle Array with Whole Numbers," *Friend of Man*, April 12, 1837.

17. Green to Elizur Wright, Jr., November 21, 1837, Wright Papers, Library of Congress.

18. Green, *The Martyr: A Discourse on Commemoration of the Martyrdom of the Rev. Elijah P. Lovejoy, Delivered in Broadway Tabernacle, New York, and in the Bleecker Street Church, Utica* (New York: American Anti-Slavery Society, 1838), pp. 3-4.

19. Ibid., pp. 15-16.

20. The Dabney and Fuller quotes are from H. Shelton Smith, *In His Image But . . .: Racism in Southern Religion, 1780-1910* (Durham, N.C.: Duke University Press, 1972), pp. 133, 136.

21. Weld's analysis of slavery in the Old Testament first appeared as "Is Slavery from Above or Beneath?" *Quarterly Anti-Slavery Magazine*, II (April 1837) and finally as *The Bible Against Slavery. An Inquiry into the Patriarchal and Mosaic Systems on the Subject of Human Rights* (New York, 1838).

22. Beriah Green to Wright and Weld, October 22, 1838, *Letters of Theodore Dwight Weld, Angelina Grimké Weld, and Sarah Grimké, 1822-1844*, ed. by Gilbert H. Barnes and Dwight L. Dumond (New York: D. Appleton Century Co., 1938), II, 709.

23. Ibid., p. 710.

24. Green to Weld, November 17, 1838, *Weld-Grimké Letters*, II, 714.

25. Green, *The Chattel Principle. The Abhorrence of Jesus Christ and the Apostles: or, No Refuge for American Slavery in the New Testament* (New York: American Anti-Slavery Society, 1839), pp. 4-6.

26. Ibid., pp. 9-10.

27. Ibid., p. 14.

28. Ibid., p. 22.

29. Ibid., pp. 53-55. For a contemporary assessment of the nature of slavery in apostolic times, see S. Scott Bartchy, *First-Century Slavery and the Interpretation of 1 Corinthians 7:21* (Missoula, Mt.: Society of Biblical Literature Dissertation Series, Number Eleven, 1973), Chapter II. Bartchy writes (p. 87): "The unquestioned acceptance of the institution of slavery in the first century A.D., the improving conditions of slave-life during that period, the respective places of slaves and freedmen in society, and the slave's view of his own situation clearly indicates that the person in Greek or Roman slavery in the first century A.D. led an existence which differed in many significant ways from the slavery practiced in modern times. Perhaps the most significant differences between that ancient slavery and modern slavery was the manumission anticipated by first-century slaves."

30. Ibid., pp. 56, 59.

31. Ibid., pp. 70-71.

32. See Caroline L. Shanks, "The Biblical Anti-Slavery Argument of the Decade, 1830-1840," *Journal of Negro History*, XVI (April 1931), 132-57. Shanks mistakenly credits Green with two New Testament-based essays. She cites "Slavery not in the New Testament," from Green's *Sermons and Other Discourses* (1860), as if it were a separate document. It is merely a portion of *The Chattel Principle*. Elizur Wright, Jr., *The Sin of Slavery, and Its Remedy: Containing Some Reflections on the Moral Influence of African Colonization* (New York: Printed for the Author, 1833).

33. *The Chattel Principle* sold in 1839 for 12 1/2 cents at the Anti-Slavery Depository, a bookstore run by the New York State Anti-Slavery Society in Utica. *Friend of Man*, October 9, 1839.

34. Green, *Education of the Apostles*, p. 18.

35. Ibid., p. 29.

36. Green, letter to the Reverend Dr. Cogswell, Corresponding Secretary of the American Education Society, January 1836, in *New-York Evangelist*, February 6, 1836.

37. Green, *Education of the Apostles*, p. 31.

6—"A TROUBLER OF ISRAEL"

1. *Records of the Session of the Presbyterian Church, Whitesborough, New York*, Volume III, February 7, 1826-December 30, 1850, passim. These are in the possession of the congregation. Hereafter cited as Session Minutes.

2. Minutes, June 26, 1834, *Oneida Presbytery Records*, Volume VI, 1833-1838, Presbyterian Historical Society, Philadelphia. Hereafter cited as Presbytery Minutes. The Synod of Utica also voiced concern over slavery in 1834, but it did little more than urge that the matter by prayed upon. See P. H. Fowler, *Historical Sketch of Presbyterianism Within the Bounds of the Synod of Central New York* (Utica, N. Y.: Curtis and Childs, 1877), p. 155.

3. Whitney Cross, *The Burned-over District: The Social and Intellectual History of Enthusiastic Religion in Western New York, 1800-1850* (Ithaca: Cornell University Press, 1950), p. 226.

4. Session Minutes, December 11, 1835.

5. Presbytery Minutes, February 3, 1836.

6. (Beriah Green), *Reply of the Congregational Church in Whitesboro, to a Question of the Oneida Presbytery* (Whitesboro: Press of the Oneida Institute, 1839), p. 5.

7. David L. Ogden, *Review of a Pamphlet Entitled "Reply of the Congregational Church in Whitesboro to a Question of the Oneida Presbytery"* (Utica: R. Northway, 1839), p. 7.

8. Ibid.

9. Ibid.

10. Ibid., p. 8.

11. Green, *Reply of the Congregational Church*, pp. 5-6.

12. Green, *Things for Northern Men to Do: A Discourse Delivered Lord's Day Evening, July 17, 1836, in the Presbyterian Church* (Whitesboro: Published by Request, 1836), p. 22. For a similar condemnation of the complicity of American churches with slavery, see James Gillespie Birney, *The American Churches: The Bulwarks of American Slavery* (Second American edition; Newburyport, Mass.: Charles Whipple, 1842).

13. Ogden, *Review of a Pamphlet*, pp. 9-10.

14. David L. Ogden, *Thoughts on Men and Things*, journals while a minister in Whitesboro, 1837-1843, Clements Library, University of Michigan, Ann Arbor. Three manuscript journals survive. Volumes two and three cover the Whitesboro years.

15. Green to Smith, August 2, 1837, Smith Papers.

16. *Friend of Man*, August 9, 1837.

17. *Friend of Man*, August 17, 23, 30, September 6, 1837.

18. *Friend of Man*, September 20, October 11, 1837.

19. Ogden, *Thoughts on Men and Things*, August 2, 1837.

20. Ibid., August 3, 1837.

21. Ibid., August 8, 1837.

22. Ibid., September 11, 1837. Frances (Fanny) Wright, a Scotswoman, came to the United States to lecture on feminism, utopianism, and, according to her detractors, free love and atheism. The Locofocos were Democratic extremists who opposed the granting of corporate privileges or any form of monopoly and regarded the state as the natural enemy of individual "equal rights."

23. Ibid., September 14, 1837.

24. Ibid., September 16, 18, 1837.

25. *New York Observer*, September 30, 1837. West's letter is reprinted in *Friend of Man*, November 15, 1837.

26. Gerrit Smith to Beriah Green, October 5, 1837, Letter Copybook, Smith Papers. Green to Smith, October 18, 1837, Smith Papers.

27. *Friend of Man*, November 15, 1837.

28. Session Minutes, November 10, 1837.

29. Ibid., November 21-December 26, 1837. Ogden, *Review of a Pamphlet*, p. 11.

30. Green to Smith, January 6, 1836, Simon Gratz Collection, Pennsylvania Historical Collection, Philadelphia.

31. Green, *Reply of the Congregational Church*, p. 10.

32. Ogden, *Thoughts on Men and Things*, April 7, 1838.

33. Ibid., April 7, 1838. An opponent of all forms of ultraism, Ogden wrote, "tetotalism turns the good cause of Temperance into ridicule." Ibid., July 5, 1839.

34. Presbytery Minutes, February 22, 1838; March 13, 14, 1839.

35. Green, *Reply of the Congregational Church*, p. 3.

36. For the Constitution and Confession of Faith, see Beriah Green, *Sermons and Other Discourses with Brief Biographical Hints* (New York: S. W. Green, 1860), pp. 93-95.

37. Presbytery Minutes, June 16, 1840; February 1, June 15, 1841.

38. Ibid., February 21, 1837.

39. Ogden, *Thought on Men and Things*, October 10, 1839.

40. Smith's evaluation is in a letter to Charles West, October 5, 1827, Letter Copybook, Smith Papers.

41. Green to Smith, March 19, 1837, Smith Papers.

42. Green to Smith, October 2, 1837, Smith Papers.

43. Ogden, *Thoughts on Men and Things*, April 18, 1839.

44. Ibid., June 8, 1839.

45. Ibid., June 28, 1839. Ogden deplored the friendships and intimacies "being formed among those of different colors of the same sex" which he observed at Oneida Institute and feared that such social radicalism would encourage the union of blacks and whites in a "family state." He also predicted that the slaves, if freed, "would fade away like the Indians before their superiors."

46. Ibid., August 2, 1839.

47. Presbytery Minutes, February 21, 1837; March 4, 1840.

48. Green to Smith, March 19, 1839, Smith Papers.

49. Green to Smith, April 18, 1839, Smith Papers.

50. Wright to Beriah Green, December 15, 1838; Wright to Mr. and Mrs. Wright, December 5, 1839, Elizur Wright, Jr., Papers, Library of Congress.

7—"GONE, GONE, SOLD, & GONE"

1. Quoted by Ronald G. Walters, *The Antislavery Appeal* (Baltimore: John Hopkins University Press, 1978), p. 21.

2. Stanley M. Elkins, *Slavery* (New York: Grosset & Dunlap, 1963), pp. 27-30. See also, James Brewer Stewart, "Politics and Belief in Abolitionism: Stanley Elkins' Concept of Antiinstitutionalism and Recent Interpretations of American Antislavery," *South Atlantic Quarterly*, 75 (1976), 74-97.

3. Green to Gerrit Smith, February 16, June 6, 1837, Smith Papers.

4. *Catalogue of the Trustees, Faculty and Students of the Oneida Institute* (Whitesboro: Oneida Institute Press, 1837), p. 12.

5. Green to Smith, April 12, 1837; June 6, 1837; August 16, 1837, Smith Papers. Wright to Green, April 25, 1838, Elizur Wright, Jr., Papers, Library of Congress. See Green's review of the *Nineteenth Report of the American Education Society* for a summary of the abandonment of Oneida Institute by the education societies, published in the *New York Evangelist*, February 1836.

6. *Friend of Man*, September 19, 1838.

7. Green, *The American Student, A Valedictory Address to the Senior Class of the Oneida Institute, Delivered September 12, 1838* (Whitesborough: Press of the Oneida Institute, 1838), p. 23n.

8. Green to Gerrit Smith, April 18, 1839, Smith Papers.

9. Green to Smith, January 17, October 17, 24, 1839, Smith Papers.

10. Executive Committee of the Trustees, "To the Friends of Learning and Religion," Whitesboro, 1839, Smith Papers. The *Friend of Man*, August 21, 1839, reprints the 1839 catalogue and the circular from the Executive Committee.

11. Ann Green to Hannah Deming, September 28, 1839. Courtesy of Newell Green.

12. Green to Wright, June 28, 1839; Wright to Green, January 1, 1840, Wright Papers, Library of Congress.

13. Green to Phelps, April 12, 1839, Phelps Papers, Boston Public Library.

14. Green, *The Education of the Apostles: A Valedictory Address to the Senior Class of the Oneida Institute, Delivered September 12, 1839* (Whitesborough: Press of the Oneida Institute, 1839), p. 18.

15. Green to Gerrit Smith, February 26, 1840, Smith Papers.

16. Wright to Green, June 21, 1840, Wright Papers, Library of Congress. Green advocated expanded educational opportunities for women but he held to traditional views of sex role

differentiation, especially in the middle-class evangelical home. He seems to have been unable to transcend the notion that male and female roles were divinely established in the orders of Creation.

17. John Keep to Weld, January 11, 1839, *Letters of Theodore Dwight Weld, Angelina Grimké Weld, and Sarah Grimké, 1822-1844,* edited by Gilbert H. Barnes and Dwight L. Dumond (New York: D. Appleton-Century Co., 1938), II, 717-40. *Proceedings of the General Anti-Slavery Convention. Called by the Committee of the British and Foreign Anti-Slavery Society, and Held in London from Friday, June 12th to Thursday, June 23rd, 1840* (London: British and Foreign Anti-Slavery Society, 1841), p. 141.

18. Green to Phelps, July 21, 1840, Phelps Papers, Boston Public Library.

19. Ibid.

20. Green to Amos Phelps, August 1839, Phelps Papers, Boston Public Library.

21. Charles Stuart, *Oneida and Oberlin, or A Call, Addressed to British Christians and Philanthropists, Affectionately Inviting Their Sympathies, Their Prayers, and Their Assistance, in Favor of the Christians and Philanthropists of the United States of North America, for the Extirpation, By Our Aid, of that Slavery which We Introduced into those States, while They were Under our Power* (Bristol, England: Wright and Albright, 1841), pp. 12-14.

22. Ibid., pp. 16-17. Asa Mahan and John Morgan had been antislavery clergymen in Cincinnati when the Lane rebels left to form Oberlin and served on its faculty. Mahan became president of the new college and Finney taught theology.

23. Ibid., p. 20.

24. Elizur Wright, Jr., "To Those Who Know the Oneida Institute," manuscript dated August 1840, Wright Papers, Library of Congress. Henry B. Stanton, a convert of Finney, left Oneida Institute in 1832 for Lane Theological Seminary. After the Lane dispute, he served on the Executive Committee of the American Anti-Slavery Society, studied law, joined the Liberty Party and, from 1846-51, served in the New York State Senate.

25. Wright, untitled manuscript, dated August 20, 1840, Wright Papers, Library of Congress.

26. Ibid.,

27. J. B. Vashon visited Oberlin in 1840 and reported that he "saw none of that low, poor, mean, black prejudice there." Out of a total student population of 404 (in 1839), there were three female and twelve male African Americans. Vashon, who had encountered racial prejudice in efforts to enroll his son at Western Reserve College, described Oberlin as "the purest Christian College in the United States." See the letter from Vashon to Charles B. Ray in the *Colored American,* April 4, 1840.

28. Green, *A Right Minded Minority. A Valedictory Address to the Senior Class of the Oneida Institute, Delivered September 9, 1840* (Whitesboro: Press of the Oneida Institute, 1840), pp. 14-15.

29. Josiah Bushnell Grinnell, *Men and Events of Forty Years* (Boston: D. Lothrop Company, 1891), pp. 28-30. Charles E. Payne, *Josiah Bushnell Grinnell* (Iowa City: State Historical Society of Iowa, 1938), pp. 10-17.

30. Grinnell, *Men and Events,* p. 35.

31. *Freshman Gem,* I (May 1840), 14. The only issue still extant is located in the Widener Library, Harvard.

32. Green to Smith, January 1, 1841, Smith Papers.

33. Green to Smith, January 7 and 21, 1841, Smith Papers.

34. *Friend of Man,* February 23, 1841.

35. Green, *The Miscellaneous Writings of Beriah Green* (Whitesboro: Published by the Oneida Institute, 1841). The spine bears the title, *Green's Miscellanies.* Beriah's son Samuel published a second edition in 1848. Green to Smith, June 3, 1841, Smith Papers.

36. Green, *Faith and Works: A Valedictory Address to the Senior Class of the Oneida Institute, Delivered October 27, 1841* (Whitesboro: Press of the Oneida Institute, 1841), *passim*.

37. Circular by Green and Hough, dated November 1841, Whitesboro, found on the back of a letter, Green to Smith, June 21, 1842, Smith Papers.

38. Green to Smith, November 19, December 12, 1841, Smith Papers.

39. Green to Smith, December 12, 23, 1841; March 8, 1842, Smith Papers.

40. Green to Smith, April 26, 1842, Smith Papers.

41. Green to Smith, August 19, 26, 1842, Smith Papers.

42. Green, *The Divine Significance of Work. A Valedictory Address Delivered at the Anniversary of the Oneida Institute, November 2, 1842* (Whitesboro: Press of the Oneida Institute, 1842, passim.

43. Green, *Thoughts on the Atonement* (Whitesboro: Institute Press, 1842), pp. 3, 10, and *passim*. Samuel W. Green, *Beriah Green: A Memorial* (New York: S. W. Green, 1875), p. 7.

44. Green to Smith, February 8, 1843, Smith Papers.

45. Green to Smith, April 11, May 9, 1843, Smith Papers.

46. Beriah Green, *A Voice from the Oneida Institute*. Number 3, July 1843 (Whitesboro: Institute Press, 1843.), same as, "Ten Years in Oneida Institute," in *Sermons and Other Discourses with Brief Biographical Hints* (New York: S. W. Green, 1860), 164-201.

47. Green, "Ten Years in Oneida Institute," pp. 197-98.

48. Ibid., pp. 200-201.

49. Green to Smith, September 25, 1843, Smith Papers. The *Liberty Press* notified its readership, "We are happy to learn that the loss to President Green by the burning of his house, was not great, but it is something which his numerous friends would be pleased to make up to him." *Liberty Press*, October 3, 1843.

50. Green, *Success. A Valedictory Address Delivered at the Anniversary of the Oneida Institute, November 1, 1843* (Utica, N.Y.: R. W. Roberts, 1843), as included in Green's *Sermons and Other Discourses*, pp. 207-08.

51. Ibid., pp. 223-25.

52. *Liberty Press*, October 10, 1843.

53. Green to Smith, January 13, 1844, Smith Papers.

54. "Circular and Appeal in Behalf of Clinton Seminary," *Liberty Press*, January 31, 1843. Stewart report, *Liberty Press*, January 3, 1843.

55. *Liberty Press*, October 26, 1844.

56. *Fiftieth Anniversary of Whitestown Seminary, June 20, 1878* (Utica: Ellis H. Roberts & Co., 1878), p. 10.

57. Green to Smith, April 23, 1844, Smith Papers. Green to Phelps, May 22, 1844, Phelps Papers, Boston Public Library.

58. Beriah Green, *A Memorial of Ann Parker Green Hough* (Utica, N.Y.: R. W. Roberts, 1844), p. 19.

59. Ibid., p. 27.

8—THE AXE AND THE POLITICAL SCEPTER

1. *Friend of Man*, March 14, 1838.

2. Green to Smith, October 19, 1838, Smith Papers.

3. *Friend of Man*, October 31, 1838.

4. *Friend of Man*, October 17, 1838.

5. Green to Smith, November 29, 1838, Smith Papers.

6. *Friend of Man*, February 20, 1839. William Goodell, *Slavery and Anti-Slavery: A History of the Great Struggle in Both Hemispheres, with a View of the Slavery Question in the United States* (New York: William Harned, 1852), p. 469.

7. "Speech of Myron Holly at Perry, July 4, 1839," *Friend of Man*, August 14, 1839. Holly died in 1841. In 1844, Green participated in an effort to erect a monument to him in Rochester. James C. Jackson, Corresponding Secretary of the New York State Anti-Slavery Society, wrote that the monument was to "pay respect to the man who by common consent, has awarded to him the Honor of having organized and brought into shape the Liberty Party of the United States." *Albany Patriot*, April 10, 1844.

8. Cited by James B. Stewart, "The Aims and Impact of Garrisonian Abolitionism, 1840-1860," *Civil War History*, 15 (September 1969), 198.

9. Green to Smith, August 28, 1837, Smith Papers.

10. Green to Weld, April 14, 1838, *Letters of Theodore Dwight Weld, Angelina Grimké Weld, and Sarah Grimké, 1822-1844*, ed. by Gilbert H. Barnes and Dwight L. Dumond (New York: D. Appleton-Century Co., 1938), II, 755.

11. *Emancipator*, February 6, 1840.

12. *Liberator*, February 21, 1840.

13. Green to Smith, January 11, 1839, Smith Papers.

14. Green to Smith, March 26, 1840, Smith Papers.

15. Quoted in Phillip Green Wright and Elizabeth Q. Wright, *Elizur Wright, The Father of Life Insurance* (Chicago: University of Chicago Press, 1937), p. 32. Samuel J. May, one of those present at the 1833 meeting, recalled that this was the first time in his life that he had heard the voice of a woman in a public deliberative assembly and that, until Mott was invited to come forward, the women had modestly seated themselves in the rear. See May's speech in *Proceedings of the American Anti-Slavery Society, at its Second Decade, Held in the City of Philadelphia, Dec. 3d, 4th, and 5th, 1853* (New York: American Anti-Slavery Society, 1854), p. 9.

16. Green to Gerrit Smith, June 21, 1842, Smith Papers. The *Albany Patriot* of May 20, 1846 published an interesting response by Susan Ormsby to Green's refusal to extend suffrage to women.

17. Green to James G. Birney, February 27, 1840, *Letters of James Gillespie Birney, 1831-1857*, ed. by Dwight L. Dumond (New York: D. Appleton-Century Co., 1938), I, 533.

18. Green to Smith, July 9, 1840, Smith Papers.

19. *Friend of Man*, Extra, July 23, 1840.

20. Theodore C. Smith, *The Liberty and Free Soil Parties in the Northwest* (New York: Longmans, Green, 1897), p. 46.

21. Green to Smith, June 11, 1841, Smith Papers.

22. Green to Smith, June 27, 1842, Smith Papers.

23. Green to Smith, May 23, 1842, Smith Papers.

24. Green to Smith, January 6, February 8, April 1, December 1, December 6, 1843. *Liberty Press*, December 6, 1842.

25. *Christian Investigator*, September 1843. Green to Smith, April 9, 1843, Smith Papers.

26. Green to Birney, April 18, 1844, *Birney Letters*, II, 812-23.

27. Green, *Sketch of the Life and Writings of James Gillespie Birney* (Utica: Jackson and Chaplin, 1844), pp. 117-18.

28. *Liberty Press*, September 1, 1844.

29. "Speech of Beriah Green," December 4, 1844, *Albany Patriot*, December 18, 1844.

30. Alan M. Kraut, "The Forgotten Reformers: A Profile of Third Party Abolitionists in Antebellum New York," in *Anti-Slavery Reconsidered*, ed. by Lewis Perry and Michael Fellman (Baton Rouge: Louisiana State University Press, 1979), pp. 143-45.

31. Green to Gerrit Smith, Esq., and Smith to President Green, letters in *Albany Patriot*, February 19, 1845.

32. Green to Smith, September 15, 1846, Smith Papers.

33. Green to Birney, September 23, 1846, *Birney Letters*, II, 1027. See also Green's extensive critique of Stewart and those in the state society who refused to go beyond one-ideaism in the *Albany Patriot*, October 21, 28, and November 4, 1846.

34. Green to Smith, November 10, 1846, Smith Papers.

35. Green to Smith October 16, 1846, Smith Papers. Jonathan S. Green to Lewis Tappan, May 11, 1846, in *American Missionary*, I (March 1847), 1-2. Green's letter of resignation appears in the *Liberator*, November 13, 1846.

36. Green to Smith, August 2, 1838, Smith Papers. Green to Weld, July 13, 1841, *Weld-Grimké Letters*, II, 870. Green to Smith, December 30, 1845, Smith Papers.

37. Only scattered issues of the *Weekly Chronotype* have survived. The whole debate can be followed more conveniently in the *Albany Patriot*, May 6, May 20, June 3, and June 10, 1846.

38. Carlyle to Emerson, July 17, 1846, in *The Correspondence of Emerson and Carlyle*, ed. by Joseph Slater (New York: Columbia University Press, 1964), p. 406. Carlyle's letter to his wife is cited on p. 406, note 3.

39. Green to Birney, September 23, 1846, *Birney Letters*, II, 1028. W. O. Duvall had advocated a coalition of Libertymen and Whigs until he heard Green speak at Port Byron in March 1846. Duvall testified: "President Green's speech on the subject of 'civil government' was so different, in many points, from any I had ever listened to, that at the close of it I almost found myself ready again to enroll myself among the political hosts. He proved nearly to my satisfaction, that a just civil government may exist without the *yielding up of one natural right*. Knowing that no civil government ever *had* existed without taking from the citizen some of his natural rights, I had reasoned that none *could* exist on any other condition. He also proved conclusive to my mind, that both the great political parties in this nation are nothing more nor less than 'bloody conspiracies against justice, freedom, and philanthropy.' He also convinced me of another thing, *viz.*, that in view of the radical reform necessary in bringing government back to its legitimate objects and uses, Negro suffrage almost sinks into insignificance. There is vastly too much *white* suffrage. *Conspirators* are unfit to wield that important trust." Letter to *Albany Patriot*, March 25, 1846.

40. Green to Birney, April 23-May 5, 1847, *Birney Letters*, II, 1067.

41. Ibid.

42. Ibid. Green's mention of "the Investigator" had to do with Goodell's paper *The Christian Investigator*, begun in 1841 when Goodell was still in Whitesboro. The paper promoted the "free church" or "Christian union" movement of the Christian abolitionists in which Green participated. For Goodell's criticism's of Carlyle, see "Abolitionism and the Doctors—Thomas Carlyle," *Albany Patriot*, June 10, 1846.

43. Green, "The Foundation of Civil Government," *Albany Patriot*, June 2, 1847, and three essays entitled, "The 'Declaration' of the Callers of the Macedon-Lock Convention," *Albany Patriot*, June 9, 16, 23, 1847.

44. J. C. Jackson, "To the Agents of the Liberty League," *Albany Patriot*, October 7, 1846.

45. William Wiecek, *The Sources of Anti-slavery Constitutionalism in America, 1760-1848* (Ithaca: Cornell University Press, 1977) p. 250.

46. Green to Birney, August 2, 1847, *Birney Letters*, II, 1081.

47. Green to Birney, April 23, 1847, *Birney Letters*, II, 1065.

48. Green to Smith, November 9, 1847, Smith Papers.

49. *Albany Patriot*, May 10, 1848.

50. "Speech of Beriah Green," *Proceedings of the National Liberty Convention, Held at Buffalo, N. Y, June 14 and 15, 1848* (Utica: S. W. Green, 1848), pp. 35-36.

51. Ibid., p. 37.

52. Green to Smith, August 28, 1848, Smith Papers.

53. Green, *To the Surviving Members of the Liberty Party* (Whitesboro: n. p., 1848), pp. 3-5.

54. Ibid., p. 3.

55. Lewis Perry, *Radical Abolitionism: Anarchy and the Government of God in Anti-slavery Thought* (Ithaca, N. Y.: Cornell University Press, 1973), p. 5.

56. Green, "Speech of Beriah Green," pp. 37, 41.

57. Green to Birney, September 23, 1846, *Birney Letters*, II, 1027.

58. Perry, *Radical Abolitionism*, p. 173.

59. I have borrowed this concept from Michael Walzer, "Puritanism as a Revolutionary Ideology," *History and Theory*, 3 (1964), 79-88.

9—"A VOICE IN THE WILDERNESS"

1. *Model Worker*, July 21, 1848.

2. Samuel W. Green to Gerrit Smith, April 11, 1849; September 23, 1850, Letter Copybook, Smith Papers.

3. Smith to Green, April 4, 1842, Letter Copybook, Smith Papers. Beriah's namesake is sometimes referred to as Greene Smith, as on his grave marker in the Peterboro cemetery, but Smith clearly meant his son to be called "Green." To the embarrassment of his father and the disappointment of his namesake, Green Smith was an indifferent student. Gerrit sent his son to the "Weld Institute" run by Theodore Dwight Weld, his wife Angelina and her sister Sarah, in the hope that he would develop character. Young Green came home pretending to be a spiritualist medium. Shortly before the Civil War, Gerrit was forced to call his son back to Peterboro from Cambridge, Massachusetts, where he was preparing for college, because of reports of "bad conduct" associated with liquor and tobacco. In later life, Green Smith became a respected amateur ornithologist. Beriah's son Charles Stuart Green exhibited similar errant ways. He was not fond of studying and took to training and racing horses, not a vocation that his father approved of. Smith to Green, June 5, 1853, Smith Papers.

4. Smith to President Green, Whitesboro, April 4, 1849, Smith Papers. The circular elaborates on criticisms Smith leveled at Green subsequent to his address at the Buffalo Liberty Party convention in 1848. Smith originally published them in the *Model Worker*, August 11, 1848.

5. Ibid. Smith was basically a Jeffersonian Democrat who held to the view that a limited government best served the public.

6. Green to Smith, May 1, 1839, Smith Papers.

7. Smith to Green, May 3, 1849, note in Smith's handwriting appended to Green to Smith, May 1, 1849, Smith Papers.

8. Green to Smith, December 26, 1849, Smith Papers.

9. Ibid.

10. Smith to Green, January 15, 1850, Letter Copybook, Smith Papers. Smith to Green, February 23, 1850, Smith Papers.

11. Green to Smith, February 15, August 8, 1850, Smith Papers.

12. Smith to Green, August 4, 1850, Letter Copybook, Smith Papers.

13. Green to Birney, April 6, 1852, *Letters of James Gillespie Birney, 1831-1857*, ed. by Dwight L. Dumond (New York: D. Appleton-Century Co., 1938), II, 1142-44.

14. Smith to Jonathan S. Green, March 5, 1853, Smith Papers. Smith quotes Jonathan's earlier letter.

15. Green to Smith, February 12, 1833; June 27, 1854, Smith Papers.

16. Green, *Faith and Infidelity—A Sermon, at Whitesboro, 1853. Delivered in the Congregational Church at Whitesboro and Elsewhere* (New York: S. W. Green, 1853), as republished in Green's *Sermons and Other Discourses with Brief Biographical Hints* (New York: S. W. Green, 1860), pp. 309-12, 391.

17. Green, "Redemption," sermon republished in *Sermons and Other Discourses*, pp. 535-56.

18. Green to Birney, August 2, 1847, *Birney Letters*, II, 1078-79.

19. Samuel W. Green, *Beriah Green: A Memorial* (New York: S. W. Green, 1875), p. 10.

20. Green, "The Liar," sermon republished in *Sermons and Other Discourses*, p. 515.

21. Samuel Green, *Beriah Green*, pp. 10-11. In this memorial Samuel claims that his father viewed the Bible as an Oriental production and "looked for the essential fact under the eastern allegory. Jesus was wholly a man, whatever else he might be, and was the normally produced son of Joseph and Mary" (p. 9).

22. Donald M. Scott, *From Office to Profession* (Philadelphia: University of Pennsylvania Press, 1978), p. 152.

23. The controversy can be followed in Green to Smith, February 19, 23, April 23, 1853, Smith Papers.

24. Green to Smith, May 27, 1853, Smith Papers.

25. Green to Smith, October 26, November 28, 1853, Smith Papers.

26. Green, "Personality and Property," in *Sermons and Other Discourses*, pp. 399-400.

27. William M. Wiecek, *The Sources of Antislavery Constitutionalism in America. 1760-1848* (Ithaca, N.Y.: Cornell University Press, 1977), p. 274.

28. *Radical Abolitionist*, I (June 1856), 93-94.

29. Green to Smith, March 30, 1854, Smith Papers. See also September 19, December 11, 19, 1854, Smith Papers.

30. Green to Smith, March 30, 1854, Smith Papers.

31. *Radical Abolitionist*, I (August 1855), 7.

32. *Liberator*, February 5, 1858. *Radical Abolitionist*, I (December 1856), 44.

33. Green to Smith, September 23-24, 1857, Smith Papers.

34. Green to Smith, September 30, 1857, Smith Papers. See December 22, 1857; January 2 and 5, 1858 for more on the Green-Stuart controversy.

35. Green to Smith, February 2, 1858, Smith Papers.

36. Green to Smith, April 16, 1858, Smith Papers. Green, "The Light of Loyalty," Republished in *Sermons and Other Discourses*, pp. 444-46.

37. Green to Emerson, May 31, 1858, Emerson Papers, Houghton Library, Harvard University.

38. No new material appeared in either the 1861 or 1872 editions. The 1860 edition includes a photograph of Beriah and has the following dedication: "To All the Names, Dear and

Cherished, which Filially Gather, As they may Find Opportunity, Around the Hearthstone and Table of the Old Hive. I leave you here a little Book for you to look upon that you may see your Father's face when he is dead and gone."

39. Green to Phillips, December 29, 1859, Phillips Papers, Houghton Library, Harvard University. For Phillips' speech at North Elba, see *Wendell Phillips on Civil Rights and Freedom*, ed. by Louis Filler (New York: Hill and Wang, 1965), pp. 95-113.

40. Green to Smith, July 12, 1860, Smith Papers. On Smith's foreknowledge of John Brown's plans, see F. B. Sanford, *The Life and Letters of John Brown, Liberator of Kansas, and Martyr of Virginia* (Concord, Mass.: F. B. Sanborn, 1865), p. 458.

41. Quoted in Philip G. Wright and Elizabeth Q. Wright, *Elizur Wright, the Father of Life Insurance* (Chicago: University of Chicago Press, 1937), p. 212.

42. Wright to Green, October 8, 1860, Wright Papers, Library of Congress.

43. Green to Wright, October 31, 1860, Wright Papers, Library of Congress.

44. Green, "Let the Dead Bury Their Dead," published in *Sermons and Other Discourses*, p. 463.

10—STAYED ON RIGHTEOUSNESS

1. Green to Smith, March 16, 1860, Smith Papers.

2. *Liberator*, April 19, 1860.

3. Green to Smith, August 7, 15, 1861; January 7, 10, 1862, Smith Papers.

4. Green to Smith, January 14, 1862, Smith Papers.

5. Green to Smith, September 3, October 14, 1862, Smith Papers.

6. Green to Smith, October 14, December 6, 1862, Smith Papers.

7. Green's anti Johnson views are reported in Henry Highland Garnet to Gerrit Smith, October 23, 1865, Smith Papers.

8. Green to Ann Lander Green, March 3, 1865. Courtesy of William D. Green.

9. Green to Smith, March 19, 1867, Smith Papers.

10. Green to Smith, March 22, 1867, Smith Papers.

11. Green to Elizur Wright, Jr., Wright Papers, Library of Congress, Washington, D. C.

12. Green to Smith, May 10, 1871, Smith Papers.

13. Green to Smith, May 23, 1872, Smith Papers.

14. *Utica Weekly Herald*, May 5, 1874. Green left little in the way of an estate. A house and lot of about four acres in Twinsburg, Ohio, went to his sisters, Laura and Rhoda, who never married. He left his wife Daraxa four thousand dollars and whatever she wanted of his furniture, books, and papers. Elizabeth, who had cared for her elderly parents many years, received two thousand dollars. Beriah's three sons, Samuel, Jonathan, and Charles, were given one hundred dollars, while his daughters Mary, Ruth, Clara, and Marcia received four hundred dollars. A granddaughter, Annie (née Green) Stanley of Chicago, received three hundred dollars. Daraxa Green died in 1885. The last of Green's descendants to be buried in the family plot in Grand View Cemetery, Whitesboro, was Beriah Green Underwood (d. 1917), a grandson. *Wills and Testaments*, No. 25, Oneida County, New York.

15. The epitaph is derived from 1 John 3.7, which in the King James version reads in full: "Little children, let no man deceive you: he that doeth righteousness is righteous, even as he is righteous."

16. Cited in "Beriah Green," undated clipping from the Utica press, probably February 1904. Courtesy of Betsy H. Woodman.

17. (Elizur Wright, Jr.) "Finding a Man," originally in Wright's *Chronotype*, reprinted in *Model Worker*, August 11, 1848.

18. Ibid.

19. William G. Allen, *The American Prejudice Against Color, An Authentic Narrative, Showing how Easily the Nation Got into an Uproar. By W. G. Allen, a Refugee from American Despotism* (London: W. and F. G. Cash, 1853), pp. 13-14.

20. Wright, "Finding a Man," *Model Worker*.

21. Green, *Iniquity and a Meeting: A Discourse delivered in the Congregational Church, Whitesboro, Lord's Day, January 31, 1841* (Whitesboro: Press of the Oneida Institute, 1841), republished in Beriah Green, *Sermons and Other Discourses with Brief Biographical Hints* (New York: S. W. Green, 1860), p. 255.

22. Josiah Bushnell Grinnell, *Men and Events of Forty Years* (Boston: D. Lothrop Company, 1891), pp. 34-35.

23. Lawrence J. Friedman, *Gregarious Saints* (New York: Cambridge University Press, 1982), p. 54.

24. Quoted by M. L. Witcher, *A Few Stray Leaves in the History of Whitesboro by a Villager* (Utica, N.Y.: T. J. Griffiths, 1884), p. 35.

25. *Liberator*, April 12, 1861.

26. Samuel W. Green, *Beriah Green: A Memorial* (New York: W. S. Green, 1875), pp. 12-13.

27. Green to Weld, July 11, 1843, Theodore Dwight Weld Papers, Library of Congress, Washington, D. C.

28. John Greenleaf Whittier, "Thomas Carlyle on the Slave Question" (1849), in *The Writings of John Greenleaf Whittier in Seven Volumes* (Riverside edition; Boston: Houghton, Mifflin and Company, 1889), VII, 144, incorrectly dated 1846. See also Roland H. Woodell, "Whittier and Carlyle," in *Memorabilia of John Greenleaf Whittier*, ed. by John B. Pickard (Hartford, Ct.: The Emerson Society, undated typescript), p. 44.

29. *Liberty Leaguer*, May 1849. Goodell added, "I cannot reproach myself with having cut the cord of cooperation with my old friend Pres. Green, and his pupils. I left the Liberty Party, as he well knows, on far other grounds, than the differences between us. . . . My relations to Pres. Green, I had always supposed to be those of a man to his brother man not those of a mere servile 'supporter and admirer.' . . . I am as ready to be cooperative with him, wherein we are agreed, as I ever was—and am as little disposed as I ever was, to recognize him, or any other mere human being, as a Messiah, a king."

30. Ibid.

31. Green to Weld, April 14, 1839, *Letters of Theodore Dwight Weld, Angelina Grimké Weld, and Sarah Grimké, 1822-1844*, ed. by Gilbert H. Barnes and Dwight L. Dumond (New York: D. Appleton-Century Co., 1938), II, 755.

32. Wright to Green, November 3, 1860, Wright Papers, Library of Congress.

33. Ibid.

34. R. W. B. Lewis, *The American Adam* (Chicago: University of Chicago Press, 1955), p. 21.

35. Wright, "Finding a Man," *Model Worker*.

36. *Frederick Douglass' Paper*, November 16, 1855.

37. Jane H. Pease and William H. Pease, *Bound With Them in Chains* (Westport, Ct.: Greenwood Press, 1972), p. 299.

38. Cited in James B. Stewart, *Holy Warriors* (New York: Hill and Wang, 1976), pp. 202-203.

39. Cited in James M. McPherson, *The Abolitionist Legacy* (Princeton, N. J.: Princeton University Press, 1975), p. 391.

BIBLIOGRAPHY

BERIAH GREEN'S WRITINGS

Thighis is a chronological listing of Green's published essays, sermons, addresses, pamphlets, and books. Though many items appear in his collected works, I searched for and used originals whenever possible. Green often employed only excerpts, added footnotes, or made editorial changes when including a particular item in his collected writings. For references to his many published letters in the religious and abolitionist press, see the chapter notes. Several of the following titles could not be dated. An "M" indicates that a particular title later appeared in *The Miscellaneous Writings of Beriah Green* (1841). An "S" refers to *Sermons and Other Discourses with Brief Biographical Hints* (1860, first ed.).

182- *Duty to the Heathen.* (also) *A Christian decides to do his duty to the heathen.* N.p., T. R. Marvin, Printer.

1824 "Review of Ware's 'Hints on Extemporaneous Preaching,' " *Boston Telegraph.* (M. 1-17)

1826 *A Sermon, Preached in Poultney, June 19, 1826, at the First Annual Meeting of the Rutland County Foreign Missionary Society.* Castleton, Vt.: Published by Order of the Society.

1826 *An Oration, Pronounced at Middlebury, Before Associated Alumni of the College, on the Evening of Commencement, August 16th, 1826.* Castleton, Vt.: Ovid Miner.

1827 "Family Worship." *Vermont Chronicle.* (M, 18-19)

1827 "Christian Friendship." *Vermont Chronicle.* (M, 20-23)

1827 *"Consecration to Christ,"* A Speech Delivered at the Second Annual Meeting of the Rutland County Foreign Missionary Society, June 28, 1827. (M, 24-34)

1827 "A Fragment." (On the peace-killing tendencies of skepticism). *Vermont Chronicle.* (M, 34-38)

1827 "Hume and the Puritans." (M, 39-40)

1827 *A Sermon Preached at Brandon, Vermont, October 3, 1827, at the Ordination of the Rev. Messrs. Jonathan S. Green and Ephraim W. Clark, as Missionaries to the Sandwich Islands, by Beriah Green, Pastor of the Congregational Church in Brandon.* Middlebury, Vt.: J. W. Copeland.

1828 "An Address of the Rev. Beriah Green of Vermont." *The Home Missionary and American Pastor's Journal,* I (June 1828), 25-28

1828 "The Fishermen of Galilee." *Vermont Chronicle.* (M, 42-44)

1828 "Letters on Agencies." *Vermont Chronicle.* (M, 45-48)

1828 "Leaves of a Minister's Journal." *Vermont Chronicle.* (M, 49-51)

1828 "Eastern Customs." *Vermont Chronicle.* (M, 52-53)

1828 "The Taste of the Times." *Vermont Chronicle.* (M, 54-56)

1828 "On Using Saxon English in Giving Public Religious Instruction." *Vermont Chronicle.* (M, 57-58)

1829 "The Long Forbearance of God toward Sinners." *The National Preacher,* VII (February 1829), 129-35.

1829 "Evangelical Truths Offensive to the Unrenewed, But Joyous to the Believer." *The National Preacher,* VII (February 1829), 135-44. (M, 151-67)

1829 "An Address, Adapted to the Monthly Concert for Prayer." *The Home Missionary and American Pastor's Journal,* II (July 1, 1829), 41-43. (M, 69-74)

1829 "Review of the *Memoirs of the Life, Times and Writings of Thomas Boston.*" *The Quarterly Christian Spectator,* I (December 1829), 585-92. (M, 87-105)

1830 "Dogmatism of Boasted Ignorance—Remarks on Judge Hopkinson's Letter." *Spirit of the Pilgrims,* III (June 1830), 294-301. (M, 75-76)

1830 "Natural Affections not Holiness." (Not located)

1830 "Review of *Letters on Missions by William Swan, Missionary to Siberia, with an introductory preface by William Orne, foreign secretary to the London Missionary Society, London, 1830.*" *The Quarterly Christian Spectator,* II (December 1830), 632-46. (M, 106-29)

1831 "Review of the Fifth Report of the American Home Mission Society." *The Quarterly Christian Spectator,* III (June 1831) (M, 130-50)

1832 "Christian Obligations." *The National Preacher,* VI (April 1832), 353-62.(M, 168-87; S, 8-28)

1832 "Claims of the Prison Discipline Society to the Support of Christians." *The National Preacher,* VI (April 1832), 362-68. (M, 188-204)

1833 "Letter" in (Timothy Dwight Weld), *First Annual Report of the Society for Promoting Manual Labor in Literary Institutions including The Report of Their General Agent, January 28, 1833.* New York: S. W. Benedict, pp. 111-13.

1833 *Four Sermons, Preached in the Chapel of the Western Reserve College, on Lord's Days November 18th and 25th, and December 2nd and 9th, 1832 by Beriah Green.* Cleveland: Printed at the Office of the Herald. (M, 323-408) Extracted as "Negro Colonization and Slavery Abolition," *The Abolitionist*, 1 (August 1833).

1833 *An Address, Delivered at Whitesborough, New York, September 5, 1833, by Beriah Green, President of the Oneida Institute.* Utica: William Williams. (M, 227-48)

1834 *A Sketch of the Condition and Prospects of the Oneida Institute . . . by the Board of Instruction and Government.* Utica: Bennett and Bright. (Extracts in M, 249-265; S, 77-87)

1834 *Ancient Classics, Letters I to IX.* (M, 266-300)

1835 *To the Friends of Immediate and Universal Emancipation, October 22, 1835.* (Not located)

1835 "A Review—The Principles of Reform, Art. X On Political and Ecclesiastical Reform of Wood's *Literary and Theological Review.*" No. VI in *The Quarterly Anti-Slavery Magazine*, I (October 1835), 34-67.

1836 *The Savior's Arms Open to Little Children. A Discourse, Delivered Sabbath Evening, Nov. 8, 1835, in the Broad Street Church, Utica, Before the Association of Sabbath School Teachers.* Utica: Bennett and Bright. (M, 205-24)

1836 "Radicalism—In Reply to the *Literary and Theological Review.*" *Quarterly Anti-Slavery Magazine*, I (January 1836), 156-61.

1836 "Letter to the Minister of the Gospel." (The Relation of the Pulpit to Slavery) *Quarterly Anti-Slavery Magazine*, I (July 1836), 333-40. Also in *The Emancipator*, July 14, 1836.

1836 *Things for Northern Men to Do: A Discourse Delivered Lord's Day Evening, July 17, 1836, in the Presbyterian Church, Whitesboro, N. Y.* New York: Published by request.

1836 *The Church Carried Along, or the Opinions of a Doctor of Divinity on American Slavery.* New York: S. W. Dorr, 1836. Also in *Quarterly Anti-Slavery Magazine*, II (October 1836), 41-61.

1837 *The Basis of a Sound Reputation: A Valedictory Address to the Senior Class of the Oneida Institute. Delivered September 13, 1837 by Beriah Green.* Whitesboro: Press of the Friend of Man.

1837 "Letter on Education." (Letter to Angela Grimké on his theory of Education) *National Enquirer*, I (January 21, 1837), 77.

1837 "No Principle at Strife with Principles; or, Ciphers in Battle Array with Whole Numbers." Reprinted in *The Friend of Man*, April 12, 1837. (Original not located).

1838 *The Martyr: A Discourse on Commemoration of the Martyrdom of the Rev. Elijah P. Lovejoy, Delivered in Broadway Tabernacle, New York; and in the Bleecker Street Church, Utica.* New York: American Anti-Slavery Society.

1838 *The American Student. A Valedictory Address to the Senior Class of the Oneida Institute, Delivered September 12, 1838.* Whitesboro: Press of the Oneida Institute.

1839 *The Education of the Apostles. A Valedictory Address to the Senior Class of the Oneida Institute, Delivered September 10, 1839.* Whitesboro: Press of the Oneida Institute.

1839 *Reply of the Congregational Church in Whitesboro, To a Question of the Oneida Presbytery.* Whitesboro: Press of the Oneida Institute. (S, 230-41)

1839 *The Chattel Principle. The Abhorrence of Jesus Christ and the Apostles; or, No Refuge for American Slavery in the New Testament.* New York: American Anti-Slavery Society, 1839. (S, 265-851). Also published as *Anti-Slavery Examiner,* No. 7.

184- "God and Humanity." (S, 90-104)

184- "The Great Conspiracy." (S, 127-43)

184- "The Staff of Accomplishment." (S, 144-63)

1840 *A Right Minded Minority. A Valedictory Address to the Senior Class of the Oneida Institute, Delivered September 9, 1840.* Whitesboro: Press of the Oneida Institute. Reprinted in *The Model Worker,* June 14, 1848.

1841 *Faith and Works. A Valedictory Address to the Senior Class of Oneida Institute. Delivered October 17, 1841.* Whitesboro: Press of the Oneida Institute.

1841 *Iniquity and a Meeting. A Discourse delivered in the Congregational Church, Whitesboro, Lord's Day, January 31, 1841.* Whitesboro: Press of the Oneida Institute. Second ed. 1842. Also published as Vol. I, No. 1 of the *Tract Distributors* (March, 1844). (S, 243-64)

1841 *The Miscellaneous Writings of Beriah Green.* Whitesboro: Published by the Oneida Institute. Second ed. 1848.

1842 *Thoughts on the Atonement.* Whitesboro: Oneida Institute Press.

1842 *The Divine Significance of Work. A Valedictory Address delivered at the Anniversary of the Oneida Institute, November 2, 1842.* Whitesboro: Press of the Oneida Institute.

1843 *A Voice From the Oneida Institute, July 1843.* Whitesboro: Institute Press. (S, 164-201 as "Ten Years in Oneida Institute")

1843 *Success. A Valedictory Address Delivered at the Anniversary of the Oneida Institute, November 1, 1843.* Utica: R. W. Roberts.

1844 *Belief Without Confession, A Sermon Preached at Whitesboro, N.Y.* Utica: J. C. Jackson.

1844 *A Memorial of Ann Parker Green Hough.* Utica: R. W. Roberts.

1844 *Sketches of the Life and Writings of James Gillespie Birney.* Utica: Jackson and Chaplin.

184(4?) *The Counsel of Caiaphas, or a Sermon, John XI, 47-50,63.* N.p., n.p.

1846 *Work and Wages. A Sermon Preached at Whitesboro, N.Y., Nov. 1846.* Extracted as, "The Gospel Demands a Radical, and Universal Revolution in Human Society." Also in *The Harbinger,* V (June 26, 1847). (S, 106-25)

1848 "Speech of Beriah Green" (on Civil Government). In *Proceedings of the National Liberty Convention, Held at Buffalo, N.Y., June 14 and 15, 1848. Including the Resolutions and Addresses Adopted by that Body, and the Speeches of Beriah Green and Gerrit Smith in that Session.* Utica: S. W. Green, pp. 33-45.

1848 *To the Surviving Members of the Liberty Party.* Whitesboro: n.p.

1853 *Faith and Infidelity—A Sermon, at Whitesboro, 1853, Delivered in the Congregational Church at Whitesboro and Elsewhere.* New York: S. W. Green. (S, 309-32)

1858 *Sermon at the Funeral of Henry D. Ward, July 24, 1858.* Rome, N.Y.: R. R. Meridith

18— "Slavery." (S, 359-79) Note: This and the following eight items, mostly sermons, are undated but appear to be from the 1850s.

18— "Personality and Property." (S, 380-400)

18— "Ideas and Phenomena." (S, 401-23)

18— "The Light of Loyalty," John 7:17. (S, 424-49)

18— "Let the Dead Bury the Dead," Luke 9:59, 60. (S, 450-81)

18— "Office of Faith," 2 Cor. 5:7. (S, 482-506)

18— "The Liar," 1 John 2:22. (S, 507-29)

18— "Redemption," 1 John 1:7. (S, 530-56)

18— *The True Test of Sound Character. Adapted to and designed for the Human Family.* N.p., n.p.

1860 *Sermons and Other Discourses with Brief Biographical Hints.* New York: S. W. Green, 1860. Second ed. 1861. Third ed. 1872.

A NOTE ON PRIMARY SOURCES

In addition to Green's writings, I have used a wide variety of published and unpublished primary sources. Of the twenty manuscript collections consulted, none proved more helpful than the Gerrit Smith Papers in the George Arents Research Library at Syracuse University. Unless otherwise noted, all references to the Smith Papers in the notes refer to this invaluable collection. The contemporary religious and abolitionist press yielded up much that was useful after painstaking searches. Of the thirty papers consulted, those that proved most generous were the *Albany Patriot* (1843-48), *Christian Investigator* (1842-48), *Friend of Man* (1836-41), *Liberator* (1831-65), *Liberty Press* (1842-49), *Model Worker* (1848-52), Hudson's *Observer and Telegraph* (1834-35), and the *Radical Abolitionist* (1855-58). Important primary sources also included the published proceedings and reports of reform and abolitionist societies, the records of First Presbyterian, Whitesboro, and of the Oneida Presbytery, catalogues of Oneida Institute, and books and articles by Green's contemporaries. I found the published letters of Theodore Dwight Weld and James Birney very helpful. The microfilm collection of the Black Abolitionist Papers also yielded important information. In the interests of economy of space, primary sources other than Green's published writings, listed above, are cited in full only in the chapter notes.

SELECT SECONDARY SOURCES

With the exception of direct quotes, I have generally not cited secondary sources in the notes. Published literature on American abolitionism and related reform and religious topics is immense. The following items have been selected in order to point readers to authors who have been especially helpful, either by providing incidental facts, historical background, or insightful perspectives.

Dissertations and Theses

Block, Muriel. "Beriah Green, the Reformer." M.A. thesis, Syracuse University, 1935.

Britt, Joseph J., Jr. "The Gospel Ministry: The Oneida Institute and the Rise of Abolitionism in the United States." Honors Thesis, Boston College, 1970.

French, David Charles. "The Conversion of an American Radical: Elizur Wright, Jr., and the Abolitionist Commitment." Ph.D. dissertation, Case Western Reserve University, 1970.

Goodheart, Lawrence Barr. "Elizur Wright, Jr., and the Abolitionist Movement, 1820-1860." Ph.D. dissertation, University of Connecticut, 1978.

Henderson, Alice. "The History of the New York State Anti-Slavery Society." Ph.D. dissertation, University of Michigan, 1963.

Howard, Victor B. "The Anti-Slavery Movement in the Presbyterian Church, 1835-1861." Ph.D. dissertation, Ohio State University, 1961.

Kraut, Alan Morton. "The Liberty Men of New York: Political Abolitionism in New York State, 1840-1848." Ph.D dissertation, Cornell University, 1975.

Lamb, Wallace G. "George Washington Gale: Theologian and Educator." Ph.D. dissertation, Syracuse University, 1949.

McManis, Michael A. "Range Ten, Town Four: A Social History of Hudson, Ohio 1799-1840." Ph.D. dissertation, Case Western Reserve University, 1976.

Somerville, Scott. "The Bible and the Moral Government of God: The Abolitionist Thought of Beriah Green." M. Divinity Thesis, Union Theological Seminary, New York, 1978.

Articles and Essays

Allmendinger, David F., Jr. "The Strangeness of the American Education Society: Indigent Students and the New Charity, 1815-1840." *History of Education Quarterly*, XL (Spring 1971), 3-22.

Anderson, Lewis Flint. "The Manual Labor School Movement." *Educational Review*, 46 (November 1913), 369-86.

Banner, Lois. "Religion and Reform in the Early Republic: The Role of Youth." *American Quarterly*, 23 (December 1971), 677-95.

Barker, Anthony J. "Captain Charles Stuart and the British and American Abolition Movements: 1830-34." *Slavery and Abolition*, I (May 1980), 46-63.

Bartor, Ron. "American Views on 'Biblical Slavery': 1835-1865, A Comparative Study." *Slavery and Abolition*, 4 (May 1983), 41-63.

Bigglestone, William E. "Straightening A Fold in the Record." *Oberlin Alumni Magazine*, 68 (May/June 1977), 11.

Blackett, R. J. M. "William G. Allen: The Forgotten Professor." *Civil War History*, XXVI (March 1980), 38-52.

Blight, David W. "Perceptions of Southern Intransigence and the Rise of Radical Antislavery Thought 1816-1830." *Journal of the Early Republic*, 3 (Summer 1983), 139-63.

Brewer, W. M. "Henry Highland Garnet." *Journal of Negro History*, XIII (January 1928), 44-47.

Burke, Ronald K. "The Anti-Slavery Activities of Samuel Ringgold Ward in New York State." *Afro-Americans in New York Life and History*, 2 (1978), 17-28.

Carwardine, Richard. "Evangelicals, Whigs and The Election of William Henry Harrison." *Journal of American Studies*, 17 (April 1983), 47-75.

Coates, Charles P. "From George Gale to Arthur Morgan." *Educational Review*, LXXXI (1926), 53-55.

Cooper, Frederick. "Elevating the Race: The Social Thought of Black Leaders, 1827-50." *American Quarterly*, 24 (December 1972), 602-25.

Dyson, Zita. "Gerrit Smith's Effort in Behalf of the Negroes in New York." *Journal of Negro History*, III (October 1918), 354-59.

Ellis, David Maldwyn. "The Yankee Invasion of New York, 1783-1860." *New York History*, XXXII (January 1951), 3-17.

Essig, James David. "The Lord's Free Man: Charles G. Finney and His Abolitionism." *Civil War History*, XXIV (January 1978), 25-45.

French, David. "Elizur Wright, Jr., and the Emergence of Anti-Colonization Sentiments on the Connecticut Western Reserve." *Ohio History*, 85 (Winter 1976), 49-66.

Friedman, Lawrence J. "The Gerrit Smith Circle: Abolitionism in the Burned-Over District." *Civil War History*, 26 (1980), 18-38.

_____. "Historical topics Sometimes Run Dry: The State of Abolitionist Studies." *Historian*, 43 (February 1981), 177-94.

Geiser, Karl F. "The Western Reserve in the Anti-Slavery Movement, 1840-1860." *Proceedings of the Mississippi Valley Historical Association*, 5 (1911-12), 73-98.

Goen, C. C. "Broken churches, Broken Nation: Regional Religion and North-South Alienation in Antebellum America." *Church History*, 52 (March 1983), 21-35.

Goodheart, Lawrence B. "Abolitionists As Academics: The Controversy at Western Reserve College, 1832-1833." *History of Education Quarterly*, 22 (Winter 1982), 421-33.

_____. "The Chronicles of Kidnapping in New York: Resistance to the Fugitive Slave Law, 1834-1835." *Afro-Americans in New York Life and History*, 8 (January 1984), 7-15.

Harlow, Ralph Volney. "Gerrit Smith and the Free Church Movement." *New York History*, XVIII (July 1937), 269-87.

Hirsch, Leo H. Jr. "The Negro and New York, 1783-1865." *Journal of Negro History*, XVI (October 1931), 382-463.

Kett, Joseph. "Growing up in Rural New England." In *Anonymous Americans: Explorations in Nineteenth-Century Social History*. Ed. by Tamara K. Hareven. Englewood Cliffs, N. J.: Prentice-Hall, 1971. Pp. 1-16.

Kraut, Alan M. "The Forgotten Reformers: A Profile of Third Party Abolitionists in Antebellum New York." In *Anti-Slavery Reconsidered: New Perspectives on the Abolitionists*. Ed. by Lewis Perry and Michael Fellman. Baton Rouge: Louisiana State University Press, 1979. Pp. 119-45.

Lawson, Ellen N., and Merrill, Marlene. "The Antebellum 'Talented Thousandth': Black College Students at Oberlin Before the Civil War." *Journal of Negro Education*, 52 (1983), 142-55.

Litwack, Leon F. "The Abolitionist Dilemma: The Antislavery Movement and the Northern Negro." *New England Quarterly*, XXXIV (March 1961), 50-73.

McKivigan, John R. "The Antislavery 'Comeouter' Sects: A Neglected Dimension of the Abolitionist Movement." *Civil War History*, XXVI (1980), 142-60.

Mahler, Frederick. "Beriah Green, Chair and Cabinetmaker." *Spinning Wheel*, (March 1978), 32-34.

Maynard, Douglas H. "The World's Anti-Slavery Convention of 1840." *Mississippi Valley Historical Review*, 47 (December 1960), 452-71.

Meyers, John L. "The Beginning of Anti-Slavery Agencies in New York State, 1833-1836." *New York History*, XLIII (April 1962), 149-81.

_____. "The Major Effort of Anti-Slavery Agencies in New York, 1836-1837." *New York History*, XLVI (1965), 162-86.

Morrison, Howard Alexander. "The Finney Takeover of the Second Great Awakening During the Oneida Revivals of 1825-1827." *New York History*, LVIX (January 1978), 27-53.

_____. "Gentlemen of Proper Understanding: A Closer Look at Utica's Anti-Abolitionist Mob." *New York History*, 62 (January 1981), 61-82.

Moses, Wilson J. "Civilizing Missionary: A Study of Alexander Crummell." *Journal of Negro History*, LX (April 1975), 229-51.

Perkal, M. Leon. "American Abolition Society: A Viable Alternative to the Republican Party?" *Journal of Negro History*, 65 (1980), 57-71.

_____. "William Goodell: Radical Abolitionist." *Centerpoint*, 2 (Spring 1977), 17-25.

Reed, Harry A. "The Slave as Abolitionist: Henry Highland Garnet's Address to the Slaves of the United States of America." *Centennial Review*, 20 (1976), 385-94.

Scott, Donald M. "Abolition as a Sacred Vocation." In *Anti-Slavery Reconsidered: New Perspectives on the Abolitionists*, ed. by Lewis Perry and Michael Fellman. Baton Rouge: Louisiana State University Press, 1979, pp. 51-74.

Scruggs, Otey M. "We the Children of Africa in this Land: Alexander Crummell." In *Africa and Afro-American Experience: Eight Essays*. Ed. by Lorraine A. Williams. Washington, D. C.: Howard University Press, 1977. Pp. 77-95.

Sernett, Milton C. "The Efficacy of Religious Participation in the National Debates over Abolitionism and Abortion." *Journal of Religion*, 64 (April 1984), 205-20.

_____. "First Honor: Oneida Institute's Role in the Fight Against Racism and Slavery." *New York History*, LXVI (April 1985), 197-209.

_____. "Lutheran Abolitionism in New York State: A Problem in Historical Explication." *Essays and Reports, Lutheran Historical Conference, 1982*, X (1984), 16-37.

_____. "The Odd Couple: The Antislavery Alliance of Gerrit Smith and Beriah Green." *Syracuse University Library Associates Courier*, XXI (Fall 1986).

Sevitsh, Benjamin. "The Well-Planned Riot of October 21, 1835: Utica's Answer to Abolitionism" *New York History*, 50 (July 1969), 251-63.

Shanks, Caroline L. "The Biblical Anti-Slavery Argument of the Decade 1830-1840." *Journal of Negro History*, XVI (April 1931), 132-57.

Short, Kenneth R. "New York Central College: A Baptist Experiment in Integrated Higher Education, 1848-61." *Foundations*, 3 (July 1962), 250-56.

Sokolaw, Jayme A. "The Jerry McHenry Rescue and The Growth of Northern Anti-Slavery Sentiment during the 1850s." *Journal of American Studies*, 16 (December 1982): 427-45.

Stewart, James B. "The Aims and Impact of Garrisonian Abolitionism, 1840-1860." *Civil War History*, 15 (September 1969), 197-209.

_____. "Peaceful Hopes and Violent Experiences: The Evolution of Reforming and Radical Abolitionism, 1831-1857." *Civil War History*, XVII (December 1971), 293-309.

_____. "Politics and Belief in Abolitionism: Stanley Elkins' Concept of Antiinstitutionalism and Recent Interpretations of American Antislavery." *South Atlantic Quarterly*, 75 (1976), 74-97.

Swift, David. "O! This Heartless Prejudice." *Wesleyan*, LXVII (Spring 1984), 13-17.

Thompson, J. Earl, Jr. "Abolitionism and Theological Education at Andover." *New England Quarterly*, 47 (1974), 238-61.

Walzer, Michael. "Puritanism as a Revolutionary Ideology." *History and Theory*, 3 (1964), 79-88.

Warner, Robert A. "Amos Gerry Beman—1812-74, A Memoir of a Forgotten Leader." *Journal of Negro History*, 22 (April 1937), 200-21.

Walters, Ronald. "The Erotic South: Civilization and Sexuality in American Abolitionism." *American Quarterly*, 25 (Winter 1973), 177-201.

Wesley, Charles H. "The Negroes of New York in the Emancipation Movement." *Journal of Negro History*, XXIV (January 1939), 65-103.

_____. "The Participation of Negroes in Antislavery Political Parties." *Journal of Negro History*, XXIX (January 1944), 32-74.

Wyatt-Brown, Bertram. "Conscience and Career: Young Abolitionists and Missionaries." In *Anti-Slavery, Religion and Reform: Essays in Memory of Roger Anstey*, ed. by Christine Bolt and Seymour Drescher, Folkestone, Kent, England: Wm. Dawson and Sons, 1980, pp. 183-203.

Books

Abzug, Robert H. *Passionate Liberator: Theodore Dwight Weld and the Dilemma of Reform*. New York: Oxford University Press, 1980.

Allmendinger, David F., Jr. *Paupers and Scholars: The Transformation of Student Life in Nineteenth Century New England*. New York: St. Martin's Press, 1975.

Barnes, Gilbert H. *The Antislavery Impulse 1830-1844*. 1933. Reprint, Gloucester, Mass.: Peter Smith, 1973.

Bartchy, S. Scott. *First-Century Slavery and the Interpretation of 1 Corinthians 7:21*. Missoula, Mt.: The Society of Biblical Literature, 1973.

Barth, J. Robert, S. J. *Coleridge and Christian Doctrine*. Cambridge, Mass.: Harvard University Press, 1969.

Behnken, Eloise M. *Thomas Carlyle: "Calvinist Without the Theology."* Columbia, Mo.: University of Missouri Press, 1978.

Benson, Lee. *The Concept of Jacksonian Democracy: New York as a Test Case*. Princeton, N.J.: Princeton University Press, 1961.

Bodo, John R. *The Protestant Clergy and Public Issues, 1812-1848*. Princeton, N.J.: Princeton University Press, 1954.

Bolt, Christine, and Drescher, Seymour, eds. *Anti-Slavery, Religion and Reform: Essays in Memory of Roger Anstey*. Folkestone, Kent, England: Wm. Dawson and Sons, 1980.

Brown, Jerry Wayne. *The Rise of Biblical Criticism in America, 1800-1870, The New England Scholars*. Middletown, Conn.: Wesleyan University Press, 1969.

Bushman, Richard L. *From Puritan to Yankee: Character and the Social Order in Connecticut, 1690-1765*. Cambridge, Mass.: Harvard University Press, 1967.

Case, Lora. *Hudson of Long Ago*. 1897. Reprint, Hudson, Ohio: Hudson Library and Historical Society, 1963.

Cole, Charles C., Jr. *The Social Ideas of the Northern Evangelists, 1826-1860*. New York: Columbia University Press, 1954.

Conforti, Joseph A. *Samuel Hopkins and the New Divinity Movement*. Grand Rapids, Mich.: Wm. B. Eerdmans Publishing Co., 1982.

Cramer, C. H. *Case Western Reserve: A History of the University, 1826-1976*. Boston: Little, Brown, 1976.

Cross, Whitney, R. *The Burned-over District: The Social and Intellectual History of Enthusiastic Religion in Western New York, 1800-1850*. Ithaca, N.Y.: Cornell University Press, 1950.

Cutler, Carroll. *A History of Western Reserve College, 1826-1876*. Cleveland: Crocker Publishing House, 1876.

Duberman, Martin, ed. *The Antislavery Vanguard*. Princeton, N.J.: Princeton University Press, 1965.

Du Bois, W. E. Burghardt. *The Souls of Black Folk*. 1903. Republished, New York: Fawcett Publications, Inc., 1961.

Dumond, Dwight L. *Antislavery: The Crusade for Freedom in America*. Ann Arbor: University of Michigan Press, 1961.

Durant, Samuel W. *History of Oneida County, New York*. Philadelphia: Everts and Fariss, 1878.

Elkins, Stanley. *Slavery: A Problem in American Institutional and Intellectual Life*. Chicago: University of Chicago Press, 1959.

Essig, James D. *The Bonds of Wickedness: American Evangelicals against Slavery, 1770-1808*. Philadelphia: Temple University Press, 1982.

Field, Phyllis F. *The Politics of Race in New York*. Ithaca, N.Y.: Cornell University Press, 1982.

Fladeland, Betty. *James Gillespie Birney: From Slaveholder to Abolitionist*. Ithaca, N.Y.: Cornell University Press, 1955.

_____. *Men & Brothers: Anglo-American Antislavery Cooperation*. Urbana: University of Illinois Press, 1972.

Fletcher, Robert S. *A History of Oberlin College from its Foundation through the Civil War*. 2 vols. Oberlin, Ohio: Oberlin College, 1943.

Foster, C. I. *An Errand of Mercy: The Evangelical United Front, 1790-1837*. Chapel Hill: University of North Carolina Press, 1960.

Fowler, P. H. *Historical Sketch of Presbyterianism Within the Bounds of the Synod of Western New York*. Utica, N.Y.: Cross and Childs, 1877.

Fox, Dixon Ryan. *Yankees and Yorkers*. New York: New York University Press, 1940.

Foner, Eric C. *Politics and Ideology in the Age of the Civil War*. New York: Oxford University Press, 1980.

Friedman, Lawrence J. *Gregarious Saints: Self and Community in American Abolitionism, 1830-1870*. New York: Cambridge University Press, 1982.

Frothingham, Octavius Brooks. *Gerrit Smith. A Biography*. New York: G. P. Putnam and Son, 1909.

Green, Samuel W. *Beriah Green: A Memorial*. New York: S. W. Green, 1875.

Greven, Philip. *The Protestant Temperament: Patterns of Child-Rearing, Religious Experience, and the Self in Early America*. New York: Alfred A. Knopf, 1977.

Griffin, Clifford S. *Their Brother's Keeper, Moral Stewardship in the United States, 1800-1865*. New Brunswick, N.J.: Rutgers University Press, 1960.

Hammond, John L. *The Politics of Benevolence: Revival Religion and American Voting Behavior*. Norwood, N.J.: Ablex, 1979.

Harlow, Ralph V. *Gerrit Smith, Philanthropist and Reformer*. New York: Holt, Rinehart, and Winston, 1939.

Hareven, Tamara K., ed. *Anonymous Americans: Explorations in Nineteenth-Century Social History*. Englewood Cliffs, N.J.: Prentice-Hall, 1971.

Hatcher, Harlen. *The Western Reserve: The Story of New Connecticut in Ohio*. Indianapolis: Bobbs-Merrill, Inc., 1949.

Hawaiian Mission Children's Society. *Jubilee Celebration of the Arrival of the Missionary Reinforcement of 1837*. Honolulu: Daily Bulletin Steam Print, 1887.

_____. *Missionary Album: Portraits and Biographical Sketches of the American*

Protestant Missionaries to the Hawaiian Island. Enlarged from the 1937 ed. Honolulu: Hawaiian Mission Children's Society, 1969.

Hemenway, Abby Maria, ed. *Orleans and Rutland Counties.* Vol. III of *The Vermont Historical Gazetteer.* Claremont, N.H.: The Claremont Manufacturing Company, 1877.

Johnson, Oliver. *William Lloyd Garrison and His Times.* Boston: Houghton Mifflin, 1881.

Keller, Charles S. *The Second Great Awakening in Connecticut.* New Haven: Yale University Press, 1942.

Kennedy, William S. *The Plan of Union: or, A History of the Presbyterian and Congregational Churches in the Western Reserve.* Hudson, Ohio: Pentagon Steam Press, 1856.

Kitzmiller, Helen H. *One Hundred Years of Western Reserve.* Hudson, Ohio: The James Ellsworth Foundation, 1926.

Kraditor, Aileen S. *Means and Ends in American Abolitionism.* New York: Vintage Books, 1970.

Lesick, Lawrence T. *The Lane Rebels: Evangelicalism and Antislavery in Antebellum America.* Metuchen, N.J.: Scarecrow Press, 1980.

Litwack, Leon F. *North of Slavery.* Chicago: University of Chicago Press, 1961.

Lockridge, Laurence S. *Coleridge the Moralist.* Ithaca, N.Y.: Cornell University Press, 1977.

Mabee, Carleton. *Black Education in New York State.* Syracuse: Syracuse University Press, 1979.

_____. *Black Freedom: The Nonviolent Abolitionists from 1830 through the Civil War.* London: Macmillan, 1970.

McKivigan, John R. *The War against Proslavery Religion: Abolition and the Northern Churches, 1830-1865.* Ithaca, N.Y.: Cornell University Press, 1984.

McManus, Edger J. *A History of Negro Slavery in New York.* Syracuse, N.Y.: Syracuse University Press, 1970.

McPherson, James M. *The Abolitionist Legacy: From Reconstruction to the NAACP.* Princeton, N.J.: Princeton University Press, 1975.

Marini, Stephen. *Radical Sects of Revolutionary New England.* Cambridge, Mass.: Harvard University Press, 1982.

Marsden, George M. *The Evangelical Mind and the New School Presbyterian Experience.* New Haven, Conn.: Yale University Press, 1970.

Mathews, Alfred. *Ohio and Her Western Reserve with a Story of Three States.* New York: D. Appleton, 1902.

Meyer, D. H. *The Instructed Conscience: The Shaping of the American National Ethic.* Philadelphia: University of Pennsylvania Press, 1972.

Muelder, Hermann R. *Fighters for Freedom: The History of the Anti-slavery Activities of Men and Women Associated with Knox College.* New York: Columbia University Press, 1959.

Nichols, Robert Hastings. *Presbyterianism in New York State.* Ed. by James Hastings Nichols. Philadelphia: Westminster Press, 1963.

Ofari, Earl. *"Let Your Motto Be RESISTANCE": The Life and Thought of Henry Highland Garnet.* Boston: Beacon Press, 1972.

Payne, Charles E. *Josiah Bushnell Grinnell.* Iowa City: The State Historical Society of Iowa, 1938.

Pease, Jane H., and Pease, William H. *Bound with Them in Chains: A Biographical History of the Antislavery Movement.* Westport, Conn.: Greenwood Press, Inc., 1972.

_____. *They Who Would Be Free: Blacks' Search for Freedom, 1830-1861.* New York: Atheneum, 1974.

Perry, Lewis. *Radical Abolitionism: Anarchy and the Government of God in Antislavery Thought.* Ithaca, N.Y.: Cornell University Press, 1973.

Perry, Lewis, and Fellman, Michael, eds. *Anti-Slavery Reconsidered: New Perspectives on the Abolitionists.* Baton Rouge: Louisiana State University Press, 1979.

Quarles, Benjamin. *Black Abolitionists.* New York: Oxford University Press, 1969.

Quillin, Frank. *The Color Line in Ohio.* Ann Arbor, Mich.: George Wahr, 1913.

Ratner, Lorman. *Powder Keg: Northern Opposition to the Antislavery Movement, 1831-1840.* New York: Basic Books, 1968.

Richards, Leonard L. *"Gentlemen of Property and Standing": Anti-Abolition Mobs in Jacksonian America.* New York: Oxford University Press, 1970.

Rohman, D. Gordon. *Here's Whitesboro.* New York: Stratford House, 1949.

Rosenburg, Philip. *The Seventh Hero: Thomas Carlyle and the Theory of Radical Activism.* Cambridge, Mass.: Harvard University Press, 1974.

Rowe, Henry K. *History of Andover Theological Seminary.* Newton, Mass.: N.p., 1933.

Ryan, Mary P. *Cradle of the Middle Class: The Family in Oneida County, New York, 1790-1865.* New York: Cambridge University Press, 1981.

Schor, Joel. *Henry Highland Garnet: A Voice of Black Radicalism in the Nineteenth Century.* Westport, Ct.: Greenwood, 1977.

Scott, Donald M. *From Office to Profession: The New England Ministry, 1750-1850.* Philadelphia: University of Pennsylvania Press, 1978.

Sewell, Richard H. *Ballots for Freedom: Antislavery Politics in the United States, 1837-1860.* New York: Oxford University Press, 1976.

Smith, H.P., and Rann, W.S., eds. *History of Rutland County, Vermont.* Syracuse, N.Y.: Mason, 1866.

Smith, Theodore Clarke. *The Liberty and Free Soil Parties in the Northeast.* New York: Longmans, Green, 1897.

Smith, Timothy L. *Revivalism and Social Reform: American Protestantism on the Eve of the Civil War.* 1957. Reprint, New York: Harper & Row, 1965.

Sorin, Gerald. *The New York Abolitionists: A Case Study of Political Radicalism.* Westport, Conn.: Greenwood, 1971.

Sperry, Earl E. *The Jerry Rescue.* Syracuse, N.Y.: Onondaga Historical Association, 1924.

Staudenraus, Philip J. *The African Colonization Movement: 1816-1865.* New York:

Columbia University Press, 1961.

Stewart, James B. *Holy Warriors: The Abolitionists and American Slavery*. New York: Hill and Wang, 1976.

Thomas, Benjamin. *Theodore Dwight Weld, Crusader for Freedom*. New Brunswick, N.J.: Rutgers University Press, 1950.

Thompson, John L. *The Liberator: William Lloyd Garrison*. Boston: Little, Brown, 1963.

Thompson, Zadock. *History of Vermont, Natural, Civil and Statistical*. Burlington, Vt.: Chauncy Goodrich, 1842.

Waite, Frederick C. *Western Reserve University: The Hudson Era*. Cleveland: Western Reserve University Press, 1943.

Walters, Ronald G. *The Antislavery Appeal: American Abolitionism after 1830*. Baltimore: The Johns Hopkins Press, 1978.

Wiecek, William M. *The Sources of Antislavery Constitutionalism in America, 1760-1848*. Ithaca, N.Y.: Cornell University Press, 1977.

Wishy, Bernard. *The Child and the Republic: The Dawn of Modern American Child Nurture*. Philadelphia: University of Pennsylvania Press, 1968.

Witcher, M. L. *A Few Stray Leaves in the History of Whitesboro by a Villager*. Utica, N.Y.: T. J. Griffith, 1884.

Wright, Philip G., and Wright, Elizabeth Q. *Elizur Wright, the Father of Life Insurance*. Chicago: University of Chicago Press, 1937.

Wyatt-Brown, Bertram. *Lewis Tappan and the Evangelical War Against Slavery*. New York: Atheneum, 1971.

Zilversmit, Arthur. *The First Emancipation: The Abolition of Slavery in the North*. Chicago: The University of Chicago Press, 1967.

INDEX